**A pocket-sized encyclopedia
for those who are
serious about developing
wilderness skills**

"FASCINATING...

"SKILLS FOR TAMING THE WILDS is
just about the last word in the way of guid-
ance for the outdoorsman."
—*San Rafael Independent-Journal*

SKILLS FOR TAMING THE WILDS
was originally published by
Stackpole Books.

OTHER BOOKS BY BRADFORD ANGIER

FREE FOR THE EATING
HOME IN YOUR PACK
MISTER RIFLEMAN
    (with Colonel Townsend Whelen)
WE LIKE IT WILD
WILDERNESS COOKERY
HOW TO GO LIVE IN THE WOODS ON $10 A WEEK
ON YOUR OWN IN THE WILDERNESS
    (with Colonel Townsend Whelen)
LIVING OFF THE COUNTRY
HOW TO BUILD YOUR HOME IN THE WOODS
AT HOME IN THE WOODS

SKILLS FOR TAMING THE WILDS

A Handbook of Woodcraft Wisdom

by Bradford Angier

PUBLISHED BY POCKET BOOKS NEW YORK

SKILLS FOR TAMING THE WILDS

Stackpole edition published May, 1967

POCKET BOOK edition published March, 1972

This POCKET BOOK edition includes every word
contained in the original, higher-priced edition. It is printed
from brand-new plates made from completely reset, clear, easy-to-read
type. POCKET BOOK editions are published by POCKET BOOKS, a division
of Simon & Schuster, Inc., 630 Fifth Avenue, New York, N.Y. 10020.
Trademarks registered in the United States and other countries.

L

For my Boston friend of many years
GEORGE VIRTUE

The author is indebted for some of the illustrations to: Andy Emert, New York State College of Agriculture at Cornell University and their bulletin *Wild Foods* by Eva L. Gordon, and Vena Angier.

CONTENTS

one to start each fire, protecting them from moisture and accidental combustion—Cold weather procedure—Building fires without exertion—Making fires without matches by striking spark in tinder, focusing light rays with water and ice, shooting a firearm, using bow and drill—Minimizing smoke while maximizing warmth—How to use stones as hot water bottles—Ready-made fires—Safety precautions

16   EATING WELL IN THE WILDS   230

Boiled onions—Roast corn—Treats for the sweet
tooth (ice cream, maple syrup substitute, applesauce from dried apples, stewed prunes and
apricots, fruit and dumplings, Hudson's Bay
Company plum pudding)

SKILLS
FOR TAMING
THE WILDS

Chapter 1

ENJOYING THE
WILDS NEAR
YOUR DOORSTEP

THROUGHOUT this country there are vast stretches of unspoiled and practically uninhabited wilderness. Here you can take your pack. You can fish and photograph and live with nature for almost as long as you will, and have a glorious and totally different adventure you'll never forget.

All this can be done at hardly any expense. The most costly factor, as a matter of fact, is time. Once you have assembled a small outfit and reached a jumping-off place, you can journey and sight-see at no further outlay than for the food you'd eat anyway, for less than the cost of living at home.

Furthermore, you are completely footloose and independent, free to roam and sleep where you will. You need rely on no one, and there is none of the care and cost of boats, cycles, automobiles, and pack animals.

"Hiking a ridge, a meadow, or a river bottom, is as healthy a form of exercise as one can get," says Supreme Court Justice William O. Douglas. "Hiking seems to put all the body cells back into rhythm. Ten to twenty miles on a trail puts one to bed with his cares unraveled. Hiking—and climbing, too— are man's most natural exercises. They introduce him again to the wonders of nature and teach him the beauty of the woods and fields in winter as well as in spring. They also teach him

1

how to take care of himself and his neighbors in times of adversity.

"We need exercise as individuals. We need to keep physically fit and alert as people . . . 'History is the sound of heavy boots going upstairs and the rustle of satin slippers coming down.' Nations that are soft and sleek—people who get all their exercise and athletics vicariously—will not survive when the competition is severe and adversity is at hand. It is imperative that America stay fit. For today we face as great a danger, as fearsome a risk, as any people in history."

Although modern equipment and improved methods have been developed that ease hiking of its drudgery and hard physical work, and open it to all ages, there is nothing new about hiking and camping with only what can be easily packed on one's back. Our early frontiersmen traveled that way whenever they entered the wilderness. Daniel Boone spent two whole years more or less alone in the virgin wilderness of Kentucky, living off the country, with no outfit except that which he had been carrying when he left.

Those who have never done any backpacking in the right manner, with a good outfit, have the idea that it is the toughest kind of toil. One often hears the expression, "I don't propose to make a packhorse of myself." Many who have attempted such a vacation never repeat it because they have found it too much like hard work. Any resemblance to hard work, however, is due entirely to improper equipment and mistaken technique. Done right, there is nothing hard about vacationing with a packsack. You wander free and unfettered, with just enough exercise in the pure air to make life thoroughly enjoyable.

Those who have adopted the best methods of backpacking (described in Chapter 4), formerly known to a few, are returning regularly to the trails and bringing others with them. Many are combining the satisfaction of hiking with camping and fishing in unspoiled wilderness, all this at costs they could not even approximate in any other form of diversion.

Such trips are for anyone healthy and fairly vigorous. They can be enjoyed equally by parents, by teenagers of both sexes, elderly people in good health, and certainly by children. One of the most important sidelines of some of the packsack companies is child carriers, some designed so the youngster riding an adult's back, something like a papoose of yore, can be carried either forward or—especially in bush country—backwards.

Today only two things are essential for backpacking vacations: drinking water, which you can purify if need be, and country where you can walk without trespassing.

WHERE TO GO

Within the 154 national forests in thirty-nine states and Puerto Rico are 182,000,000 such acres and more than 105,000 miles of trails, all open to backpacking. National parks are crisscrossed with thousands of miles of maintained trails. Innumerable public campgrounds are enmeshed by well-marked webs of hiking paths which lead to every type of attraction. Considerable undeveloped countryside everywhere, within easy reach of even the largest cities, calls for exploration on foot.

Toting everything you need, you can rove in the woods of all our Atlantic states; in the forests of northern Michigan, Wisconsin, and Minnesota; in the Ozark Mountains; and in the piñon and cactus highlands around Taos, New Mexico, where Kit Carson made his camps earlier.

If you live near crowded New York, there are the Catskill Mountains only three hours away by car. North of Boston, beyond the inviting backways of Essex and Gloucester, are the White Mountains, with the Little Imp and other unforgettable trails. Just east of Philadelphia are the South Jersey pine barrens. From the capital of our country, the cloud-scoured Blue Ridge is only two hours distant.

TRAILS

HIKING THE LONG TRAIL. Vermont's Long Trail is a wilderness footpath for hikers. Extending from Canada to Massachusetts, it winds along or near the crest of the state's historic Green Mountains. Some ninety side trails, together with frequent crossings of country roads, provide such frequent access to supplies that it's possible to make this trip with ultra-light equipment. All you have to do is crisscross the route beforehand in an automobile and cache food, preferably contained in large cans for easy storage and preparation, in convenient places such as under rock shelves. The fact that there

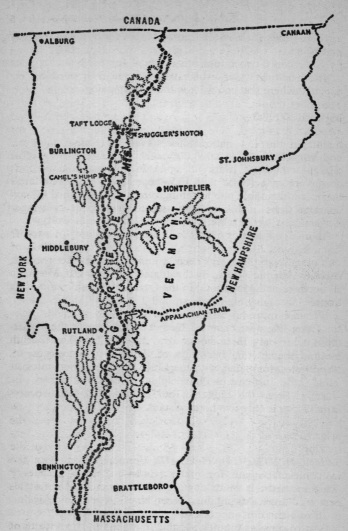

Vermont's Long Trail. This trail, over 255 miles long, roughly coincides with the Appalachian Trail between the Massachusetts border and a point slightly northeast of Rutland, where the latter trail branches off to the east.

are some sixty-three shelters, open or enclosed, along the way makes such a lightweight trip even more practical. These havens are never more than a day's hike apart.

The length of the Long Trail is a fraction over 255 miles, approximately a hundred miles longer than Vermont itself. The more than ninety side trails add another 170 miles, making a total of about 425 miles for the complete Long Trail system. Of this, the Green Mountain Club is responsible for maintaining a total of 265 miles, 175 miles of the Long Trail and 90 miles of side trails. The U. S. Forest Service is in charge of 80 miles of the Long Trail and of the largest part of the remaining side trails. The portion of the Long Trail between Vermont 100, near Sherburne Pass, and Massachusetts 2 at Blackinton, is associated with the younger Appalachian Trail.

There is one shelter for about every four miles of trail. If you'd like to earn the right to join the End-to-End Club of one of this country's major trails, here's a good place to start. Incidentally, the way to walk all these north-south footpaths is northward, if possible. Then you are considerably less troubled by sun in the eyes.

Detailed information on the Long Trail is available from the Green Mountain Club, 108 Merchants Row, Rutland, Vermont, which puts out an up-to-date guidebook to this footpath in the wilderness. This easily packed booklet gives the mapped, step-by-step story. Some other publications also are available.

RIDING AND HIKING TRAIL. With nationwide interest in wilderness hiking increasing at a remarkable rate, big new trail systems are still being developed. One of these is the projected 3000-mile California Riding and Hiking Trail, extending from San Ysidro near Mexico northward through the Tehachapi Mountains and the Sierra Nevada to near the Oregon line, and returning in a long loop through the breezy coast mountains. Something over a thousand miles of this new trail have already been completed and are being enthusiastically used.

Construction specifications call for a minimum trail width of thirty inches to be built through a twenty-foot right of way. A system of overnight camps has been started. Units are to be spaced some fifteen to twenty miles apart, with facilities consisting of stoves, tables, water, sanitation, and corrals. Numerous secondary trails are already planned. All in all, the wilderness through which these three thousand miles loop is among the most magnificent in the West.

Although in several counties the trail is complete and in use, in some others the acquisition of rights of way has just been started. Where the trail goes through federal lands, construction and maintenance are being handled by the U. S. Forest Service and the National Park Service. In other areas the construction and maintenance are under the supervision of the Department of Parks and Recreation in Sacramento, California, from which current information is available.

THE BIG ONES. Then there is the 1,995-mile footpath known as the Appalachian Trail, with its chain of free lean-tos and fireplaces, which twists from Mount Katahdin in Maine to Springer Mountain in Georgia. On the other side of the continent, the rugged 2,156-mile Pacific Crest Trail extends from Canada to Mexico in a country-long slash from near Mount Baker in Washington to Campo in San Diego County, California. Both are enlivened by hundreds of miles of secondary trails that invite side excursions.

The Appalachian Trail is a free, serene, slightly incredible footpath that crosses the sparkling lake and mountain country south of Maine, goes through the Green and White Mountains and the Berkshire Hills, and finally leads through the restful wild areas along the crests of the Catskill, Allegheny, Blue Ridge, and the Great Smoky mountains to its southern terminus.

Among the feeder paths to this great wilderness thoroughfare is the Horseshoe Trail, which starts at the historic Valley Forge battlefield and joins the main Appalachian Trail at Manada Gap, Pennsylvania. The Horseshoe, unlike the parent route, is a riding lane as well as a footpath. There also are numerous motor roads that cross the summits of these mountains, thus tapping the Trail and providing easy access to it from any of the eastern states.

The wilderness way twines, for the most part, at elevations of 2,000-5,000 feet through high wooded mountains with many open crests. It passes through a well-watered country. There are campgrounds with fireplaces and a large number of lean-tos along it for those who do not choose to pack their

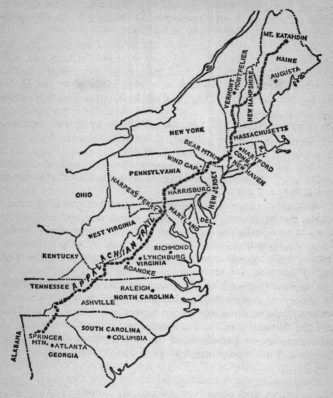

The Appalachian Trail. Popular with hikers, this famous trail extends from Maine to Georgia.

own shelter. Innumerable camp spots exist everywhere for the more experienced.

Weather and travel conditions are best from about the middle of June to late September. The climate at these generally high altitudes is a relief during the summer months from the swelter of the lowlands—and from the noise and grime of nervous vacation traffic. Hiking and camping under nearly

The Pacific Crest Trail. This rugged trail, extending from Canada to Mexico, is, for the most part, a wilderness route for expert outdoorsmen.

arctic conditions is possible for the more strenuous during the snowy months.

Here and there along the Appalachian Trail will be found an occasional lodge and small vacation resort. As a rule, however, it is still all wilderness. Those who plan to take fullest advantage of the outdoor opportunities the country affords must pack shelter and food on their backs, as it is a hiker's route and not a horse trail.

It is unnecessary to overburden oneself with weighty equipment and food. The mild summer nights demand a minimum of bedding, except in the White Mountains area above timberline, where the weather is unpredictable. A very light down bag is ideal. Every three or four hiking days along the Trail there are branch paths, and sometimes roads, winding down to farming land and small villages where country stores afford a chance to replenish food supplies. Good fishing abounds in many of the streams that splash from the crests.

The Appalachian Trail is a volunteer recreational project. It is supervised and maintained by the Appalachian Trail Conference, with headquarters at 1916 Sunderland Place, N. W., Washington 20036, D.C. This is a federation of organizations, mainly outing clubs, and individuals interested in the footpath. Its activities and objectives are entirely voluntary. Having no salaried employees, it furnishes complete information about the trail by means of its pamphlets, guidebooks, bulletins, and maps. A small charge is made for these. The funds so derived are used to republish the literature.

The Pacific Crest Trail extends from Canada to Mexico along the crests of the Cascade, Sierra Nevada, and Sierra Madre mountains. It incorporates seven major units, largely built and maintained by the National Park Service. These are almost entirely within government parks and forests. Only some 160 miles, in fact, lie outside these public lands.

The long path, skirting such famous mountains as Rainier, Adams, Hood, Shasta, and towering Whitney, is not a rustic

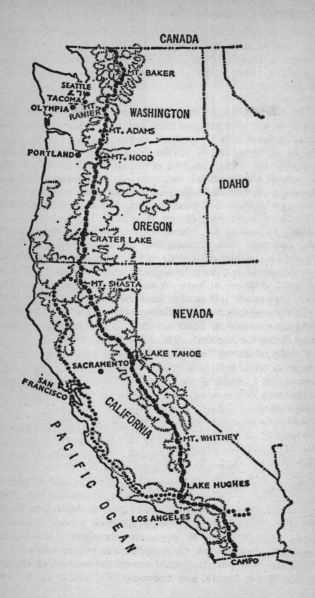

lane for picnic parties. It is, in its rugged course from lodge-pole pine to dusty cactus, a wilderness route for expert out-doorsmen. This does not imply that numerous scenic portions of the Trail, particularly in California, are not entirely feasible for families with eight-year-old children and eighty-year-old grandparents. They are.

The Sierra Club, Mills Tower, San Francisco 94104, California, is the organization that has done the most work in bringing the Pacific Crest Trail to the attention of the public and in fostering all it stands for. Founded in 1892 with naturalist John Muir its first president, the Sierra Club with its present thousands of members each year organizes trips into the high hills and along the star-scouring routes where it maintains numerous campsites, huts, and cheerful lean-tos.

Much of the robust course is suitable for well-shod pack animals as well as for hikers. Most of it passes through very wild country with considerable distances between supply points. This is higher, steeper in spots, than the Appalachian Trail. Some of it zigzags to altitudes one and two miles above sea level. Because of snow in the high country, portions are not always penetrable until at least well into July.

Only a few railroads and highways cross the main Trail. All along the mountains, however, there are numerous roads entering from the lowlands. These bring you to it after one or two days of travel from traffic-clogged highways. Some of these side trails are, as a matter of fact, equal in scenic and recreational features to the north-south wilderness path itself. At the ends of many of these approaches will be found out-fitters with pack animals and supplies for trail travel.

You can arrange, if you want, for a packer with his train to take you along the trail as far as you wish, perhaps going in over one lateral road and coming out along another. The more popular plan, when you aren't going to do all the walking, though, is to have an outfitter pack your duffle into a more or less permanent camp in some favorably situated locality, and then pick you up to go out on some pre-arranged date. In the meantime, you can explore the region with a back pack. The country is so vast, and in most areas the scenery is so varied and grand, that you can easily spend a month or more taking short trips from an established camp and never exhaust the possibilities for variety and enjoyment.

The Pacific Crest Trail is the roughest of the four. Too, the nights there are apt to be cooler than on the East's Appalachian Trail and the Long Trail. In the West, therefore, depending, of course, on where you hike, some of your equipment may well approach that of the Alpinist. Strong mountain shoes, preferably with cleated rubber soles that will cut through gravel and give you sure footing on rocks, are highly desirable. You'll probably appreciate a warm jacket, shirt, or sweater for the evenings. Bedding in general should be a little heavier than along the Atlantic heights of the continent. A down sleeping bag, a mummy type weighing not over five pounds, will be excellent.

Along neither route is a regular tent essential during moderate weather. A compact plastic poncho, weighing less than a pound, will pinch-hit perfectly for both raincoat and shelter.

A compass is always desirable, as it is everywhere in wild places. Although the main wilderness trails are well marked, it is easy to get mixed up on directions in the haze and clouds often encountered at high altitudes.

AVAILABLE MAPS

The trail organizations mentioned have available sometimes extremely detailed maps of their routes with, in some accompanying guide publications, almost step-by-step directions.

The best Pacific Crest Trail maps are those published by the U.S. Forest Service, Washington, D.C. If you will mention the particular sections of the trail in which you are interested, this division of the Department of Agriculture will suggest the names and the very low prices of the maps showing these.

The supervisors of the various national forests can furnish both planimetric maps of their areas and the names of outfitters in the regions you wish to penetrate. The two U. S. Forest Service regional headquarter offices covering the Trail area are located at 630 Sansome Street, San Francisco, California, 94111 and in the Post Office Building, Portland, Oregon 97208.

As none of these many widespread routes nor the regions adjacent to them can be reasonably negotiated nor thoroughly enjoyed without backpacking, a readily carried outfit containing equipment and food for each person is indispensable (see Chapter 4). Large tents and other heavy rigging are both unsuitable and handicapping, except for extended and rather expensive pack train trips. For backpacking, everything should be cut down in weight and bulk to absolute essentials. Food should be largely water-free.

ENCHANTED AND ENCHANTING

And so, at the end of the paved road—shouldering your pack and striding into enchanted and enchanting country— you leave behind the unhealthy tension, bustle, noises, fumes, expense, and frustrations of civilization. There is no other kind of vacation that can compare to these backpacking trips, none that will take you so close to peace and utter freedom.

And when you return, what a tale you'll have to tell about this entirely different world in which you've been. Everyone who has made such a lightweight hike, and has sat at night by crackling campfires deep in the wilderness, wants to go back.

Chapter 2

LEARNING NATURE'S WEATHER SIGNS

KNOWING what nature and the woods are saying about the weather is a skill essential to feeling and staying at home in the wilds.

Despite the innumerable legends that have built up around them over the centuries, animals are worthless as long-term weather forecasters. Their actions, however, often give a clue to the immediate climate.

Spiders show a most delicate apprehension of what weather conditions will be within the next few hours. When the day is to be fair and comparatively windless, they will spin long filaments over which they scout persistently. When precipitation is imminent, they shorten and tighten their snares and drowse dully in their centers. One of the best fair-weather signs is the familiar profusion of fresh webs over grass and shrubbery.

Insects are especially annoying before a storm. At such times they also cling vexingly to shelter canvas and to the screened windows of log cabins.

Too, insects do not fly as high as usual when bad weather is breeding, a fact you can verify by the heights at which the birds that feed on them soar. Swallows are especially good indicators.

If bees are swarming, fair weather will continue for at least the next half-day.

CLUES FROM ANIMAL BEHAVIOR

Elk particularly have built-in barometers. In the fall they will migrate suddenly out of high country just before heavy snows cover their feed and block the passes.

In moose and deer country, you can tell when a big storm is on the way by the unusually heavy feeding activity. The animals then lie up in cover until the bad weather is nearly over, whereupon they again feed vigorously.

In the snowy north, the wilderness becomes alive with tracks, and both wild and domestic animals become youthfully frisky before a chinook, the hot, dry west wind that sometimes lifts temperatures close to 100° within an hour and which the Indians call "snow eater."

But long-term weather proverbs involving the animal kingdom are just so much fiction. Goose bones or, for that matter, the thickness of hickory shells, have no bearing on what the weather will be. As far as that goes, neither does the thickness of fur. The depth of a bear's den means nothing weatherwise. And when bruin emerges earlier than usual in the spring, only to return to his bed, it doesn't indicate more wintry weather, but merely that there is not yet enough food to satisfy his huge appetite.

If the groundhog does not see his shadow on February 2, winter is not necessarily over. When squirrels lay in heavy caches of food, it does not follow that a severe winter will ensue.

Night birds call every night, although it is true that their sound carries farther just before a storm. Other birds, such as waterfowl, cannot sense the weather more than a few hours ahead, or so many thousands would not be entrapped and killed by storms or by returning north too far in advance of the tardy spring.

OTHER NATURAL SIGNS

There are certain time-tested and accurate signs by which the woodsman, especially when he balances one against another, can forecast the immediate weather. However, two companion proverbs should always be considered. In dry weather all signs fail. In wet weather it rains without half trying.

When campfire or cabin smoke, after lifting a short distance with the heated air, beats downward, it is a sign of approaching storm. On the other hand, steadily rising smoke prognosticates fair weather.

A red sun or sky in the morning indicates nearing rain. When forest fires are burning, this effect can be deceptive because of smoke. The redness, however, is still deepened by the tell-tale presence of excessive moisture in the atmosphere.

A red evening sky shows that the air contains so little moisture that rain within the next twenty-four hours is highly improbable.

A gray, overcast evening sky shows that the moisture-carrying dust particles in the atmosphere have become so overloaded with water that conditions favor rain.

A gray morning sky, implying dry air above the haze caused by the collecting of dew on the dust in the lower atmosphere, justifies the expectation of a fair day.

When sudden green light slants from the late afternoon sun as it sinks behind a clear horizon, fair weather is probable for at least the next twenty-four hours.

A rainbow late in the afternoon indicates fair weather ahead. However, rainbow in the morning, woodsman, take warning.

A corona is the circle that appears around the sun or moon when either shines through clouds. When this corona grows larger and larger, it shows that the drops of water in the atmosphere are evaporating and that the weather probably will be clear. When a corona shrinks by the hour, it means that the water drops in the clouds are becoming so large that rain is almost sure to fall.

When the breeze is such that leaves show their undersides, a storm is in the offing.

When you are in the mountains, the sight of morning mist rising from ravines is an excellent sign of clear weather.

In fair weather, as any hunter can tell you, air currents flow down streams and hillsides in the early morning. They start drifting back towards sunset. Any reversal of these directions warns of a nearing storm.

The higher the clouds, the better the weather. Prospects are even finer when scattered clouds, preferably decreasing in numbers, are separated by brilliant clear blue. The combining of clouds, especially in a milky sky, does not augur so well.

A night sky alive with stars is a good sign. Except near the coast where fog may give a deceptive picture, when only a few stars gleam the clear weather is about over.

When thin but tight cloud cover slowly blankets the moon, the spell of fair weather is coming to an end.

Dew and frost occur abundantly only when the atmosphere is such that rain and snow can scarcely fall. On calm nights, one or the other, depending on the season, fails to form only when conditions favor precipitation.

Anyone who has a touch of rheumatism can forecast approaching bad weather by the onset of increasing discomfort.

When sound travels more distinctly, and you are able to hear distant noises such as woodchopping more clearly, stormy weather is coming.

You also can smell an approaching storm in that ground, swamp, muskeg, and tideland smells become more noticeable.

Another sign of the approaching storm is the increase of high wind and its gradual extension to lower and lower air, causing the forest to murmur and the mountains to roar.

As the air grows damper and stormy weather comes nearer, canvas, hemp rope, and ax heads tighten; camp salt picks up moisture; and curly hair, whether in humans or animals, becomes more unruly.

CLOUDS

When moist air is cooled, water molecules condense on dust and other particles in the atmosphere. As more and more of these molecules collect, they form drops of water. When enough of these drops float together, they combine into a cloud.

Still other clouds, massing together at subfreezing heights, are made up of ice.

Clouds provide the most accurate signposts for wilderness weather forecasting. It is necessary to keep watching them, however. Even more important than momentarily predominant cloud formations is the way they change.

CUMULUS. Cumulus clouds are fair weather clouds. Too, clear nights usually follow days when cumulus clouds drift dramatically and picturesquely through the sky.

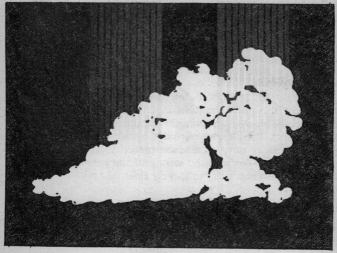

Cumulus Cloud

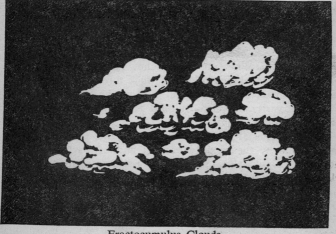

Fractocumulus Clouds

Cumulus clouds, which grow as warmed air soars skyward until its water vapor cools into drops of moisture, heap themselves into flatbottomed piles. Towards evening, when this process slows, they become small or even non-existent. At their heights, they measure from about a thousand feet to more than a mile thick from puffy tops to flattened bases.

FRACTOCUMULUS. Being formed when strong overhead gales blow the fluffy cumulus clouds into shreds that hurtle across the heavens, fractocumulus clouds indicate the presence of high wind. Their speed helps distinguish them from younger clouds that have not yet reached maturity. In late afternoon when the winds die with the setting of the sun, fractocumulus formations also ebb away to leave a clear fair sky.

STRATOCUMULUS. Although light showers may slant down from stratocumulus clouds, these formations generally thin to cumulus or fractocumulus by the middle afternoon and later disappear entirely, leaving a clear night sky. They also form at sunset when cumulus clouds blend into one another before dissipating. Spreading in irregular patches or layers, stratocumulus clouds are not as fluffy as cumulus.

STRATUS. Stratus clouds of themselves often bring light drizzle but seldom rain. When thin stratus clouds form during the night to cover the morning sun, they usually mean a warm clear day.

Stratus clouds are layers of water particles, flat on top as well as bottom. When one approaches, its edge appears to be nearly straight and almost equally thick throughout. Although some are small, others cover all that can be seen of the sky. Thickness varies, too, from almost a quarter of a mile to a few, sun-filtered feet.

The high coastal fogs of California, Maine, and Newfoundland, made by the mixture of cold and of warm moist air above the mingling ocean currents, are stratus clouds that form close to a thousand feet above the surface of the Earth and thicken downward. Such fogs customarily dissipate in sunlit skies.

However, pure stratus is the predominant cloud when the center of a low-pressure area is approaching. When this is the

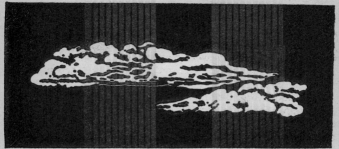

Stratocumulus Clouds

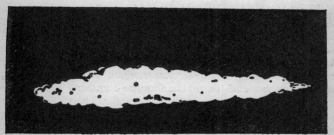

Stratus Cloud

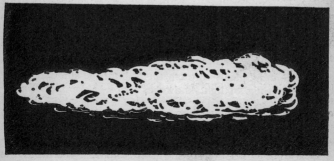

Nimbostratus Cloud

case, the stratus generally gives way to the denser nimbo-stratus, which is characterized by rain or snow. When the low is passing, the nimbostratus may revert again to stratus or to the wind-churned fractostratus. This latter usually disappears to leave a clear sky alive with cirrus tufts.

NIMBOSTRATUS. Nimbostratus clouds in three out of four instances indicate rain or snow within four or five hours. The duration of such storms varies, but in winter snow often lines down from them for about eight hours.

These layers of gray rain or snow clouds, darkening the day, many times sheet the sky for miles. Although their average height is about 3,500 feet, some almost scrape the treetops, while others soar nearly three miles high. Rags of clouds that move beneath them, dangling like torn remnants, are known as scud.

CIRRUS. When the sky is brilliantly blue above cirrus, the clouds will probably dissipate during the morning, leaving clear skies. This happens when the heat of the forenoon sun, attacking the floating ice of these clouds which form some five to seven miles above the earth, changes them again to vapor.

Cirrus clouds resemble thin curls and wisps of soft hair. Some are straightened by the wind except for a twirl at one end, while others are filigreed in silvery nets that nearly enclose the sky. Those that are blown into wispy streaks are called mares' tails.

CIRROSTRATUS. When the sky is grayish above cirrus, the clouds likely will thicken to cirrostratus, as rain or snow is probably on the move. Cirrostratus clouds almost always indicate that a storm is no more than a day away.

Cirrostratus clouds, which are made up of ice particles, look like white veils, often decorated with milky streaks and patches. Shining hazily through them, both the sun and moon form misty rings of light known as halos. These clouds may float as high as the loftiest cirrus, but the biggest and densest of them usually are no more than about 18,000 feet above the ground.

ALTOSTRATUS. As the storm area approaches, the cirro-stratus clouds thicken and lower to altostratus which either

Cirrus Cloud

Cirrostratus Cloud

completely hide the sun and moon or let their light through in shapeless blobs. Altostratus clouds look like gray or dull blue haze, banded or spotted with thick streaks or patches. The rain or snow that usually follows generally is steady but not very hard. These clouds range in height from some two to three and one half miles.

CIRROCUMULUS. Cirrocumulus clouds are almost always a sign of fair weather. They commonly appear the first or second morning following a storm, usually dissolving that fore-noon to leave a flawless, deeply azure sky.

So-called mackerel skies, resembling the patterns on this fish's back, are the result of floating rows of cirrocumulus. Being made of ice, inasmuch as they form at heights of from three to five miles, cirrocumulus clouds are about midway between puffy cumulus and wispy cirrus. They are seen near cirrus and cirrostratus. They are so thin and shadowless that diffused sunlight beams through them cheerily.

ALTOCUMULUS. The altocumulus is another fair weather cloud, usually showing itself on the first day following a storm or forming above the breaking stratus. However, when these clouds take on the aspect of towers and castles, they generally mean that showers will be arriving in eight hours.

These small, high, white clouds often tag one another so closely that the sky seems packed with tightly massed white mounds. Floating from one to four miles high, they are some-times assailed by up-and-down currents that divide them into flakes resembling those of a mackerel sky. The lower portions of these clouds often are gray, however, and the larger ones run their shadows across the ground.

CUMULONIMBUS. These towering piles of rain clouds, usually forming on moist hot days, often cause hail as well as rain. Since they contain lightning and thunder as well, they are commonly called thunderheads, even when they do not result in precipitation.

Thunderheads start out as puffy cumulus clouds some 2,000 feet above the earth, piling and towering into dramatically ominous heaps up to seven miles high. When these gleaming white masses are toward the southwest, they can be expected to

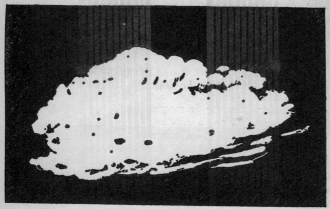

Altostratus Cloud

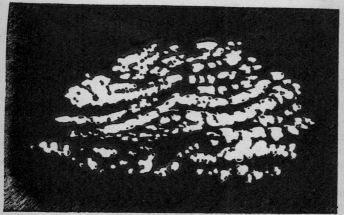

Cirrocumulus Clouds

approach steadily, darkening to blue, purple, and even green, as they do so. Sheets of rain often can be seen in the distance. Then the day suddenly chills and darkens.

Afterwards, the precipitation abruptly slackens. The thunder again becomes a distant rumble. Fresh wind, cool and invigorating, blows out of the west.

Being in the wilderness during the height of the most spectacular thunder storm of the season is far less dangerous than

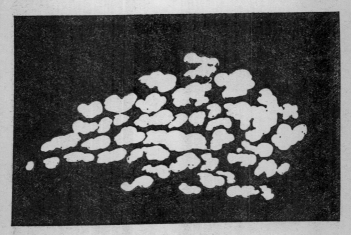

Altocumulus Cloud

driving downtown to the store. Taking certain precautions will lessen even this very small amount of peril.

Although it is natural to seek shelter from the rain, the worst refuge you can pick is a tall, isolated tree. Small evergreen growth offers much better, as well as comparatively safe, protection. So does a cave or a niche among overhanging rocks. If you come upon a barn, stay out of it, as the mass of dry, warm air within invites the passage of electrical bolts. It is best to lay down such natural lightning rods as metal fishing rods. If you are caught in the open, your safest procedure will be to lie flat.

Cumulonimbus Cloud

HOW TO READ A BAROMETER

A small aneroid (without fluid) barometer, whose rising needle is so handy for prognosticating the best fishing days, can be of considerable help in weather forecasting when you are away from newspapers and radios.

Unless you are traveling particularly light, a good one is a wise addition to most wilderness outfits. The following facts will help you read it in the United States and Canada.

BAROMETER	WIND	WEATHER
High, steady	S.W. to N.W.	Fair with little temperature change for one to two days
High, rising rapidly	S.W. to N.W.	Fair with warmer weather and rain within two days
High, falling rapidly	E. to N.E.	Summer: rain in 12 to 24 hrs. Winter: snow or rain with increasing wind
Very high, falling slowly	S.W. to N.W.	Fair, with slowly rising temperatures, for two days
High, falling rapidly	S. to S.E.	Rain, with increasing wind, in 12 to 24 hrs.
High, falling slowly	S. to S.E.	Rain within 24 hrs.
High, falling slowly	E. to N.E.	Summer: light winds, fair Winter: precipitation in 24 hrs.
High, falling slowly	S.W. to N.W.	Rain within 24 to 36 hrs.
Low, rising rapidly	Shifting to W.	Colder and clearing
Low, rising slowly	S. to S.W.	Clearing soon and fair for several days
Low, falling slowly	S.E. to N.E.	Rain for one or two more days
Low, falling rapidly	E. to N.	Northeast winds with heavy rain or snow, followed in winter by cold

GAUGING WIND SPEED

The wind, the moisture content of the air, and the sun all make weather. Of these, the wind is many times the most interesting, especially in the wilderness. When you are bucking it in a canoe or trying to keep out of the way of toppling branches, you often wonder exactly how fast it is blowing. The following table will then be of use:

Beaufort Scale	Wind Velocity (mph)	Air	Signs
0	0-1	Calm	Smoke rises straight up
1	1-3	Light air	Wind direction shown by drifting smoke, but not by waves
2	4-7	Slight breeze	Wind felt on face, leaves rustle, ordinary waves moved by wind
3	8-12	Gentle breeze	Leaves and twigs move constantly, flag extends
4	13-18	Moderate breeze	Dust and small branches are moved
5	19-24	Fresh breeze	Small-leafed trees start to sway
6	25-31	Strong breeze	Large branches move
7	32-38	Moderate gale	Whole trees in motion
8	39-46	Fresh gale	Twigs break off; hard to walk
9	47-54	Strong gale	Slight structural damage occurs
10	55-63	Whole gale	Trees uprooted, considerable structural damage
11	64-72	Storm	Widespread damage, very rarely experienced
12	73 up	Hurricane	Devastation occurs

Chapter 3

DRESSING FOR
WOODLAND COMFORT

HE WHO tames the wilds begins with meeting the wilds on even terms by dressing for the occasion.

The boot, where the woodsman and the wilderness meet, is the most important part of the clothing category. Poorly fitted and chosen footwear has taken the edge off far too many outdoor vacations.

The matter is a serious one. The individual taking to the woods for the first time on a trip that requires long and difficult foot travel is apt to discover, when it's too late, that he is committed to footwear that will handicap or badly cripple him, thus ruining the grand outing he has possibly been planning for years.

The shoe size you wear in the city, and the one the ordinary salesman there will measure you for, will, perhaps, do well enough for the several miles of walking which is all many of us cover on a usual outing. But beware of this size for a daily tramp of eight or more miles over wild country, especially if it is hilly.

One such excursion in city-size footwear will almost certainly lay you up with blisters and abrasions. After three or four miles of hiking over rugged terrain, feet swell considerably because of the repeated and varying pressure of walking, and because of the increased blood supply that is pumped into them by the stimulation of exercise. The shoes you select must be large enough to remain comfortable when your feet are in this enlarged condition.

ASSURING FOOT COMFORT

SOCKS

The simple but all-important formula for wilderness walking is heavy socks and big shoes. Regardless of heat or cold, dryness or wet, only wool socks are suitable for long hikes, although nylon reinforcements at toes and heels may help to extend their lives. These socks may vary from thin to medium during the summer and from medium to heavy during the frosty months.

Throughout the year, however, wear only top quality, finely processed, and well-made woolens. Don't have anything to do with shoddy products if you can possibly avoid it. Poor woolens mat. They contain impurities that irritate the feet. They wear poorly. As for loosely and skimpily knit socks, these are an abomination from the first day you put them on.

A few individuals' feet seem to be allergic to wool. Such hikers often can wear thin socks of some other material under the wool with advantage. These may be made of cotton. Some select nylon, which certainly is long-wearing but which, for many, is a lot too slippery unless either worn too tightly or gartered in some manner, neither of which practice is compatible with the outdoor routine.

Wear only well-fitting and fairly new socks with no rough seams nor unduly harsh darned spots. If your feet are tender, dust both them and your socks the first week with foot powder. Giving them alcohol baths at supply points will help toughen them.

In any event, wash your feet at least every night and change your socks daily. When the going is rough, it is refreshing to stop, when possible, during the day and bathe the feet. When afoot, many carry an extra pair of socks on the outside of the pack to switch to at that time. Actually, when the way is hot and you're perspiring considerably, the thing to do is to change socks frequently, hanging the damp socks on the outside of the pack where they can dry.

Good woolen socks are easily washed without shrinking, with soap and barely warm water. They should be rinsed, gently squeezed reasonably free of moisture without wringing, and stretched back into shape to dry slowly, preferably in the open breeze, but, in any event, well back from the campfire.

SELECTING PROPER SIZE OF FOOTWEAR

Taking the thickness of your socks into consideration, here is a general rule you can apply in selecting the ideal size of footwear for hard outdoor wear. With one pair of thin or medium wool socks, have your shoes one full size longer and one full size wider than your proper fit in city shoes. For heavy socks, have them one and one-half sizes larger. If half sizes are not available, increase to the next full size.

For the additional pair of socks that may be desirable in extremely cold weather, experiment to get the same comparative freedom of fit as above. Incidentally, three closely packed pairs of socks afford less warmth than do two loose pairs. Aside from the fact that circulation is impeded by such a tight fit, the resulting compression of the fibers cuts down on the insulative dead air space.

What some bushmen do is purchase woolen tubing similar to elongated stocking legs. All they have to do is tie pieces of string around the bottoms of two such tubes and draw them on like ordinary stockings.

When what amounts to the heel of one tube wears through, standard operating procedure is to twist it around so the hole is over the instep. Using the initial hole as a guide and subsequently turning the tube first to one side and later to the other, one can wear each tube in four different positions without mending. Nor, in many cases, is that all. The woodsman finally cuts off the entire section that had served as the foot, reties the string, and begins the process anew.

Because the same principle also can be employed with ordinary stockings, it is not a bad dodge to remember in an emergency.

AVOIDING COLD FEET

There is an entirely different way to combat cold feet, inasmuch as limits of effective insulation on the feet are rather quickly reached. This is a reason why the answer to cold feet isn't necessarily thicker and warmer footwear. Oddly enough, it is an extra shirt or some other additional insulation around the waist, chest, and back that may warm the feet without any alteration of footwear.

Depending on the requirements, the body is always regulating its heat, either warming or cooling itself. In the preceding instance, the accumulation of excess heat in the torso results in a cooling requirement. This is achieved by the directing of the overwarm blood to the extremities. As a consequence, these act as radiators and, incidentally, are kept warm themselves. This effect can be concentrated in the feet, of course, by keeping the head and hands extra warm.

INSOLES

Insoles frequently are added to provide additional insulation, cushioning, arch support, and a more comfortable fit. They are most frequently made of leather, felt, and lambskin, all of which pick up moisture and should be taken out periodically for drying separately. Insoles also are obtainable in woven synthetic fiber, non-absorbent and non-matting, whose loose structure helps ventilate the feet.

BREAKING IN FOOTWEAR

It is highly important that you break in new footwear well in advance of a trip. Some have feet that are shaped different from normal, and some have deformities probably more or less caused by past improper, if stylish, fittings of city shoes. The lasts on which good outdoor shoes are made, changing as foot sizes themselves have enlarged over the generations, are designed for normal extremities. When shoes are new, even when correctly fitted, they may bring undue pressure on parts of your feet. The new footwear will gradually stretch at those points, however, if broken in slowly and easily.

There are two functional ways of breaking in new leather shoes. You can do it gradually by hiking two miles the first day, three miles the second, and so on up to five miles, by which time the process should be completed. The second method consists of standing in four inches of water for fifteen minutes and then hiking until the shoes dry on your feet.

TYPES OF FOOTWEAR AND THEIR USES

HIGH-TOP BOOTS. High tops almost always sag and wrinkle more or less at the ankle. This can bring pressure on the Achilles tendon at the back of your ankle. It is true that this becomes negligible in the case of gradually softened and well broken-in leather tops, and that in the case of any boot, it can be offset to a large extent by the insertion of some stiffener, such as folded heavy paper or a piece of birch bark.

Unless there is a definite and valid reason for high tops, however, the fact remains that this pressure, if not relieved, will set up a painful inflammation of the sheath through which this greatest tendon of our body runs. Medically, this is known as synovitis. The only cure for this is ten days off the feet.

There also is the weight factor. A boot with a ten-inch top will weigh about eight ounces more than one which is six inches high. This is an additional half-pound to be lifted three inches high and to be carried 28 inches ahead about 2,500 times every mile. Such additional expenditure of energy really accumulates on a long, all-day tramp.

CANVAS SNEAKERS. Ordinary rubber-soled sneakers and basketball shoes are popular along fairly smooth wilderness ways, such as the Appalachian Trail, and in comparatively dry country, such as found along stretches of the Sierra Trail. For rugged use, don't buy the low ones, however. Rather, select those with tops about six inches high. The rubber soles should be roughly corrugated or substantially cleated as a safeguard against slipping.

The chief advantage afforded by such footwear is that of lightness, which is a joy. Although a hundred miles over rough terrain is about the limit for most, they offer an inexpensive way to outfit the growing children in a family. They are worn best with one pair of medium-weight woolen socks.

They soon wet through in rain and even in morning dew. This makes no particular difference, however, for they dry out quickly and without becoming stiff.

RUBBER BOTTOMS AND LEATHER TOPS. Boots with leather tops and rubber bottoms are popular especially when it's wet underfoot. For practically all wear, unless there is a definite reason to the contrary, they should be purchased with tops only six or eight inches high.

These boots should be worn with one or two pairs of wool socks and with insoles. For those who do not care for the flat-footed sensation that is characteristic of most such rubbers, leather insoles with arch supports are available. For very cold weather, these may be secured with clipped lambskin next to the feet.

The better boots of this sort are ideal for all expeditions except in the steepest country, because they are almost noiseless and because they can be kept water-repellent clear to the top. They're not good for wear in the very steep mountains of the West, particularly not on abrupt, snow-covered slopes. However, they can be very comfortably used in winter down to about twenty degrees below zero, although they get pretty frosty below that range. If worn with adequate insoles and not laced too tightly, the insoles and socks compress with each step and pump air in and out, ventilating the feet and making these boots excellent for summers where, even in fair weather, the ground is often wet with dew and there are swamplands.

HIKING BOOTS. The proven favorites among most trail veterans, especially in the West, are the special boots for hiking, both imported and domestic, stocked by the big catalog-issuing sporting goods dealers. Equipped with the best of rubber lug soles, these afford high traction and long wear. They are safe, comfortable, and quiet, but not inexpensive. However, with reasonable care, they will be good for years, especially as they can be resoled when necessary.

If your sporting goods dealer cannot readily obtain these for you locally, it is practical to order them by mail, as a proper fit is guaranteed. To measure your feet, put on the socks you intend to wear on the trail. Then stand on a piece of paper, distributing your weight equally on both feet. Holding a pencil vertically, clearly make the outline of each foot. Send these outlines to the outfitter, along with a notation of the length and width of your normal dress shoes.

SOLES FOR TRACTION

Neoprene rubber cleated soles are available which will grip on almost everything except glare ice and ice-covered rock.

These soles are the same type that are to be found on many of the best trail boots. Not only do they make resoling of regular mountain boots possible, but they can be attached to other shoes.

This makes it possible to turn a favorite pair of leather work or hunting boots into good trail performers, at the same time saving money. It is not practical, however, to buy such boots for this purpose, as, for very little more money, you can purchase ready-made boots especially designed for trail work.

These soles are generally available in two treads. One of these types of soles, of which there are different makes, has a deeper cleat for longer and more useful life during general hiking. A lighter model has a shallower cleat designed more particularly for rock climbing.

HOBNAILS. Hobnails, although noisy and requiring skillful use on smooth rock, still have their advocates. They are better than rubber on ice, crusted snow, and wet, mossy slants.

HOW TO MAKE MOCCASINS

If you have animal skins, you can make moccasins. You also can fashion moccasins from such fabrics as blankets, but in ordinary circumstances, these will seldom wear long enough to merit the trouble. Nor are excessively perishable hides worth bothering with for moccasins.

Soft tanned leather provides an easily worked and comfortably light material for moccasin-making, but it soon wears out in rough or wet going. In such places as the Continental Northwest, where this type of foot covering is worn a great deal, the ordinary practice is to protect moccasins from dampness with store rubbers and overshoes.

For a more enduring moccasin which will give the feet stauncher protection, it is best, especially under rugged conditions, to use as stiff and tough a chunk of hide as possible. In preparing the green skin, you should not take any steps to soften it. Not only should you not tan it, but you should scrape it only enough to smooth out any irregularities that might hurt the feet. The hair can be left facing inward.

One moccasin pattern which is as practical as it is simple is shown by the accompanying illustration. You can fit the pattern to your size by standing on the material to be used, or on a more easily manipulated sample, and first drawing an oval around the foot. Do not attempt to trace closely to the ends of the toes, in order to allow sufficient room for free movement.

You can then add about three inches all around for the sides of the moccasin. Or, if you have plenty of leather, you may want to bring these high around the ankle in two flaps, which can be tied by wrapping them with several turns of lacing.

You can save yourself work in the beginning by making, to start with, a trial moccasin from a correspondingly thick piece of fabric. Two of these can be used later, incidentally, as linings or slippers.

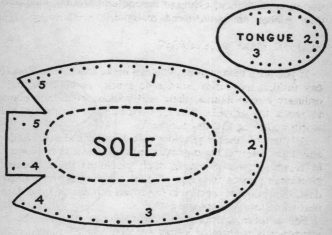

Moccasin Pattern

Once the pieces of the moccasin are cut, punch or slit holes around the edges, as shown in the drawing. Thongs can easily be made from odd bits of leather by cutting them around and around, as later described. These, or some other lacing should be run through the holes so as to join the parts as marked.

MAKING THE LACING

A thong or lace can be cut from something such as an old moccasin top or odd piece of rawhide. If you have a sharp knife, one method is to find a smooth log with a stub or branch sticking up for use as a guide. A nail or peg may also serve for this purpose.

Suppose you want a lace one-quarter of an inch thick? First, round any square corners from the leather. Second, start the lace, making one or two inches by severing a narrow strip of the correct width from the main stock.

Now comes the mechanics. Using a billet of wood, tap the knife point-first into the log so the blade is facing away from you one-fourth of an inch from the projection. Then place the lace between this guide and the knife. By pulling the lace and turning the leather, you can cut around and around, manufacturing as long a thong as there is material.

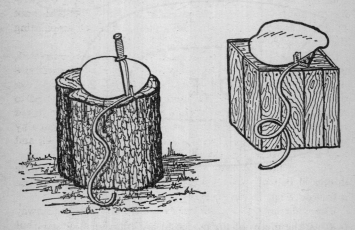

Making Lacing. As these drawings show, various implements may be used, but the basic technique remains the same. *Left:* using stump, knife, and peg. *Right:* using crate, razor blade, and wedge.

TANNING

Tanning is simple enough, like starting a fire with bow and drill, but it requires considerable work and infinite patience. If you do need leather instead of rawhide, if someone has just secured an animal such as a deer, and if you are staying in one place without too much else to occupy you, here is one of the primitive ways to go about the task.

Skin the animal carefully, taking care not to nick and cut the hide any more than necessary. With a sharp knife or similar instrument, working over your knee, if you want, remove as much flesh and fat as possible. Then weigh the skin down in water for several days, until patches of hair slip out when you give them an easy tug.

Upon retrieving the hide, lay it on a log, the bark of which you have removed, if that is necessary, for smoothness. Scrape one side and then the other, removing hair and grain. Many consider it best to complete this process in one operation before the hide dries. It can be redampened, however. By driving the point of the longest knife you have into a smooth knot of wood, you can provide an additional hold for manipulating the graining tool with both hands.

When this labor of eradicating hair and grain is completed, the still moist hide may be thoroughly rubbed with a mixture of, for instance, the animal's fat and brains that have been simmered together in equal amounts. The hide is allowed to remain in this state for several days. Then it should be washed as clean as possible. Wring it as well as you can, perhaps by rolling it loosely around two poles that are lying parallel, and then turning these in opposite directions.

The skin must then be pulled, rubbed, and stretched while drying, if you don't want it to become stiff. If you plan to use it for footwear, however, any rigidity will be a virtue.

The hide finally may be smoked by hanging it well away from the campfire for a few days, within reach of smoke, but not of heat. Or you can make a special smudge with green or rotten wood, taking the same precaution regarding warmth. The sweet oily fumes produced by birch achieve a particularly pleasing effect.

TREATING RAWHIDE

Rawhide is prepared more easily. You can dry the green skin in the shade, at odd moments scraping the flesh side as clean as possible with any dull instrument such as a piece of rock or bone, flattened on one side. A knife can be used, too, of course. The skin may be conveniently held by stretching across the knee that portion that is being worked. Or, like many, you may prefer to leave it tacked or pegged to some smooth surface where hungry birds will aid your efforts.

If you want the rawhide to be soft, you probably will have to wet the flesh side, allow it to dry, and then rescrape the skin, doing this as many times as may be necessary until the hide is satisfactorily pliable.

Care must be taken not to dampen the other side if retention of hair or fur is desired. If this is too long, it may be clipped. If you want it off entirely, this can be accomplished easily enough when the pelt is first secured by wetting the coat until it starts to slip, whereupon you can scrape it off in great clumps.

CARING FOR LEATHER

Wet leather footwear can be very quickly ruined if dried out near a campfire or stove. The best treatment is to scrape and wash off any dirt and mud, wipe off any free moisture, and then allow the gear to dry slowly in the air. If the bottoms are leather, shape will be better retained if the boots are first straightened and then stuffed with something, such as paper, dry clothing, or moss.

If any artificial warmth at all is used, it should be extremely mild. Even the natural enough procedure of hanging footwear at the far end of a hot cabin can very easily stiffen, shrink, crack, and ruin the leather. It is often well enough to be philosophical at the end of the day about wet shoes, figuring that if the woods are wet, they'll soon be soaked again anyway.

After footwear is nearly dry, and in any event periodically, they should be rubbed with neat's-foot oil or any good boot conditioner. These will go on easier and penetrate better if the leather is slightly warm. They should be rubbed with particular energy into wrinkles, stitchings, and the partition between the upper and the sole.

WEATHERPROOFING LEATHER FOOTWEAR

Leather footwear cannot be made entirely waterproof, nor would this be desirable. It then would defeat its own purpose by trapping perspiration and soon making the feet more uncomfortably wet than, under ordinary conditions, would be the case with leather that could breathe.

Boots may be fairly waterproof when new. After a few miles of hiking they will leak more or less at the seams, however, while, during continued immersion, some water will work through the leather. If dubbing is then worked thoroughly into the seams, they will again be fairly waterproof for a little while until the preparation wears off. This is one reason why leather footwear should be well treated about once a week when in use. Treating them more often can make them too soft.

When boots are to be put away until the next season, scrape all dirt or mud from them with a flat stick or brush. Wash with a mild soap and very little water, using a small hand brush. Remove all suds and wipe the insides dry with a clean cloth. It is a good idea to keep them in shape, either with boot trees or by stuffing them with crumpled newspapers. Then grease them and store them, away from pests, in a reasonably cool and dry place.

COMFORTABLE CLOTHING

This varies drastically, depending on the climate, and you will do well to make particular inquiries about what most often is worn where you plan to camp. One thing always holds true, however. Wear comfortable undergarments that will not bind or chafe. Cotton is a common choice.

Generally speaking, a woodsman perspires freely at times, and, under exertion, his clothing becomes more or less wet. Cotton garments are best for all hot and warm climates, since they are coolest. The perspiration which they absorb, however, makes them so cold that they can chill one as soon as this function slows down. When cotton is worn, the outdoorsman should have a rubdown and change to dry clothing as soon as he gets to camp. At least, if he is at all chilly, he should put on a woolen shirt or some other warm garment when he stops for the night.

For a cold or even chilly climate, all but the underclothing should be light wool throughout. Wool also gets wet from perspiration, but much of the water passes through it to be evaporated on the outside. Wet wool, moreover, does not feel particularly cold. It does not chill like wet cotton except when the wind is blowing very strongly. Under these circumstances, common in high country, a closely woven but still porous outside jacket of thin cotton should be taken for slipping on as a windbreak.

Wool is warm chiefly because of the insulating effect of the dead air held in the numerous tiny spaces among its fibers. A pair of light wool garments are warmer than a heavy one of the same total weight because of the additional air contained between the two of them.

THE LAYER SYSTEM OF WEARING CLOTHING

In extremely cold weather one can freeze quickly in wet clothing. It is very necessary under such circumstances to keep from perspiring excessively. This you can accomplish by shedding layers of clothing as you warm up, thereby always remaining moderately cool.

In fact, the layer system is best in the wilderness. In the chill of the morning, no matter if you are on the quickly varying desert or high on a northern range, many like to start with everything on. In any event, shed layers as the sun climbs higher. There is one thing to watch out for, though, and that is not to carry this too far. In the thin dry air of upper altitudes the sun burns deeply, even through a basic low-country tan. Back and shoulders, so important if you're backpacking, are especially vulnerable.

Another thing. It always is best to anticipate heat changes whenever possible and to open the clothing before you actually start to perspire and to close it again before really feeling chilly. This takes a certain amount of experience, of course, and often is one of the signs that a beginner is maturing into a veteran.

Be sure that clothing is not too tight or restrictive. Knees in particular should work freely. Incidentally, many like to have dirt-collecting cuffs removed and trousers staged about three inches shorter than city trousers. Otherwise, the trousers' legs, especially if they are at all full, have the habit of catching on snags and tripping one.

Picking out clothing with fast bright colors has several virtues. You are less likely to strike camp and leave some article behind drying on a bush. There is the factor of safety if you travel during hunting seasons, which, with some species, often last the year round. Too, such a selection can do a lot for color photography.

EIDERDOWN JACKET

A light eiderdown jacket is one of the most comfortable garments to draw on when you stop, tired but enthusiastic, for the night. They are even handy on the desert, as most such country gets surprisingly cold as soon as the sun sinks and the heat, with little moisture in the atmosphere to beat it back, radiates out of sand and rocks. Nights, when you bask in front of your campfire, one is luxurious against your otherwise chilly back. If your sleeping bag is the least bit cold, when you go to bed, spread this jacket between the robe and the mattress.

POCKETS

Pockets are so handy in the outdoors that special attention should be paid to their deepness and ruggedness when buying clothing for the woods. Because of the danger of losing your already limited essentials, it is well to get most or all of these with fasteners. Even on the side trousers pockets, for example, slide fasteners often are available, or you can install them yourself, using an especially smooth and husky zipper.

No compromise should be made with shirt pockets. Flap closures, buttoned or otherwise secured, are best. But if you have an old shirt that you plan to wear out on the trip and it has open pockets, either install flaps, or at the very least, snaps. With the latter arrangement, you'll have to secure the contents further as with a handkerchief wadded across the top of the opening.

The side trousers pockets should not be loaded, as often is done, in such a way that they interfere with free leg motion. As for pockets low in the legs, the feature of some older military surplus clothing, experiments have shown that it is three times more tiring to carry anything here than on the back.

RAINWEAR

A poncho is good for foul weather wear, except in thick going. It has the added virtue of performing as ground sheet, shelter, and other functions. When it is worn during rain, it is loose enough to permit ventilation. Admittedly, this looseness can be a problem on a windy day, but it is preferable to encasing the body in closely fitting rainwear that soon soaks one with perspiration.

Waterproof raiment, as, for example, an oil-silk shirt so thin that it may easily be carried in a breast pocket, can, if you are at all active, make you a lot more uncomfortably wet in a very short time than you'd get by staying out in the rain for a much longer period in an ordinary mackinaw.

Except in cold weather, when such a result can be fatal, or under circumstances when, by undermining strength, it can be dangerous, the matter has to do with individual ideas of comparative disagreeableness and is one of personal choice.

TREATING CLOTHING FOR WATER REPELLENCY. It is not uncommon for individuals to make such garments as stag shirts water-resistant by rubbing them with hands dipped in oil of one kind or another. If intense cold is a threat, however, such a practice can be dangerous in the extreme for two reasons: Grease directly and indirectly reduces the warming qualities of a garment by itself conducting body heat rapidly away, and by filling the inert air spaces in a fabric which otherwise provide most of its insulating characteristics.

WINDBREAKER

Although loose layers of clothing add up to the most efficient insulation for their weight, the air currents set up by body motion and those from the outside can still take away most of the garb's insulative value by preventing the establishment of dead air. Something must be provided to keep cooler air from constantly replacing this insulation of inert air. The easiest way to do this is to don a windbreaker. This should be as thin as durability will permit. The fabric, often poplin or something similar, should be woven as tightly as possible, while still permitting the necessary dissipation of body vapor.

INSULATIVE UNDERWEAR FOR COLD WEATHER COMFORT

No matter where you go, you'll do well to take the best of outdoor clothing, bought specifically for where you are going. The neatest trick for cold country comfort lies in some of the recently developed insulative underwear.

You have to be careful what you buy, however. Garments made from some of the synthetics trap perspiration as tightly as rubber. In weather that is at all warm, you might as well be traveling in a portable steam bath. In really cold going, more than just discomfort is at stake. Some entrapped perspiration freezes, and if you keep on trying to bull it through, so may you.

The difficulty at the subzero temperature encountered on some winter trails is not so much keeping warm, but doing so without too much weight and constraint while maintaining body ventilation. One garment which does this job is a light undersuit made with dacron polyester insulation quilted inside a nylon shell and lining. The considerably more expensive eiderdown, being lighter and more compressible, is even better.

Like eiderdown, though, this crimped dacron seems to have a built-in thermostat that adjusts it to widely varying temperatures. The easiest way to give this an assist in ordinary cold going? Just unzip the garment, as much and for as long as comfortable. Many find this satisfactory in temperatures ranging from —50° up to about 0°. When the weather becomes balmier, this undersuit generally becomes too warm.

The solution when you are on the trail and the weather gets too warm? Just take off either or both of the two parts and stow them in your pack. Together, they're far lighter and more compact than one ordinary heavy sweater.

During winter in most wilderness, winds have to be combatted in addition to cold temperatures. In a twenty-mile-per-hour head-on wind, regular woolen clothing loses about 55 per cent of the warmth it maintains in still air. Get a much faster wind in weather 30° below, and unless you put on windproofs, you feel as if you're wearing burlap. Dacron-insulated nylon checks the wind more effectively than most other satisfactory fabrics not built especially for this purpose. To get the fullest benefit from such an undersuit, however, you still need a windbreaker.

A fringe benefit is that such a suit can be worn effectively on cold nights as a second sleeping bag inside the regular combination.

MULTIPURPOSE BELTS

It is reasonable to desire every article selected for wilderness use to be functional in as many ways as feasible. An example is the belt which, although suspenders are admittedly more comfortable for supporting the heavier loads one pockets in the woods, most choose to hold up trousers and breeches.

A light, dressy band will serve the primary purpose. But a more rugged article with a stoutly attached buckle may one day be invaluable for lowering one safely from a precarious foothold, for strapping several saplings together for use as an emergency shelter, and for the numerous other odd tasks that arise when one is in the wilderness.

GLOVES OR MITTS

You may want a light pair of leather or woolen gloves to protect the hands. If warmth is an important factor, woolen mittens will be more satisfactory, especially if they extend high enough to shield the particularly vulnerable wrists, and if their tops also fit sufficiently close to exclude snow and debris which might otherwise necessitate frequent removals.

Those who have much reason to use mitts in the wilderness have found it suitable to have a slit made in the palm of one and a knitted flap added to cover that opening when it is not in use. With such a mitt on the master hand, one is enabled to bare the fingers quickly whenever this may become expedient.

In very cold weather, you may wish to add outer mitts. These may be of some windproof material such as tightly woven cotton, light and porous enough to maintain a circulation of air adequate to keep perspiration from collecting. An especially handy technique in this instance, in reasonably open country, is to join these mitts with a cord long enough to loop around the neck. Then, protected against loss by the cord, you can yank either hand bare in an instant with your teeth.

DRYING CLOTHING

Damp clothing taken into the sleeping bag will be largely dried by body heat. There are very great disadvantages to this practice, however, if it is overdone. For one thing, heat is consumed that otherwise would be used in keeping the body warm, and this may make you cold, especially when your metabolism is at its lowest ebb. For another, much of the moisture is picked up by the bag itself, increasing weight and decreasing warmth. Finally, it's uncomfortable to have any amount of damp clothing in the bag with you.

The best procedure, when at all possible, is to dry the clothing in the warmth of a stove or a crackling campfire. When this cannot be done, it may be just as well to be philosophical about the whole thing. If the clothing is the right sort, it will only be clammy and really uncomfortable when you first put it on in the morning. In any event, dripping shrubbery along the trail likely will soon wet it again, anyway.

Chapter 4

THE LOWDOWN
ON BACKPACKING

ONLY two packs are really satisfactory for the backpacking vacation. One is the alpine type of frame rucksack, usually with a single large and several smaller fabric compartments built around a strong, light, metal frame to which shoulder straps are fastened. The other is the pack board, basically a rectangular frame over which fabric is so tightly doubled and laced that a bundle lashed to it never touches the hiker's back. Both are obtainable in different sizes.

The best packs in the world for this type of recreation are variations of the pack board made in the United States and available in stores throughout the country.

Light, strong, and durable, such pack boards are made, in the main, of tough aluminum tubing, although such materials as nylon keep all hard surfaces away from the back. Carrying bags, obtainable from the same sources, fit to the frames. The result is utility plus convenience and comfort. Anyone planning to cover very many miles of recreational backpacking would do well, everything else being equal, to make such a pack the nucleus of his outfit. The wrong pack has ruined more such vacations than any other single item.

FRAME RUCKSACK

Whereas the aforementioned packs are in their present forms essentially American, although of course they evolved from the primitive backpacking experience both among the Indians and peoples the world over, the alpine type of frame rucksack is a European development. It largely replaced the pack board in Europe among those interested in packing as a recreation. This has been in part because of fashion, but it's also the result of the low center of gravity provided by such frame rucksacks as the Bergans variety, which makes them particularly adapted to such prime European sports as climbing and skiing. In recent years, however, the American pack boards have been making increasing inroads in Europe.

Frame rucksacks are, indeed, extremely comfortable with light loads. Their multipocketed sacks, whose utility is widely incorporated in the American packs, are certainly handy when you want to get at various parts of the load without unpacking the whole outfit. Besides dividing the sack into convenient compartments, these partitions also help the sack to keep its functional shape. The rucksacks' design, with the top of the sack hanging away from the back, makes them cool and keeps the point of gravity low.

This latter characteristic becomes a disadvantage, however, when heavy loads are carried. The backward tilt of the sack then becomes a drag on the hips and legs, at the same time pulling the body off balance. Another disadvantage of this

Bergan-Meis Frame Pack. A comfortable imported pack originating in Norway. Bag is mounted on a light tubular-steel framework, bow-shaped at the bottom. (*Abercrombie and Fitch, N.Y.C.*)

Lightweight Rucksack for Day Trips. Weighing only 2¼ pounds, this rucksack has a light metal frame and a sack size 12″ × 14″ × 5″—a typical rucksack adapted to short trips.

pack with heavy loads is its increased tendency to sway, further disrupting the balance.

Frame rucksacks, then, are functional for ordinary trail carrying only when the loads are relatively light. Lightness, of course, is a relative thing, being largely dependent on an individual's body weight. To sum up, it might be generalized that the Bergans type of frame rucksack is not the best choice for day-after-day trail packing when the load is more than 25 pounds.

PACK BOARDS

The usual loads carried during backpacking vacations are more comfortably supported the length of the back, rather than hanging away from it, and with the center of gravity over the hips. A pack frame, either with a convenient sack or with the fabric-wrapped load attached to the frame itself, is therefore recommended. It's true that the ordinary outfit will lighten as you eat your way along the trail. Experience, however, has shown that it is most practical to buy a pack for the heaviest loads that will be carried in it.

The pack board frame, with either a solid backing such as canvas, or with several large fabric bands top and bottom, will hold the properly packed load comfortably the length of the back and not just against the lower part. The best sacks, when one of these is used, are designed so the outfit will be packed close to the body and high. Then, leaning slightly forward places the center of the weight directly above the hips where it can be balanced with the least physical exertion.

The arrangement of the straps and the other components of this type of pack all combine to keep the weight so centered. However, the pack still must be advantageously packed. With too high a load, you tire yourself in all but the most even of terrain by constantly shifting the muscles to regain balance. A

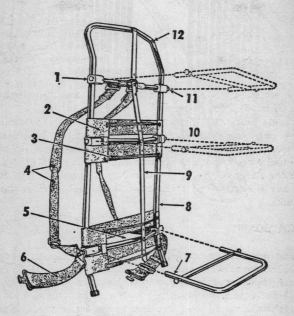

Features of a Modern Pack Frame. The Himalayan Sierra Pak #322 has /1—Magnesium locks /2—Nylon webbing /3—Self-locking laces /4—3-way control harness /5—Double space support /6—Quick release belt /7—Optional loading platform and optional platform locations /8—Titanium-aluminum space saver (frame can carry ½-pint of liquid; crossbars can carry matches, lines, hooks, etc.) /9—Bowrib /10—Nylon webbing /11—Six lash points /12—Smooth frame.

load with the weight too far back will drag backward on the shoulders.

Trailwise Pack Bag Model 71. This pack, featuring a contoured frame and handy patch-type map pocket, is suitable for an extended outing. (*The Ski Hut, 1615 University Ave., Berkeley, Calif. 94703*)

Himalayan Sierra Pak. The #322 Sierra Pak with #126 Summit Bag and #22 Stuff Bag. (*Himalayan Industries*)

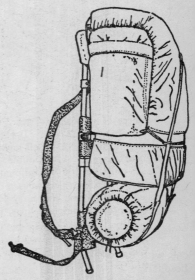

ALASKAN PACK BOARD

Another type of pack board that has been found eminently satisfactory is the Alaskan variety. The nucleus of this is a rectangular frame of wood or some other rigid material about 15 inches wide by 30 inches long, over which a canvas is doubled and tautly laced. There is about a 2½-inch space betwixt the two expanses of canvas which, because only one surface of canvas rests against the back, insures a free circulation of air. The effect is exactly as though you were lying on your back on a canvas cot.

There are two cross members to this frame, the top being about six inches below the top of the form. To it are attached, closely together, the two broad shoulder straps. These

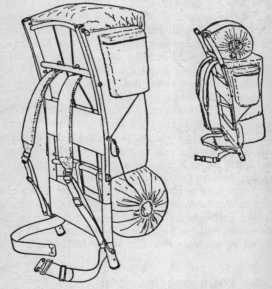

Kelty Mountaineer Pack. A comfortable, energy-conserving posture can be maintained for long-distance heavy packing with this Kelty model. (*A. I. Kelty Mfg. Co., P.O. Box 3453, Glendale, Calif. 91201*)

pass through a slit in the canvas on the side toward the back. Their lower ends are fastened to the lower outside corners of the frame.

Your outfit and food are tightly wrapped in a tarpaulin or other covering so a compact bundle is formed, depending on what you have, some 15 inches wide and about 30 inches long. This is lashed to the outside of the pack board. Because the load does not touch the back at all, being held away by the space between the two coverings of canvas, you can pack anything from a sack of fossils to an outboard motor without chafing or bruising.

The pack board should have its shoulder straps so adjusted that it sags just enough to rest some of the weight on the hips. The shoulder straps will then bear straight down on the top of the shoulders instead of pulling them uncomfortably backwards.

The commercial model of this type of pack, known as the Trapper Nelson Pack Board, can be obtained from almost all dealers in camp equipment. Three sizes are now made. The medium size, with a 26-inch by 14½-inch frame, is right for the average hiker. The small size, 24 inches by 13 inches, is excellent for women and youths. There also is a large size for heavy work, 30 inches by 14½ inches.

It can be had with a large canvas dunnage bag that laces to the frame. For lightweight packing with this type of pack, though, it is only extra weight. If you are going to get this sort of pack, it is generally best to obtain it without the bag and to tie your outfit on in a cover that has some other use, such as shelter, and so pays for its weight and bulk.

The Army used a similar pack board for heavy mountain carrying in World War II. This is strongly and substantially made over a fiberboard frame. Some still can be found in surplus stores. Although excellent for the stress of military use, though, these are unnecessarily heavy for backpacking vacations.

MAKING YOUR OWN PACK BOARD

If you'd like the fun of a personal project, or if perhaps you have to fit packs to a family and could use the resulting savings elsewhere, it's possible to build your own pack board of this type.

Procure some strips of Sitka spruce, oak, or other strong wood, 2¼ inches wide by ½ inch thick. Cut two strips 28 inches long for the sides of the frame. Round the top ends, but leave the bottom ends square.

Cut two other strips for the crosspieces, one 12 inches long and the other 15½ inches long. Join the two sidepieces by the two crosspieces, making a frame as shown in Fig. 1. The top of the upper cross member should come six inches down from the top ends of the sidepieces. The bottom of the lower cross member should be three inches above the bottom ends of the sidepieces.

The edge of the sidepieces and the flat of the crosspieces face the packer's back. Notice that the crosspieces are flush with the edge of the sidepieces farthest from the packer's back.

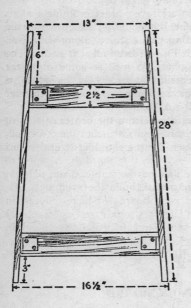

Figure 1. Frame dimensions and layout of homemade pack board.

The crosspieces must be fastened to the sidepieces very accurately and strongly. Use angle irons with wood screws in each face of the irons. Any machinist, or blacksmith, if you happen to live where one is handy, can make these bent pieces of metal in a very few minutes.

The resulting frame will be 13 inches wide at the top, 16½ inches wide at the bottom, 28 inches high, and 2½ inches thick. Using the same proportions, you can design as many different sizes as you need. Children, as well as adults, find these packs very rugged and comfortable. When the youngest member of the family finally outgrows his, so little money will be tied up in it that it can be passed along to some other young hiker without a qualm as to expense.

Over this frame lace a cover of, say, 12-ounce canvas, cut and made as shown in Fig. 2. This is, in this instance, 28 inches wide at the top, 35 inches at the bottom, and 25 inches high. It covers the frame to within 1½ inches of the top and bottom.

Hem it all around and insert seven brass grommets along each side edge to accommodate the lacing. These grommets are obtainable from many sporting goods stores, along with inexpensive tools for inserting them, and from all tent and awning makers. The latter two suppliers, as well as some outfitters, will insert them for a few cents if you prefer. On the side edge, hem the cover with two folds, fastening the grommets through both folds so they won't pull out.

Three and one-half inches down from the center of the top edge there should be a horizontal slit, 8 inches long, strongly reinforced at the edges. This is for the shoulder straps to pass through.

This canvas cover is laced around the frame, drum tight, by means of strong cod line, passed through the grommets. The

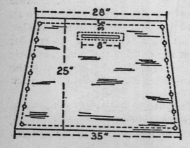

Figure 2. Layout for the pack board cover.

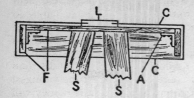

Figure 3. Top cross section of cover installation. *F*-Wooden frame. *A*-Angle iron (or aluminum angle strips for less weight). *C*-Canvas cover. *L*-Lacing. *S*-Shoulder straps.

slit comes on the side toward the packer's back. The lacing is done on the side of the frame where the crosspieces are flush with the edges of the sidepieces (see Fig. 3). The edges with the grommets should not meet by about two inches, so the canvas can be laced very tightly.

It should be mentioned in passing that some packers do away with the canvas entirely, lacing these and similar frames with long cord zigzagged ba k and forth through holes drilled about an inch apart along the sidepieces. This decreases the weight and increases the coolness, but the result is not so stable as canvas and will not hold up under heavier loads.

The upper ends of the shoulder straps are secured around the top crosspiece of the frame at the center. They pass through the slit in the canvas, then around and over the packer's shoulders, and finally are secured to the outside of the sidepieces of the frame six inches above the lower ends of these members as shown in Fig. 4. A piece of leather with a one-inch buckle is screwed to each of the sidepieces for this purpose.

The straps are best made of heavy, chrome-tanned leather, saturated with neat's-foot oil. They should be two inches wide at the top and where they go over the shoulders, tapering to an inch wide at the bottom where they are secured to the buckles. Too wide a strap passing through the armpits makes for chafing. Holes are punched in the straps to provide for their adjustment in length. If you will install these straps with the smooth side of the leather contacting the shoulders, the pack will be easier to slip on and off.

These days, it should be mentioned, firm wide nylon webbing is available, both in surplus stores and from outfitters, that can be tapered for the installation of buckles. Such webbing is excellent for use as straps. In either event, you will probably appreciate the use of shoulder pads, available so inexpensively that it's hardly worthwhile to bother trying to sew them at home. In a pinch, too, something such as heavy gloves shoved between strap and shoulder will make all the difference.

PUTTING ON THE PACK BOARD

In any event, after the straps have been adjusted for length, they can be slipped over the shoulders most conveniently, just as one puts on coat or suspenders. If you are alone and no elevated surface such as a stump or log is available, merely stand the loaded pack board upright on the ground. Sit down and place your arms through the straps. Run your thumbs under the straps to make sure they snuggle flatly into the shoulders. Then stand up.

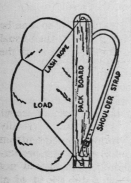

Figure 4. Side view of pack board with shoulder straps installed.

Figure 3 shows a section of this pack board as viewed looking down from the top. Figure 4 presents a side view with the shoulder straps in position and with a load lashed on the board. For this last, holes are drilled in the top and bottom of the sidepieces of the frame through which to attach the lashing ropes.

TUMP LINES

Tump lines and backpacking vacations don't really go together. The tump line, whereby part of the weight is supported by the head or forehead by means of a wide band attached by two lines to the load, is common to primitive freighting. In canoe country, too, where the freighting is over portages seldom as long as a mile, the tump line is common (see Chapter 11), often supporting one or more tarp-wrapped bundles, or taking part of the weight of a large, frameless pack, such as the Duluth, off the shoulders.

But such a pack heats and galls the back after an hour or more of packing. With head and neck immobilized by tump line, you cannot look around, enjoy the scenery, nor even properly survey the country ahead to pick out the best way. Your eyes are glued to the portage trail, and for the time being you are just a beast of burden with the tump line a tight band over your head.

WAIST BELT

A waist belt, weighing only some three ounces or so, can be welcome when you are starting out with a heavier-than-usual pack, both stabilizing the load and transferring some of the weight from the shoulders to the slope of the buttocks.

HOW TO PACK A LOAD

Briefly, the total weight of the backpack for mountain travel should not exceed about 35 pounds for young and physically fit men. This maximum should be pared down to some fifteen to twenty-five pounds for juniors and women. As for proportions, the equipment proper in the largest pack should not weigh over fifteen pounds, thus allowing a food load of at least twenty pounds.

In these days of lightweight grub, one can take off for a month at a time and have fun doing it. Furthermore, this time can be stretched when rations are supplemented with wild edibles like fish and berries as one goes along (see Chapters 9, 10, 11, and 24).

With loads changing constantly as food is used, packing is a matter of day-by-day ingenuity. There is something else, too, that should be emphasized. Packing always remains pretty much an individual affair. In other words, experiment until you find out what arrangement suits you best.

There are certain general fundamentals, however, that may serve as a basis for your trials. These differ somewhat, depending on the country. For example, too high a load will work against you two ways if you have to do much climbing. It's easy to overbalance in strenuous going, and such a load under these circumstances will tire you out just trying to keep it balanced. Secondly, when a load is packed high under such circumstances, it's difficult to get your head back to see where you're going.

The ideal, again, is to keep the weight tight to the body and comparatively high. The light sleeping bag, then, will probably go at the bottom, either in the sack, or wrapped separately below it. The lighter objects will graduate up from the bottom and will be placed at the front of the pack to press the heavier impediments toward your back.

That's really about all there is to it. Personal trials will do the rest. A couple of things. The load should ordinarily be packed so it's narrow enough not to interfere with the natural swing of the arms. Flat objects should be placed at the very back so parts of the load will not prod the spine.

A BASIC PACK

Pack	3 lbs.	12 oz.
Plastic tarp and poncho	1 lb.	5 oz.
Sleeping bag	3 lbs.	8 oz.
Cooking utensils*	1 lb.	12 oz.
First aid kit*		4 oz.
Underwear and socks		12 oz.
Wool shirt, jacket, or sweater	1 lb.	8 oz.
Toilet articles		8 oz.
Knife, whetstone		8 oz.
Flashlight		15 oz.
Needles, thread, buttons, personals		4 oz.
Total weight, without food	15 lbs.	

* In a party of two or more, these articles will be used in common, each individual carrying his share. Add a plate, cup, and spoon to cooking utensils for each additional hiker.

Chapter 5

GETTING THE MOST OUT OF FIRES

WHAT often remains most fondly in our minds after a wilderness trip are the campfires: the handful of crackling twigs that boils the kettle at noon; the cooking coals at the end of the day's fun, when odors build up in such a way that you can scarcely wait for that steak or flaky trout: the cheerful flames behind whose sanctuary you sit, while the darkening forest comes to life, and we watch moonlit magnificences reserved for those who venture into distant and deserted places.

Then there is that unforgettable first fire at dawn. Because of the air currents set into motion by the blending of day and night, it's colder now than it was during total darkness. The cook perhaps deposits an old pine stump, saved for the purpose, in the center of the fading overnight embers. This gives him a blaze like the light of a pressure lantern, and it also helps him to get some warmth into his extended fingers. Pretty soon he's thawed out enough to shove a pot grumpily into the heat. He then begins banging pans around, a little more expressively than necessary. Further sleep soon becomes impossible. The smells are too good, particularly the aroma of flapjacks and bacon.

Much of the success of a wilderness trip, as well as a great deal of the pleasure, is going to depend on your having the right kinds of fires. This does not mean, certainly, that camp-fires should be built in just one way. It all depends on where you are, what you have, and whether your most pressing need at the moment is warmth, light, or nourishment.

The principles governing outdoor fires do not change, however. In the realm of woodsmanship there probably is no one set of essentials so often mismanaged. A poor fire can cause a multitude of troubles. A good one is a joy to all around it.

WOODS TO BURN

When you want to start those food smells tantalizing your sensibilities in a hurry, the various dry softwoods, especially when split, will chortle into a quickly flaring blaze. For steadier and more conservative heat, the hardwoods are more satisfactory. For an enduring expanse of glowing coals, you will probably choose, when possible, such fuels as oak, hickory, and ash. Or perhaps you'll split up one of the sweetly black-smoking birches with its inherently hot enthusiasm even when green.

The difference between softwoods and hardwoods is botanical. The evergreens are called softwoods. Hardwoods come from trees that have various types of flat leaves instead of needles or scales.

Generally speaking, the resinous softwoods, when dry, make the quickest kindling. They flare up quickly. They are smoky, however, quick to throw sparks, and not very long-lived. The seasoned hardwoods, as well as a few green hardwoods such as birch and ash, burn longer and more steadily. It is these that break up into the bright hot coals that furnish the even heat desirable for boiling and other such forms of cookery.

The woods that spark most, roughly in the order of their doing so, are: white cedar, red cedar, alder, hemlock, balsam, the spruces, the soft pines, basswoods, box elder, chestnut, tulip, sassafras, and willow. Often you have to use wood that sparks because no other is conveniently available. Don't put fresh wood on the fire in front of your shelter and then go away and leave it, even for a minute, under such circumstances. Sparks don't often burn through heavy canvas, so if you have a pack cover or tarp, lay it over your sleeping bag.

One does not have to build many campfires before learning that when dry fuel is called for, fallen wood that has absorbed moisture from the ground should be avoided. About the only time this is worth bothering with, unless fuel is scarce, is when it is desirable to keep a fire going for a long period without very much heat.

Standing deadwood should be sought, ordinarily, but there are varying degrees of quality even with this. An upright stump that is rotten is of little value except to hold a fire, although occasionally you can uncover hard knots or a tough, resinous core in decayed softwood that will burn as if soaked in oil. Dead birch, on the other hand, quickly loses most heat-producing ability if the bark has remained intact to hold in the moisture.

Some of the barks, such as that of hemlock, are valuable for giving off steady warmth. Experimentation with what happens to be at hand usually seems to be the best teacher, for the same species of wood vary to some extent in different parts of the continent because of soil and atmospheric conditions. Among each family group, too, are many separate types, each with its peculiar characteristics.

Hickory leads the North American firewoods in heat-producing ability. Oak is not far behind. Beech ranks next in numerous areas, closely followed by the birches and the hard maples. Ash is a favorite with many. So is elm. Then come locust and cherry.

The above are half again as effective as short-leaf pine, western hemlock, red gum, Douglas fir, sycamore, and soft maple. They are twice as effective as cedar, redwood, poplar, catalpa, cypress, basswood, spruce, and white pine.

Much depends on where you happen to be at the moment. You'll naturally do the best you can, remembering the general rule that the heavier a wood is, the greater is its heating potential. Green wood, in general, is best mixed with dry.

OTHER FUELS

If no trees are growing where you are, driftwood may be your best fuel. If above the timber line, you still may find enough stunted bushes to serve your purpose. On the plains, utilize small brush, roots of vegetation such as mesquite, knots of grass, and dry cattle refuse, which is the modern equivalent of the pioneers' buffalo chips.

In some country it is a good habit to pocket tinder for the

next fire when you come across it, while, in a few regions, it is a good idea to gather the fuel itself whenever you happen upon it.

In some parts of the Arctic, where there does not happen to be driftwood, coal and peat are occasionally to be secured. Roots and brush frequently are available. The small heather-like evergreen known as *Cassiope* is sufficiently resinous to burn while wet and green. Moss and lichen also can be used as fuels. All may be secured from beneath the snow, if necessary.

STARTING A FIRE

A woodsman is known by the time it takes him to build his fires with whatever wilderness materials there may be at hand. If birch grows in the locality, the very best kindling is birch bark. Enough small shreds of this can be pulled off by hand so that seldom will there be any need, even deep in the woods, to disfigure the tree.

In evergreen country you needn't ever have difficulty in starting a blaze in any kind of weather. A fairly tight handful of the dead resinous twigs that abound in the lower parts of all conifers will burst readily into flame at the touch of a match. The only exception occurs in wet, cold weather in damp climates. Then freezing moisture sometimes sheathes the forest with ice. When this happens, the solution still remains simple. You have only to expose the dry oily interiors of the dead branches.

Shavings from pitch pine light very easily. So do shavings from any dead wood you find adhering to standing evergreens. If no softwood is about, look for dead wood on other trees. If you do have to use fallen litter for kindling, be sure that what you choose is firm and dry.

Fuzzsticks, when you need to bother with them, start a fire quickly. They are made by shaving a piece of wood again and again, not detaching the accumulating curls. These fuzzsticks are commonly employed instead of paper, by the way, to start stove fires in the backwoods. Light the fuzzsticks and all other kindling so the flames will be able to eat upward into the fresh fuel.

Ordinarily, dry materials are best to get the fire going. The job also can be done with live birch and live ash, by splitting out kindling and making fuzzsticks.

One way to start a campfire, then, is to bunch a few wisps of birch bark on the bare ground. Pile a handful of small, dry evergreen twigs above this. Over this nucleus, lean a few larger seasoned conifer stubs. Also in wigwam fashion, so ample oxygen will reach all parts of the heap, lay up some dead hardwood. Then ignite the birch bark so the flames will eat into the heart of the pile. Once the fire gets going well, you can shape it any way you want.

There is no time in any wooded area when a campfire cannot be built from materials at hand. You can always either find or make a sheltered nook. Even when a cold rain is freezing as it falls, shavings and kindling can be provided with a knife. If you don't have a knife, you can still shatter and splinter enough dead wood with which to kindle a blaze. If, preferably, birch bark is available, one sheet will form a dry base on which to arrange campfire makings, while other sheets angled above and about will keep off moisture until the fire is crackling.

Although campfires can be made in numerous ways, the principles remain the same. An understanding of these renders firemaking under every practical circumstance a lot more easy. Firewood, for one thing, does not itself actually burn. A gas driven from the wood by heat is what flames. To be capable of this, the gas must first combine with the oxygen in the air.

What you need for a campfire, therefore, is fuel that will give off combustible gas in sufficient quantity to be lit by the heat you are able to concentrate on it. This initial fire, in turn, must be hot and lasting enough to release and ignite more and more gas from progressively larger fuel.

MATCHES

The lighting should almost always be accomplished with a single match. Even on those occasions when plenty of matches are at hand, this slowly acquired skill may on some later day mean the difference between a warmly comfortable camp and a chilly, miserable one.

Ordinary wooden matches are best. These should be held so that any draft reaching them will feed the fire down to the stem where it will be able to keep burning. This you will accomplish in whatever way seems best at the moment. You may face the wind with both hands cupped in front of the flaming match. You may stretch out between the breeze and the carefully heaped flammables so your body acts as a shield. You may use your jacket or any other handy article, such as a large sheet of bark, to protect the first feeble flames.

You should have a waterproof container kept filled with wooden matches whenever you are in the wilderness. This should be unbreakable so that, even if you should happen to slip into a stream, the matches will remain intact. This match case, which may well include some provision whereby it can be attached to the clothing, should be stowed where it will not be lost. In sheer wilds, many figure it inexpensive insurance to carry a second filled container. Other matches may be conveniently available for ordinary use.

With any match holder, a danger to avoid is the accidental igniting of the matches within. A good idea is to be careful to stow about half of the matches with the butts up and to keep the heads of all as much apart as you can. It is thus possible to pack away more, too.

Paper matches are too often an abomination in the bush. If you ever happen to find yourself in the silent places with nothing more substantial, bend every effort toward protecting them from dampness as much as possible, both from perspiration and outer wetness. Wrapping the folder in something such as foil or a handy bit of plastic will serve to protect heads and stems as well as the integral striking surface.

COLD WEATHER PROCEDURE

During extremely cold spells, one will ordinarily be advised to find the best shelter available, and to lay up beside a fire until the frost moderates.

When vitality starts ebbing and a chill begins to spread throughout the body, one needs nourishment or rest, and preferably both. It is poor policy to keep traveling on nerve unless the distance to be traversed is short and the possible gain to be derived from covering it proportionately large. The best axiom, sourdoughs find, is to get a fire going and to eat. If food is lacking, the next best thing to do is to keep as warm and as inactive as possible until the cold breaks.

Everything should be ready for the fire before the hands are uncovered. The fingers will probably be stiff, anyway. If flames do not commence licking upward almost immediately once the hands are bared, the hands should be shoved against the skin to warm before another attempt is made. As soon as the fingers are limber enough to hold a match, the try can be made again as swiftly and certainly as possible.

BUILDING FIRES WITHOUT EXERTION

There are any number of ingenious ways to make little sticks out of big limbs without the use of either knife or ax. The point remains, however, that frequently it is easiest, and therefore—at least, under some conditions—preferable, to burn firewood in two, instead of expending energy unnecessarily in sectioning it otherwise. Another dodge is to lay the ends of long sticks in the blaze, continuing to advance them until they are consumed.

Another pertinent factor often overlooked in this connection is the fact that a long fire is very often preferable. If you want an open fire to lie beside, for example, it should be at least as long as your body.

To take advantage of the best available draft, a long fire should be laid in a line with the prevalent air currents. When a fire is confined by two logs, these may be advantageously placed in a slim V with the open end toward the wind.

MAKING FIRE BY STRIKING SPARK

Campfires can be lit without matches, just as food can be cooked without utensils. The direct spark technique is the easiest of the ancient methods.

That a suitable spark can be made by striking the back of a knife against a piece of flint is well known by everyone who has read of the pioneer uses of flint and steel. Not so generally realized is that other hard stones, such as quartz, jasper, iron pyrites, agate, and native jade, will serve instead of the traditional flint.

Nor need a knife or even steel be used. Iron, for example, will do instead. Furthermore, if only by the process of trial and error, two rocks generally can be found that, when struck together, with a brisk, stroking motion, will give off sparks.

The familiar iron pyrite called fool's gold because of the exciting yellow flecks it sometimes contains is a favorite in this respect among Eskimos, many of whom carry two fist-size chunks with them.

Sparks for starting a fire can also be secured by scratching together the negative and positive wires from a live battery. This procedure is possible whenever electrical power is at hand.

You must spread a preferably generous wad of tinder to catch the sparks, so that, when these shower into the bed of highly inflammable matter, the area can be blown to a glow and then to flame. If the tinder is placed in the wind, natural air currents may be enough to take care of this step.

Once tinder is in flames, all you have to do is shove it under fuel already laid as for any outdoor fire.

TINDERS. Tinder is highly combustible substance in which a spark can be blown to flame. Innumerable materials of this sort have been popular in different localities ever since man came groping out of the cold of fireless eons. Many of these tinders were carried, and some still are, in special containers such as tinderboxes, pouches, horns, and other such receptacles.

Birch bark can be detached in the thinnest of layers and shredded to make tinder. The barks of some of the cedars can be similarly utilized. Dry moss, lichen, grass, and dead evergreen needles are among the additional substances pulverized for tinder. Other suitable dry materials so used are obtained from abandoned nests.

The dry fuzz from pussy willows is a well-known tinder. So is wood which has dry-rotted and can be rubbed to a powder. A number of mushrooms and other fungi are dehydrated for such a purpose. The dessicated pith from the inside of elderberry shoots was employed by some Indians. So was the down from milkweed, fireweed, and like vegetation.

A handful of very dry pine needles often works. You can use the fluff of the so-called cotton grass, that of cattails, and the downy heads of such flowers as mature goldenrod. Many dry vegetable fibers serve as tinder. So do the powdery dry droppings of bats. So does the down found in some nests and on the undersides of certain birds.

LIGHTING FIRES WITH WATER AND ICE

A small magnifying glass is a convenient device with which to start a fire when there is sufficient sunlight. Similar lenses, such as those used in pocket telescopes and in binoculars, are likewise used. A piece of ordinary glass, perhaps from a broken jar, sometimes possesses in its distortions sufficient qualities of magnification.

The magnifying properties of water can be capitalized on for fire-making by, for example:

(1) holding the curved crystals of two watches or pocket compasses of about the same size back to back;

(2) filling the space between with water;

(3) directing this makeshift enlarging lens so as to converge the rays of the sun in a point sharp enough to start tinder glowing.

It is possible with ingenuity to devise other such improvisations.

A satisfactory lens also can be fashioned by experimentally shaving, and then smoothing with the warm hand, a piece of clear ice.

STARTING FIRE WITH A FIREARM

Pry a bullet from a cartridge, first loosening the case, if you want, by laying it on a rock and tapping the neck all around with the back of your knife. If you are carrying a shotgun, uncrimp the top of the shell and remove the wadding and projectiles.

Have the campfire laid with a good bed of tinder beneath. Stuff a small bit of dry, frayed cloth into what remains of the load. Fire the weapon straight up into the air. The rag, if it is not already burning when it falls nearby, should be smouldering sufficiently so that, when pressed into the tinder, it can be quickly blown into flame.

However, you may have to try more than once. Today's progressively burning powders, especially when they lack the resistance of bullet or shot to build pressure, tend to blow out of the muzzle partly unburned, instead of igniting either the forward part of the charge or the tinder.

BOW AND DRILL

Fires long have been made throughout the world from glowing embers obtained from the use of bow, drill, and fire board. Although the technique is simple, considerable diligence and effort are required. Once you've started, in other words, don't become too easily discouraged. Keep going.

You'll need a bow, with a thong long enough to loop around the dry stick that is to serve as a drill. Also a socket with which to hold the drill against a hollow in the fire board.

By moving the bow back and forth and so rotating the drill in the fire board, so much friction is caused that a spark starts glowing in tinder amassed to catch it. This spark can be blown into flame, with which the campfire is lighted.

SOCKET. The only use of the socket is to hold the drill in place while the latter is being turned. The socket, which, for this purpose, is held in one hand, can be an easily grasped knot of wood with a hollow shaped in its underneath. It can be one of the smooth stones, with a slick depression worn in one side, often found near water.

The socket may be oiled or waxed to allow the drill, whose upper end should offer as little resistance as possible, to spin more freely.

SUITABLE WOODS. Among the North American woods that are favored for making fire by friction are the poplar, tamarack, basswood, yucca, balsam, fir, red cedar, white cedar, cypress, cottonwood, linden, and willow. The drill and the fire board both are often made of a single one of the above woods.

DIMENSIONS OF DRILL. The drill may be a straight and well-seasoned stick from one-fourth to three-fourths of an inch in diameter and some twelve to fifteen inches long. The top end should be as smoothly rounded as possible so as to incur a minimum of friction. The lower end, where a maximum of friction is desired, is more blunt.

A long drill, perhaps one nearly a yard in length, is sometimes rotated between the palms rather than by a bow. The hands, maintaining as much downward pressure as possible, are rubbed back and forth over the drill so as to spin it as strongly and as swiftly as possible. The method, as can be appreciated once you try it, is not so effective as using a bow and socket.

FIRE BOARD. The dimensions of the fire board, which may be split out of a dry branch, can be a matter of convenience. The board, say, may be about an inch thick and three or four inches wide. It should be long enough to be held under the foot.

Using a knife, or perhaps a sharp stone, start a hole about three-fourths of an inch in from the edge of the board. Enlarge this hole, thus fitting it and the end of the drill at the same time, by turning the drill with the bow as later described.

Then cut a notch from the edge of the fire board through to the side of this cup. This slot, which usually is much wider and deeper at the bottom, will permit the hot black powder that is produced by the drilling to fall as quickly as possible into tinder massed at the bottom of the notch.

MAKING THE BOW. The bow is sometimes made from an easily handled stick such as those used to propel arrows. Some people, believing that the bow should have no resiliency, employ a stout section of branch with a bend already in it.

One end of the bow may have a natural crotch to facilitate the tying of the thong. The bow may merely be notched for this purpose, or perhaps drilled, if heavy enough not to split. The bow string, which may be anything from a shoe lace to a twisted length of rawhide, is tied at both ends so as to leave enough slack to allow its being twisted once around the drill.

OPERATING METHOD. When ready, the various components will roughly resemble the set shown in the drawing. They are used as illustrated, the campfire first being made ready to ignite.

The tinder is bedded under the slot in the fire board. If you're right-handed, you kneel on your right knee and place the left foot as solidly as possible on the fire board.

Take the bow in the right hand, looping the string over the drill. Set the drill in the cavity prepared in the fire board.

Pressure from the socket, which is grasped in the left hand, holds the drill in position. Probably you can grip the socket more steadily if your left wrist is kept against your left shin.

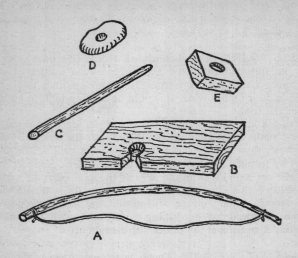

Components of the Bow and Drill. *A*-Bow, *B*-Fire board. *C*-Drill. *D*-Socket. *E*-Another type of socket.

Using Bow and Drill

Hug the left leg with the left arm. Press down on the drill, but not enough to slow it, when you commence twirling the drill by sawing back and forth with the bow.

Draw the bow smoothly back and forth in sweeps as long as the string will conveniently permit. A few grains of sand dropped into the cup helps to increase friction. At any rate, the hole will eventually commence to smoke. Work the bow even faster now, never stopping the swift even motion. Press down more assertively on the drill.

Hot black powder will begin to be ground out into the tinder. Keep on drilling, for the heartier a spark you can start glowing there, the quicker you'll be able to blow it into flame.

When everything seems right, gently remove the drill. Breathe softly into the slot until you can actually see a gleam. Then pick up both fire board and tinder if that is easiest. Press the tinder carefully around the incandescence. When the spark definitely begins spreading, get the board out of the way so you can fan the heat more freely. Carefully continue feeding oxygen to the area until the tinder bursts into flame.

Primitive peoples often carry fire so won, igniting for this purpose dry, spongy wood that, like the punk sold for setting off fireworks, smoulders over long periods of time. This fire stick they transport with them, ready to be blown into flame when the next blaze is ready to light.

MINIMIZING SMOKE

Ever notice how smoke seems to follow you around a campfire? As a matter of fact, it does follow you. The reason for this is that smoke is pulled into the partial vacuum made by any nearby object. The antidote? Create a larger attraction than that of your person. One way to go about this is by building the fire against a boulder or sandy bank.

Another method is to drive two stout stakes about a foot in back of the fire and against them pile a tier of logs two feet high. Then, no matter in what direction the wind blows, unless it is almost of hurricane force, the smoke will shoot straight up, and you can stand and work in front of the fire with no smoke nuisance at all. The wall of logs in back of a fire also can be a reserve supply of firewood.

MAXIMIZING WARMTH

Suppose you have a cooking fire (see Chapter 14) built in front of your lean-to tent, and the weather is either nippy or downright cold. When the evening meal is over, take away the pot hooks and poles. Drive a couple of stout posts about ten inches behind the backlog of your present fire, slanting them a little backwards. Pile up a wall of good stout logs, dry or green, against these. Over your cooking fire lay some smaller logs. Pretty soon you'll have quite a blaze, with the log wall in the rear reflecting the heat back into your tent—a cheerful fire before which to enjoy a frosty night.

If you will build up this fire just before turning in, you may be able to keep it going all night. It then will provide warmth while you sleep, and, in the morning, a bed of coals that will do for cooking breakfast. There is no sure formula, however, for keeping a campfire alive all night without attention. Sometimes it will hold, but if the heat is necessary for comfortable sleeping, more often than not someone has to pile out around two A.M. to freshen it.

This is not too much of a chore to an old woodsman. He lays on some logs that have already been cut, and perhaps he remains hunched up on an elbow for a few minutes. Never does smoke smell so sweet. A night bird calls. The sparks and fumes go straight up to heaven where gleams Orion's belted brightness. It's good to be awake at such a time.

SLEEPING WARM WITHOUT BEDDING

You can build a large long fire, brush it carefully to one side when ready to retire, and then stretch out on the warmed ground.

Also, you may want to consider heating stones in the fire for use as substitute hot water bottles, being wary of any stones which have been in or near water. Attractively smooth rocks from stream beds are particular offenders, the fluid often trapped within expanding to steam, thus sometimes causing dangerous explosions.

If the weather is at all cold, you owe it to yourself to take the fullest possible advantage of reflected heat. It does not take anyone long to appreciate the effectiveness of kindling a night fire against some radiating surface such as a flat boulder. Comprehending the value of having a reflector behind you usually is a matter of far greater experience.

One of the ways in the Far North to tell a "cheechako" from a sourdough is to watch how the stranger arranges his heating fire. The newcomer kindles his blaze, however expertly, against a cliff and sits in front of it. The oldtime northerner builds his fire farther away from the rock face and sits *between* the cliff and the fire.

READY-MADE FIRES

Before you turn in for the night, and certainly before you leave camp even for the day, provide a plentiful supply of fuel with which the next fire can be built. These makings may include birch bark, three or four good fuzzsticks, some split kindling, and a few pieces of larger wood. Place all these under cover where they will be sure to keep dry.

You may arrive back in camp dogtired, cold, and wet, with numb hands that will scarcely grasp a knife for whittling. Or, when your turn comes to build the morning fire, it may be raining or snowing. It won't take many such experiences to make you remember to have the makings always ready.

One of the unforgivable sins of the north woods is to quit a camp or cabin without leaving both kindling and a plentiful supply of dry firewood by the stove or fireplace.

SAFETY

Safety is of foremost concern. Never start a fire where it will spread dangerously. Wind may carry a glowing particle an unbelievable distance.

It does not pay to take chances with fire. Never kindle one on inflammable ground such as that made largely of decomposed and living vegetation. Fire will sometimes eat deep into such footing. An individual may think he has put it out, but often it may not be entirely extinct. Unseen and unsuspected, it may smoulder for days and weeks underground. It may lie nearly dormant during an entire winter. With the warmth and the increasing dryness of spring, it may regain new vigor until one hot day a strong wind may cause it to bloom into a growling, exploding, devastating forest fire.

When you leave a camp or bivouac in a potentially dangerous area for more than a few minutes, put out that fire. Saturate it with water. Stir the ground beneath and around it, working and soaking ashes and dust into mud. Dig around it until you are certain no root or humus will lead the blaze away like a fuse. Feel with your hands to make sure all heat has been safely diminished. Examine the vicinity for any activity resulting from sparks and flying embers.

Chapter 6

ENERGY-SAVING
WAYS OF TRAVEL

FEW will disagree that if you have to cover a considerable distance, the pace to take is one you will be able to follow all day and still have a reserve of energy left over. You will be apt to end up wasting time if you attempt to press.

Most find, too, that they can maintain better and therefore safer balance by keeping the feet pointed as nearly straight ahead as is comfortable. They are also able to pick up an additional inch or two per step this way. Coming up on the toes will so use these members as to afford both extra distance and impetus.

It usually requires a disproportionate amount of energy to travel straight up and down hills, as the trails of animals reveal they well know. You generally will do better in the long run either to zigzag or to slant off at a gradual pitch. Energy will be conserved if you can proceed without cutting across major drainage systems. As for resting, this is more beneficial when enjoyed frequently for brief periods. Hurrying ahead for long stretches and then taking prolonged breathing spells tends to cause the muscles to stiffen.

Anyone making a forced hike will do well to change socks around the middle of the day, if this is possible. The feet will probably be the most vulnerable part of the body in such an eventuality and should logically be attended to in ratio with their importance. The best procedure is to carry a number of small adhesive bandages whenever in the bush, and to apply one of these without delay whenever any irritation is felt.

A sensible formula, finally, to repeat to yourself and therefore to heed whenever covering wilderness afoot is: Never step on anything you can step over, and never step over anything you can step around.

NIGHT TRAVEL

Night travel is usually inadvisable. One will generally do better under a multitude of circumstances to stop about an hour before darkness, get comfortable for the night, turn in early, and then arise in time to hit the trail again as soon as there is sufficient light.

Desert travel in hot weather is an exception. Here, particularly if one is short of water, his best deal will be to keep as cool and quiet as possible during the heat of the day. If no shade is otherwise available, it will usually be worthwhile to scoop out a narrow trench in which to lie. To exclude as much heat as possible, the slit, if on a flat, should align itself with the rising and setting sun, so that during midday it will be as nearly at right angles as possible to the blazing rays.

"The temptation to stay in good country as long as light lasts is inevitable," as Colonel Townsend Whelen noted. "In the Northeast woods where white birch trees are plentiful, a birch-bark torch has often brought me safe and sound to camp.

"Strip a piece of birch bark a foot wide and about three feet long from the tree. Fold this in three folds lengthwise, making a three-fold strip about four inches by three feet. Split one end of a three-foot pole for carrying, the split of the pole engaging the bark strip about eight inches from one end and keeping it from unfolding. Light the short eight-inch end.

"If you want more light, turn the lighted end downward so the fire will burn up on the bark. If it burns too fast, turn the burning end upward. As the bark is consumed, pull more of it through the split in the stick handle. Such a strip will last fifteen to twenty minutes and will light all the ground, trees, and bushes within about twenty feet. When the bark is about half consumed, look for another tree from which to get more bark."

FOLLOWING GAME TRAILS FOR EASIER GOING

The intriguing skeins of trails worn by the feet of passing animals often make wilderness travel easier, especially when you are looking for a gradual way up or down some slope. If you are trying to hold a certain direction, however, the safest general rule is to follow a game trail only as far as it seems to be generally heading where you want to go.

It will be noticed in swampy country, especially in the north, that occasionally you will begin to encounter one game trail after another before reaching a muskeg or morass. These are made by animals seeking to avoid the wet places and to keep to easier going. In dry country, such deeply worn ruts often indicate the welcome nearness of drinking water.

RAFTING

Because rivers are the highways of many vast wilderness stretches, the knowledge of how to build and use a raft may bring you safely through hundreds of miles of primitive regions.

BUILDING A RAFT

Three long logs can be used with particular success for such a job. A raft built on such a nucleus can readily be paddled or poled, depending on the water. Drifting, it can be steered with a long oar, sweep, or some other rudder arrangement. A short, square raft, on the other hand, has too much tendency to spin.

A raft should be made, if possible, of sound, dry wood, perhaps from dead trees that still are standing. In the absence of spikes, the three logs can be lashed together with roots, vines, small limber withes, fibrous bark, or, of course, rope. With an ax, however, you can do a really professional job. A knife can be employed instead, although laboriously. In the absence of such tools, you might burn out the necessary openings.

The work may be commenced by laying the three logs in

position near the water. Two substantial crosspieces across the top, one near each end, are needed. A couple of tough, rugged poles will do. Set these in place and mark on the logs beneath where each pole is to go.

Then cut six notches so that each is narrow at the top, widening as it goes deeper into the log. When the two crosspieces are finally driven through each series of three notches, the fit should be snug. Once the raft has been allowed to soak, it then will become even more firmly interlocked.

SAFETY PRECAUTIONS FOR RAFT TRAVEL

You will be prudent if you take every possible precaution when using such a raft, however, particularly under the stress and uncertainty of emergency conditions. Keep listening and watching as far ahead as possible, for some notable patches of bad water give no warning until one is almost in them. For this reason, it is a sound idea to scout ahead whenever this is at all feasible.

If you have a rope, you may be able to line the raft through rapids while walking safely along or near shore. Otherwise, you probably will do better to let the raft go through with the idea of retrieving it later, if that is possible.

You will have to provide as well as you can for the safety of any outfit you may have along, perhaps in one of two ways: (1) by tying it securely to the raft, or (2) by packing it in as waterproof a bundle as you can manage, with some provision, such as the inclusion of a chunk of light, dry wood, so it will float.

MAKING YOUR OWN AUTOMATIC PILOT

One day you may find yourself floating along on such a raft down a broad, sluggish river like many in the Far North. A rock, pail, or old coal oil container, hung beneath the con-

Notching a Log for Use in a Raft. A crosspiece, joining this log to two similarly notched logs, fits in each notch.

veyance by a short line affixed to the front center of the raft, will automatically tend to keep your carrier in the main channel. Besides thus acting as a guide, this arrangement also can conserve energy otherwise expended on dreary hours of steering.

FINDING AN OUTLET

An old sourdough stunt used to locate the outlet of a quiet body of water is to float bannock crumbs or bits of some other light substance, such as fragmented leaves, and to observe which way they drift.

ADVANTAGES OF WINTER TRAVEL

Although the winter of fiction closes the northern wilderness, the winter of reality opens much such country, freezing streams and thus providing highways that twine enticingly through regions otherwise difficult to penetrate. Along the edges of rivers a smooth icy sidewalk often is repaved week after week by congealing overflow.

For those on snowshoes, the deepening whiteness becomes a level carpet over jackpots of brush and tangled deadfall. Because of both ice and snow, therefore, one often is able to save hours and even days of travel by proceeding in straight lines otherwise impossible on foot.

HOW TO MAKE SNOWSHOES

In winter, one often can travel much more easily by the very simple expediency of attaching broad, light evergreen boughs to the feet.

You may be able to travel without even these aids by sticking to where snow lies thinnest: along the edges of wind-scoured streams, atop northern rims and benches where the melting sun has made its influence felt, and in heavy evergreen groves where storms have not fallen so deeply. Warm, dry chinook winds, which some Indians call snow-eaters, are so pleasantly prevalent in many northern areas that there one seldom has to take to webs.

If you ever do have to improvise snowshoes, you will have a rough idea of how to proceed, if only from pictures you have seen. Where obstructions are not too thick, the circular bear-paw type will be the simplest to build and use. A narrower and longer shoe will be essential if you have to follow a tighter trail.

Frames can be made by bending live wood into the shape desired. If frozen, of course, green saplings will have to be thawed first in sunlight or near a fire.

Strips of rawhide will make satisfactory emergency webbing. You can use the green strips. These should be heavier where the foot is directly supported. In slick going, portions of hide attached beneath the snowshoes with the hair facing back may help to decrease slipping on upgrades.

Rope also is employed for webbing, although it is a nuisance in frigid going because of the manner in which it continues to stretch as cold deepens. It may have to be loosened in slushy travel, on the other hand, lest it pull and break the frames.

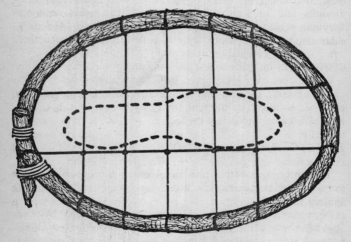

An Improvised Snowshoe

Rawhide also happens to be an annoyance under these latter conditions, sagging and stretching when wet. A possible solution? If you have any wire, string the snowshoes with this and twist rawhide strips around each strand.

The size of any snowshoes will be governed by conditions. They preferably will be as small and as light as will support one on the snow over which he has to travel. If this forest covering is deep and soft, the shoes may have to be six feet long and one foot wide. The webbing, too, should then be closer together.

Many northern outdoorsmen prefer to attach webs to their feet with a simple harness made of some fabric, lamp wicking being a favorite. You also may use a single broad strip, lacing it to the snowshoe so as to provide a loop into which the instep can be thrust. In any event, the front of the snowshoe should swing up out of the way by its own weight when the foot is lifted.

There is no intricate technique to snowshoeing. Just put them on and start walking. Various improvisations will suggest themselves according to the particular circumstances. When the going becomes tough, some old-timers help themselves along simply by knotting a line to the tip of each snowshoe so they can assist by hand the swinging of each web up and ahead each step.

BEING PREPARED TO FALL

Once one realizes that he cannot afford to have an accident, probabilities shift markedly against any mishap befalling him. Nowhere is this more apparent than under the drastic law of the wild. For what may be only a self-punishing, attention-getting, or responsibility-relieving mishap where help is at hand, can be very serious indeed when one is alone.

The only reasonable rule in remote regions anywhere is not to take unnecessary chances, weighing always the possible loss against the potential gain, and going about life with as wide a safety margin as practical.

When you are descending a cut bank or, in fact, any down-grade, for example, a basic safety principle is to control your center of gravity so that if you do fall, it will be backward in maneuverable sliding position.

The same principle holds even when you are traveling among obstructions on a flat. It is sometimes a too costly convenience to let the body drop or swing forward so as to rest a hand momentarily on a projection and vault ahead. The un-tested support to which you will then be committed may roll, slide, or give way entirely. Even though this may happen only one time in ten thousand in such a way that you will not still be able to save yourself, unless there are extenuating circumstances, the odds still will be too great to warrant taking such a gamble.

A reasonable precaution back of beyond is to expect to fall at any moment, for so realizing the possibility, you will be more likely to minimize chances of injury by: (1) avoidance of an area, (2) extreme care where it is not practical to bypass, and (3) most commonly by continually gauging beforehand where and in what manner, if you do fall, you will be able to let yourself go most safely.

Deadfalls project an especial hazard. This is greatly multiplied if the ground is at all wet. Dew can make a fallen log so slippery that the feet will fly out from beneath you so unexpectedly that any control is instantly gone. Frost imposes graver danger. Especially tricky is dead bark that, all of a sudden, turns on the trunk itself.

You can't avoid all such dangers by keeping off fallen timber, for often a downed tree is by far the most reasonable way over a ravine or flooded creek. Too, you occasionally come upon vast stretches of old burn where the only way across is atop a maze of deadfall. What you may logically choose to do, therefore, is to test such footing as carefully as possible and to proceed with maximum caution, taking secure hand holds whenever they are offered, while limiting and, when possible, excluding any tightrope walking and leaping.

FORDING

By studying the character of a stream, you most often can closely gauge how best to cross it, for, except in still water, the most shallow part is generally where the current is widest.

A stout pole can be useful during wading, both for testing the footing ahead, and for steadying one against a tugging torrent. Any packs, of course, should be held loosely enough to be swiftly disengaged, if necessary.

Despite any natural reluctance to get wet unnecessarily, no one will disagree that it often is better to wet the feet deliberately than to attempt a hazardous passage across slippery logs or unsteady stepping stones.

If there is much of a flow to be crossed, the most comfortable procedure may be to remove your clothing with the idea of keeping it dry until it can be safely donned again. It often is best, under such circumstances, to replace boots or shoes used in fording. However, when wiped out and put back on, either over dry hose or over damp woolen stockings that have been squeezed as free of water as possible, most footgear suitable for the wilderness will be no more than momentarily uncomfortable.

In connection with water, there is one special precaution that anyone venturing along a rocky open seacoast should heed. That is to hold fast at the first feasible spot upon the approach of a big wave. It is better, under such circumstances, to deliberately choose a wetting rather than to take the chance of running across uncertain footing and thus risking, in many exposed areas, the very real peril of being injured and even of being swept away.

FEELING YOUR WAY IN POOR VISIBILITY

Visibility is sometimes so deceptive and restricted in dangerous terrain that it is foolhardy to keep going (if to continue is necessary) without taking special precautions. A low, hanging cloud, sudden sleet, and the way smoke and dust sometimes swirl up in stinging particles before an eye-watering wind can make travel almost blind.

Depending on where you are, you may break off evergreen tips and keep one or two held always well ahead to mark a safe passage. This procedure you may well augment by cutting a long, dry stick, light enough to handle easily, and by poking about on all sides to minimize the possibility of stepping off into emptiness.

TRAVELING OVER ICE

Ice travel can never be considered safe. Even when temperatures drop one hundred degrees below freezing, some parts of northern rivers not only always remain open, but other portions are sheathed with ice so thin that it scarcely will support its own weight. Overflow creates other hazardous conditions. So does the dropping of water levels, leaving great sheets of ice suspended. Cracks of various widths and depths are always characteristic.

Other dangers build up when an insulating rug of snow shields ice from the hardening effects of cold, while running water beneath is eroding it. When ice is bare, its quality of magnification, which makes it possible to use a lens of ice to start a campfire, can, under the glare of sunlight, create temperature dangerously above thawing.

MINIMIZING HAZARDS OF ICE TRAVEL

Safety cannot always consist of keeping off ice. If you are making your way through a northern wilderness in winter, ice travel may very likely open the most practical routes. The solution must lie, instead, in taking all reasonable safety precautions while on ice.

CARRYING A POLE. An elementary safeguard to take, whenever you can, during ice travel is to carry a long, light pole horizontally. Then if you ever plunge unexpectedly through the ice, as is possible anywhere at any moment, this pole can serve automatically as a bridge, both checking the descent and affording a ready means of support.

The practice of bearing a slender length of dry wood becomes less a nuisance than second nature, particularly as with it you can conveniently jab at suspicious portions ahead, such as those perhaps hidden beneath snow or under a frozen skim of overflow. If you are with a companion, an alternative or additional precaution is to travel some twenty feet or so apart in single file with a rope between you.

READING STREAMS. You can read the character of a strange stream to a certain extent from the formation of its banks and thus keep, whenever possible, to shallows. Sheer banks are apt to continue their steepness beneath water, making for comparatively deep conditions nearby. A gradual bank, on the other hand, presupposes the likelihood of shoals, although there are numerous exceptions which vary for the most part according to local geology.

CANDLE ICE AND SEASONAL DANGERS. When the warm part of the year approaches, ice along the shore thaws, making the immediate problem one of reaching the still solid masses farther out. The procedure usually is to follow the shore until a jam or some other approach, such as a series of rocks is located.

Dangers of ice travel multiply rapidly at this time of the year when the sinking swish of snow enlivens the land. Not the least of the hazards then arising comes from candle ice.

Ice will still seem solid to the inexperienced eye when, as a matter of fact, it has disintegrated to candle ice so treacherous that anyone not knowing better may step on an apparently stable area and sink through it as if it were slush. The unexpectedness with which this can happen may be better appreciated when you realize that ice several feet thick often decomposes into long vertical needles, among which a testing pole can be driven all the way through in a single jab.

Candle ice, which has caused the drownings of numerous sourdoughs and natives, is best shunned entirely, particularly because of the difficulty of regaining safety after one has gotten in trouble.

If, despite following the preceding precautions, the worst happens and you do fall through the ice, apply the procedures outlined in Chapter 24 for extricating yourself and minimizing post-drenching exposure.

CONSERVING STRENGTH IN COLD WEATHER

A dangerous fallacy, practically as widespread as the mistaken idea that frostbite should be thawed by rubbing snow on the affected area, is the long-perpetuated theory that you should keep moving in cold weather lest you freeze. This universal although mistaken belief is often expressed more specifically. Don't fall asleep outdoors in very cold weather, you have probably been warned, or you'll never wake up.

The opposite is true, for why should you waste strength in moving aimlessly about when that energy can be better rationed to keep you warm? Why should you risk excessive perspiration that, freezing, could make you dangerously cold?

The best thing to do when caught out unexpectedly on a subzero night is to hole up in safe cover and get a fire going. If you can't do that, the next best procedure is to locate as sheltered a spot as you can, curl up on something dry, even though it be but spruce boughs or birch bark, and go to sleep.

You won't wake up? When the night turns cold at home, don't you awaken, if only to reach for more covers? Cold also arouses you in the bush. You stir around just enough to get warm, which, very often by changing position once or twice, is all you do in bed, and then draw yourself together again, go back to sleep if you can, or at least relax to the fullest extent possible.

This procedure can be especially important if you are short of food, as it stands to reason that the only way the body can produce the extra heat necessary to offset increased coldness is by burning additional calories. The supply of calories readily available for this function will be greatly lessened if you're also consuming them by tramping up and down.

The weaker one becomes, the less able he will be to withstand what he is up against. When he slumps down exhausted, he has probably perspired enough to rob the clothing of an important part of its warmth. The reserve strength that otherwise would have been available is too many times depleted. From that sleep of exhaustion, there often is no awakening.

Another thing to beware of when combatting cold is alcohol. Although this may bring about a deceptive sensation of agreeable warmth, it has the effect of disrupting the function of the human thermostat. It thereby drastically increases, in proportion to the amount consumed, the possibility of serious effects resulting from exposure.

Chapter 7

DEVELOPING A SENSE OF DIRECTION

ANYONE who merely happens to stray from his way is seldom faced with much of an external problem. Internal conflicts can become considerable, however, for the brain of man can impose very alarming obstacles where none have been placed by nature. Indeed, such mental blocks can prevent the individual from noticing the helpful landmarks which nature provides.

These mental, and therefore all the more unnerving, obstructions under such circumstances are most often the immediate results of either panic or pride. The first will sometimes set the ordinarily most rational of individuals running crazily. The second can, at the least, spur him to continue blundering aimlessly after dark, when there may be real danger of injury.

Just as cold actually is the lack of heat and what is known as darkness is no more than the absence of light, so is getting lost an entirely negative state of affairs. You become lost not because of anything you can do, but because of what you leave undone.

It is when you realize this that all the mysteries imputed to the procedure of finding one's way through any woods vanish. In their place appears a positive and ever intriguing problem of distances and angles. For there is just one method to keep from getting lost. That is to stay found.

You stay found by knowing approximately where you are every moment. Nor is this as complicated as it may seem at first, for anyone can keep track of his whereabouts by means of a map, compass, and pencil. Every ten or fifteen minutes, or whenever direction is changed, will not, in the beginning, be too often to bring that map up to date. Suppose you do not have a map? Then draw one as you go.

MAPS

Maps, even if they're only memorized before or during a journey or drawn during the progress thereof, are necessities for intelligent wilderness travel. It is sound procedure, for this reason, to study, whenever possible, during the course of any trip, maps of the area and to compare them to what you can see, so as to obtain at least a general picture of the vicinity.

If you don't have time to get a map or the opportunity to copy one before taking to the bush, some local inhabitant can often be found who will take pleasure in sketching a practical chart of the countryside. It is a profitable habit, in any event, to ask old inhabitants to correct and supplement local maps, especially if you are in extreme wilderness where the hardest-working and most conscientious surveyor can do only a sketchy job in the few weeks when it is possible for him to hack, blaze, perspire, and swat his way through the woods.

In any event, either be sure of basic topographical facts, or do not depend on them. Skid, tote, and other roads come to dead ends. Prominent ridges melt into level ground. Even large streams disappear underground, sometimes for miles at a time.

WHERE TO GET MAPS

Good maps are, in general, extraordinarily easy to obtain. Even the small-scale maps distributed free by gasoline stations and automobile clubs give a good general picture.

There are maps available to the passengers of most commercial planes, for example, or a supply can be picked up at terminals. Seeing where you are makes any flight more enjoyable, and even rough knowledge of this sort may help you decide more surely what to do and perhaps where to head in case of a forced landing under circumstances in which such decisions can be vital.

Sectional maps, particularly those government publications which are sold below cost, are very inexpensive. Most suppliers will furnish upon request free detailed lists of what they have available. One of these is the Superintedent of Documents, U. S. Government Printing Office, Washington, D.C. 20402.

Maps of the portions of the United States east of the Mississippi River may be obtained from the U. S. Geological Survey, Department of the Interior, Washington, D.C. Maps of areas west of the Mississippi are available from the U. S. Geological Survey, Federal Center, Denver, Colorado. Topographic maps of national park areas are available also from the map information offices there.

Canadian maps may be secured from publicity offices located in the various provincial capitals, from the Government Travel Bureau in Ottawa, and from the Map Distribution Office, Department of Mines and Technical Surveys, which also is located in Ottawa, Ontario.

For government maps of Mexico, write to Direccion de Geografia y Meteorologia, Tacubaya, D.F., Mexico. Two private sources for foreign maps are: (1) the National Geographic Society, Seventeenth and M Streets, N.W., Washington, D.C.; and (2) the International Map Company, 90 West Street, New York, N.Y.

Contour maps, when available, are by far the most valuable for wilderness use, because they indicate valleys, canyons, mountains, and other such features, in terms of elevation. Consulting such a map in strange country can save one an exhausting amount of unnecessary climbing, descending, and then climbing again. Forest Service maps rarely include contours. If you are interested in contour maps, therefore, contact the U. S. Geological Survey, Department of the Interior, Washington, D.C. This agency publishes free index sheets of individual states, and from these you can determine whether the topographic maps you want are available.

USES OF A COMPASS

It isn't so much a question of whether or not you can get along without a compass. That most can learn to do, for even in the strangest surroundings, there are numerous recognizable signs that indicate direction. Some of these are even more accurate than the wavering magnetized needle. But traveling through unmarked places without a compass is in the same unnecessarily arduous category as lighting a fire without matches.

Even the most experienced frontiersman does well to carry a compass, as well as matches, whenever in the bush, if only to save time and energy. For instance, you are on a Gaspé Peninsula knoll. The sun has set. You can glimpse smoke curling up a mile away from the tents where, all day, in a buried Dutch oven, a mulligan has been cooking. Heading directly there in the straightest possible line can mean the difference between arriving easily and safely during the remaining daylight and taking the needless chance of getting a dead branch in the eye.

So you sight over a compass. The tents lie exactly south by the needle. Once you've dropped down to the flat, the small, thick spruce is so dense that some of the time you have to crawl. Visibility is not good enough ahead to line up a straight route without a lot of time-consuming care. Checking the compass occasionally, though, assures your keeping headed along the shortest route.

Or you're on the other side of the continent, atop a Yukon mountain. A cloud swirls about you, blotting out all landmarks. Camp, you've ascertained during the climb, lies east down what is the only safe slope. The weather is thick by now. Which way is east? If you have a compass, you neither have to wait on this exposed peak for the atmosphere to clear, nor need you risk any unnecessarily dangerous scrambling.

NORTH AND MAGNETIC POLES

Compasses, as you already know, do not point true north toward the North Pole unless it be by chance. They are governed instead by the so-called magnetic pole. This magnetic field, which is energized by the earth's whirling on its axis, is situated some 1,400 miles below the North Pole near where the shallow Northwest Passage winds icily above Hudson Bay.

Even the compass line to the Magnetic Pole is not constant, as this magnetic center is drifting all the time. For all ordinary purposes of determining direction, however, a small, plain compass can be used with sufficient accuracy. The only correction usually necessary is to allow for the general declination, i.e., the difference between true north and magnetic north in a particular section, so as to read more easily the maps of that area.

Although the above is not technically exact, it is, in general, accurate enough for everyday travel. Actually, the entire earth is a magnet, causing the declination to vary at different spots. In some localities, this may be as much as fifteen degrees away from the magnetic shift indicated on ordinary maps.

DETERMINING COMPASS DECLINATION. To determine the local declination from true north with reasonable accuracy, find the North Star. This lies almost exactly over the North Pole, varying only slightly more than one degree from precise north. You then can either note immediately the variation between almost exact north and where your compass needle is pointing, or you can scratch a line pointing to the Pole Star, or indicate it by two stakes, and in daylight compare your compass to the thus established north-south mark.

The declination must be taken into consideration when you're reading a map. As a matter of fact, it is marked on many maps. If no compass directions are shown on the particular map you are using, north may be assumed to be at the top.

The compass points due north in the United States and Canada only in a narrow strip which passes through the Great Lakes, where the North and magnetic poles happen to be in line. In parts of Maine, the indicator trembles to a rest twenty-five degrees west of north. At the other side of the continent, in British Columbia, the angle is as great in an easterly direction.

However, compass correction for map reading is very simple. Suppose you are scouting over the boulder-studded hills above Ensenada in Baja California Sur. The compass declination where you are is about 14 degrees east of north. Your compass, in other words, here points 14 degrees too far east.

Watching out for cacti, you spread the map before you on the semiarid ground. An arrow marked "N" verifies that north is at the top of the chart. You move the map until the printed arrow, or until one side of the upright rectangular sheet, if there is no such mark, points 14 degrees west of compass north. For all practical purposes, you now can read the map in terms of the countryside about you.

Perhaps on the map you have there is a second arrow

marked "M" to indicate magnetic north. All you have to do in this case is move the map until this second arrow and your compass needle both head in the same direction.

All circles, no matter what their size, are divided into 360 degrees. So it is with the compass dial, where these degrees may perhaps be most easily visualized as 360 possible routes spreading out like wheel spokes from wherever you happen to be. Compass degrees are customarily numbered in a clockwise direction, starting at north.

East is one-fourth of the way around the compass dial. East in terms of degrees is, as can be seen, one-fourth of 360°, which is 90°. The distance between each of the four cardinal points—north, east, south, and west—is the same 90°. South therefore is often designated as 180° and west as 270°.

Northeast is halfway between north and east. Northeast, in terms of degrees, is therefore half of 90°, which is 45°. Half of that again, or 22.5°, is north-northeast.

COMPASS POINTS

One usually learns while a youngster that, when by standard time you stand facing the sun at noon, south is directly in front of you, and north is at your back. If you lift each arm sideways to shoulder height, your left hand will point east and your right hand west.

Halfway between north and east is called, logically, northeast. The other corresponding points are similarly determined and named: southeast, southwest, and northwest.

There may be occasions when you will want to figure direction even more finely. This you can do by using the divisions halfway between each of the already considered eight points. These additional eight points are named with equal logic. Halfway between north and northeast is north-northeast. Halfway between east and northeast is east-north-east. Each of the four cardinal points always comes first. Halfway between south and southwest is therefore south-south-west.

WHAT KIND OF COMPASS TO BUY

Any compass carried for wilderness use should have a luminous dial. Otherwise, the time may come when you will

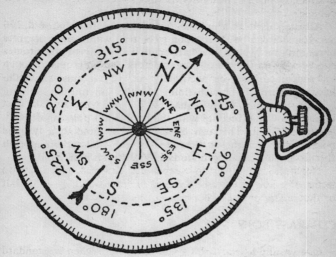

Compass Dial

be forced to sacrifice time and increasingly precious matches to maintain a compass course at night.

Also, it is no more than reasonable to expect any compass you buy to be rugged enough to stand up under rough usage, and to have some provision so it can be attached securely to the person.

Many carry a second compass. The practice is a sound one, for even if you never do lose or damage the first the bulge of a spare fastened safely in a pocket is ever reassuring.

Many also can testify to being plagued by the doubt that the compass on which they are relying may no longer be in order. An auxiliary will be welcomed at such a moment for checking purposes. If you ever do this, proceed as follows: (1) place or hold the two compasses level, (2) keep them well away from each other and from any metallic objects, and (3) make sure that the indicator of each is swinging freely on its pivot. If there should be any marked discrepancy, go by the compass whose needle oscillates more freely in gradually narrowing arcs before quivering to a stop.

USING A WATCH AS COMPASS

A watch used as a makeshift compass in the United States and Canada can be relied upon to be true within eight degrees, depending on where you happen to be in any of the fifteen-degree-wide time zones. Three factors are prerequisites: (1) the timepiece must be accurately set, (2) it must show the local standard Greenwich time, (3) the sun must be shining brightly enough to throw a shadow.

Lay the watch face up with the hour hand pointing directly toward the sun. This can be checked by holding a twig or pine needle upright at the edge of the dial, whereupon it should angle a shadow directly along this shorter hand.

Telling Direction by Watch and Sun. When the hour hand points directly toward the sun, south lies midway along the smaller arc between the hour hand and twelve o'clock.

South will then lie midway along the smaller arc between the hour hand and twelve o'clock. If such a procedure is carried out at eight o'clock in the morning, therefore, a line drawn from the center of the watch outward through the numeral ten will point south.

SETTING A WATCH BY COMPASS

By reversing the principle of using a watch to ascertain direction, you can tell time by the use of a compass. Whereas previously the timepiece had to be accurate, now it is the compass that must give the correct reading. For this purpose, local magnetic variations must be taken into account. If your maps do not indicate this, you can use the North Star as previously suggested.

If you are in the United States or Canada and want to set a watch, find by compass which way is due south. Then, using a shadow to help keep the hour hand of the watch pointed at the sun, turn the hour hand until south lies midway along the shorter arc between it and the numeral twelve. The watch will then be set to within a few minutes of the correct local standard time.

If you are in the bush with a watch but no compass, you still can proceed in the above manner by previously lining up two stakes so they point toward the North Star. Such a line will run almost exactly north and south.

IMPROVISING A COMPASS

The compass, which, along with gunpowder, was one of the wonders brought back from the Orient to Europe nearly seven centuries ago by Marco Polo, was some four thousand years earlier a chunk of magnetic ore suspended by a rawhide lace. Today the most simple compass is a magnetized needle mounted on a pivot so it can rotate freely.

You can make a temporary compass by first stroking an ordinary needle in a single direction with a piece of silk, or with the pocket magnet you may have with you, if prospecting. The next step will be to place the thus magnetized needle so that it will be free to turn. This you can accomplish a little more easily than otherwise if now you rub the needle with oil, the small amount that can be collected by passing a thumb and forefinger over the nose and forehead being sufficient.

Then take two thin bits of grass, or some other fiber, and double them to form two loops in which to suspend the needle. Lower it carefullly into still water, such as a tiny pool trapped by a stump or rock. If you are careful, the top of the water will bend noticeably under the needle, but the surface tension will still float it. The support may then be removed cautiously.

The floating needle, once freed, will turn until it is aligned with the north and south magnetic poles unless, as is the case with any compass, some metal is near enough to distract it. If you have stroked the needle from the head to the tip, the head will point north.

MEASURING DISTANCE BY TIME

By timing yourself or otherwise measuring distances, and by making either a written or mental record of all angles of travel, you can get so you can always tell just about how far away in what direction the spot from which you started lies.

The special value of a watch in the wilderness has to do with your measuring distance in the farther places less often by miles than by time. If you walk three hours along a shore, to give an example, you may not be sure if you have traversed six miles or nine. But you can be certain that if you return over the same route at about the same pace, a similar three hours will bring you close to your starting place.

Miles as such mean little in ordinary backwoods travel, for although a trail may proceed through level open country, it may as readily dip and twist down coulees and through old burns.

Suppose you ask a prospector, "How far is it along this blaze to the mine road?"

His laconic reply, "Six miles," may not give any realistic indication of what lies ahead. If instead he says, "Oh, I reckon six hours if you keep hustling," you probably will inquire if there isn't some easier approach.

CARRYING A MAP IN YOUR HEAD

Even without map, compass, or watch, it's possible to find your way. The sagest old sourdough carries his map in his head. Sun, stars, prevailing wind, landmarks, and other natural factors may be the veteran woodsman's compass under favorable conditions.

What often is regarded as a natural sense of direction is, instead, almost always the result either of (1) acquired skill apparently so effortless as to appear instinctive, or (2) familiarity with the surroundings.

The settler who lives on the edge of a clearing can be expected to become as closely acquainted with the surrounding woods as the city boy with the streets of his own neighborhood. The ruralist in a strange countryside and the urbanite in an unfamiliar metropolis will, if depending solely on familiarity, soon become lost.

Knowledge of locality becomes less and less valuable the farther you travel, for few can make a very long journey without leaving the region they know. This is a major reason why explorers the world over have been repeatedly plagued by the desertions of aborigine guides. Natives, although they may have spent their entire existences in primitive places, and, in fact, to an important extent because of the handicaps imposed by these very limitations, have, in the main, always been characteristically terrified to venture very far beyond the particular area each has come to know.

The greenest tenderfoot who learns and uses the wilderness lore set forth in this book will be able to find his way as surely in one forest as in another.

DETERMINING DIRECTION BY SUN ALONE

Suppose you've no watch. You've no compass. It's morning. The sun is shining. You want to know precisely where south is.

Drive a short pole into the ground. Observe how long a shadow the pole casts. Loop a string, lace, piece of straw, or something similar around the pole. Keep this taut, and, holding it at the desired length attached to a sharp stick, draw an arc that exactly touches the end of the shadow. Mark this point with a stake.

The shadow of the pole will keep shortening until noon standard time, when it will commence lengthening. Watch until it once more meets the arc. Mark that spot with a second stake.

A line connecting the pole with a point halfway between the first and second stakes will point due south.

The ordinary difficulty in telling direction by merely glancing at the sun is that the sun keeps rising and setting in widely different positions, appearing exactly in the east and disappearing truly in the west only two days each year. These are known as the equinoxes and fall approximately on March 21 and September 23. Even on these two annual occasions, when the sun's center crosses the equator and when night and day are therefore both twelve hours long, true east and west can be determined with certainty by the eye alone only over flat areas.

DIRECTION BY SUN OR MOON

There is a less accurate but far swifter method of telling direction any time the sun or moon is bright enough to cast a shadow. Wait five minutes or so. Then a straight line drawn from the shadow's new tip through the first mark will run roughly west.

This method is virtually accurate around noon. The line tends to shift a bit south of west in the morning, a trifle north of west in the afternoon. However, if you travel by this method all day, these variations will average out.

FINDING DIRECTION BY ANY STAR

Because of the way the earth is continually revolving, stars seem to swing from east to west in great arcs, forming the white streaks that puzzle some first looking at time-exposure pictures of the night sky. The way in which any star seems to move can furnish you, therefore, with a general idea of direction.

First of all, you have to take a sight on the star you pick, for the star's movement will be too gradual to detect just by glancing at the heavens. You will need two fixed points over which to watch. These may be two stakes, driven into the ground for the purpose and their tops lined up carefully. If you will observe a star over them for several minutes, it will seem to rise, or to move to one side or the other, or to sink.

If the star you are observing seems to be rising in the heavens, you are looking aproximately east. If it appears to be falling, it is situated generally west of you. If the star has the appearance of looping flatly toward your right, you are facing roughly south. If it gives the impression of swinging rather flatly toward your left, then you are heading just about north.

NORTH STAR

There is no more reliable way to pinpoint north, if the North Star is visible, than by consulting this star, also known as Polaris. The bright pole star seems to the naked eye to be

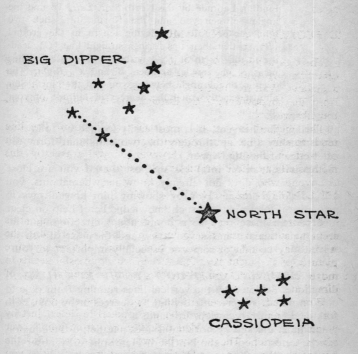

Finding the North Star. The North Star is most easily located by following an imaginary line through the two stars that form the outer edge of the Big Dipper. It lies about halfway between the Big Dipper and Cassiopeia.

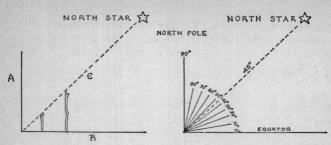

Finding Latitude by the North Star. *Left:* To find the angle between you and the North Star, stick two branches or posts of varying length in the ground (*B*), so that their tips form a straight line (*C*), leading to the North Star (*A* is the perpendicular). Then measure the angle between *B* and *C*. *Right:* The degrees of the angle between you and the North Star almost exactly equal the degrees of latitude of your location.

by itself in the heavens. It is most easily located by following an imaginary line up through the two stars that form the outer edge of the Big Dipper.

Polaris is such an infallible signpost that if you are close to anyone who does not already know its whereabouts, you will be doing him a favor by showing him how always to recognize it. Not only can such knowledge be of help on clear nights when there may be a doubt about direction, but innumerable times it has saved lives, and the next life so involved may be that of someone especially important to you.

DETERMINING LATITUDE BY THE NORTH STAR. Longitude, depicted by the vertical lines running from pole to pole on maps, is represented either by degrees or by time, both reckoned from Greenwich, England.

Latitude, marked by horizontal lines parallel to the equator, can be determined in the Northern Hemisphere by observing the North Star. Such knowledge for someone shipwrecked or down in a plane may greatly increase his chance of reaching safety. Even under normal circumstances, it makes for some very interesting experiments.

This determination of latitude is possible because of two

factors: (1) at the North Pole the North Star is located almost exactly at a 90° angle above the horizon, (2) at the equator the North Star lies on the horizon at 0°.

If you are halfway between the North Pole and the Equator on the 45th parallel, you will find, upon sighting the North Star, that it lies almost exactly at a 45° angle from you.

At whatever degree angle the North Star lies away from you, that is almost exactly also the degree of latitude. The diagram shows a practical way of making this estimation which, if only makeshift devices are at hand, can be but an approximation. But it may be enough to help you place your position on a map.

CASSIOPEIA

Most know that, depending on what time you look at them, the five stars known as Cassiopeia appear either as an M or a W. This northern constellation is always on the opposite side of the North Star from the Big Dipper and about the same distance away. By memorizing the relationship between Cassiopeia and the North Star, you can use the former for finding the pole star when the Big Dipper is not visible.

TELLING DIRECTION FROM LANDSCAPE FEATURES

Moss does grow thickest on the shadiest side of a tree. If a particular tree happens to be in the open where the sun can reach it unimpeded throughout the day, the shadiest side will be north. Also to be taken into consideration is the fact that certain growths resembling moss thrive best on the sunniest portion of the trunk.

The growth rings exposed in standing stumps tend to be widest on the sunniest side, which, under ideal conditions, is on the south. If you will examine a number of such trunks and take into account the influence of such natural factors as slope and probable shade during growth, you can make a rough approximation of where south is located.

Another valuable sign if read correctly is downfall. Trees generally fall in the direction of the strong prevailing wind. Such things as freak storms and wind deviations caused by mountains and canyons sometimes give what would seem to be false pictures, however.

The tops of such trees as hemlocks and pines naturally point toward the rising sun. They lean generally east, that is, unless the wind turns them in another direction.

Sand dunes and snowdrifts build up in such a way that they are narrower and lower to windward. This phenomenon will help to orient you, therefore, if you know from what direction the wind was blowing when the drift was formed. Usually this can be determined by a combination of signs.

Plant growth also relates its own story, being larger and therefore more open on a north slope, and smaller and consequently denser along a southern exposure.

WHAT ABOUT FOLLOWING STREAMS? The more you learn about the open spaces, the more you realize that no way of thinking or doing, however old, can be trusted without proof. Although innumerable widely accepted opinions sound reasonable enough in theory, too many of them have the often fatal tendency of not working out in practice.

An example is the counsel that following a stream downhill will eventually lead you back to civilization. In well-settled country it will, usually, if you take the often unmentioned precaution of keeping to the higher sides of any swamps. In a reasonably populous area it will, ordinarily, if you can keep going long enough through the comparatively heavy growth and downfall which characterize watercourses.

In real wilderness, particularly under the stresses imposed by emergency conditions, either real or imagined, following a strange stream with any assurance is something else again. Nor is keeping well to one side so as to have easier walking, and cutting back often enough to maintain contact, the solution.

Suppose you manage to detour impassable gorges? Suppose you are successful in circumventing morasses and marshlands? Suppose you can continue to twist and batter your way a dozen exhausting miles through alder and willow for every mile gained? The flow may very well end in some remote spot in the boondocks.

Using small streams as landmarks in strange country should be only part of one's procedure of orientation. Brooks loop around so much, for example, that when one does encounter the rill for which he has been looking, he may be thrown off by its seeming to flow in the wrong direction. Or a similar stream that runs into the first can be deceiving.

Particularly confusing is the good-sized brook which occasionally disappears underground. If one is following it, this phenomenon is simple enough to allow for. But if one is depending on cutting such a stream, he may walk right over it and not be the wiser.

WHAT ABOUT WATERSHEDS? A general way to keep track of one's whereabouts in big country is by watersheds. This is not a practice to pursue lightly, however, for flowages starting only a few feet apart can, and often do, end up several thousand miles from each other.

You're camped on a large river into which, as far as you know, all nearby streams drain. One day you don't even hike as high as usual. You cross a low saddle. It may be that all the water on the other side of this gradient trickles eventually into a brook which has no connection with the river. So, if you have fallen into the habit of following some stream back down each day until it leads you to a recognizable part of the river, you may become seriously confused by attempting this now. Such divisions are apt to be extremely abrupt in mountainous regions.

FINDING YOUR WAY BACK TO CAMP

If camp lies against some long and easily followed landmark, such as a subarctic river with a smooth, hard shore, returning there after a day afield can be practically foolproof. It is in such a place that an experienced outdoorsman will, whenever possible, be careful to locate his camp, for he will be able to find it although the weather becomes stormy and the night black.

The preceding is a broad example, for all will generally want to keep sufficient track of their whereabouts to be able to intersect such a broadside as a road or river within a reasonable distance of the spot desired. The question of which way to turn then should not be left to chance.

Coming upon an unmarked destination directly involves so much chance that it's rarely wise even to attempt it. Unless there are guiding factors such as dependable landmarks, the most expert technique by far is to bear definitely to one particular side of the target.

Then, upon reaching the trail, shore, or whatever the lateral may be, you will know at once which way to follow it.

PICKING UP TRAIL GOING AWAY

Somewhat more difficult is picking up a dead-end trail that, somewhere ahead, comes into being by running directly away from you. By adapting the lore just considered, though, you also can solve this problem handily and certainly.

You are in a level pine forest. Earlier you came to the end of a long fire lane that slashes due north and south. For three hours since you've continued to hike northward by compass, the day being cloudy and the country more enhanced by animals and singing birds than by landmarks.

You have boiled the noonday kettle, and now it is the half-way time when you should head back to camp. Because of the distance, it is preferable to return there by the much faster going of the fire lane. How to proceed?

Do you hike back southward by compass at the same pace with the idea of rejoining the trail in about the same three hours? The flaw in that procedure, you realize, is that straight lines are only a manner of speaking in ordinary bush travel. The most that you will reasonably be able to count on in that respect is that variations roughly will balance one another if, by mark or compass, you compensate for drift and keep headed in the same general direction.

But suppose you do travel south for three hours and then for one more hour at the same pace maintained throughout the day? Unless you have encountered the lane by that time, it is reasonably certain that the lane now lies either east or west.

What at that hypothetical point would be the most desirable procedure? To try going due west, say, for up to fifteen minutes with the knowledge that if you haven't cut the lane by that time, you should cross it within a half-hour by hiking back due east? Or to begin zigzagging methodically southeast and southwest, increasing these lines until the lane is reached?

All such approaches, you rightly decide, leave a great deal unnecessarily to chance. Percentages favor your reaching the trail with less time and bother if it is approached from one

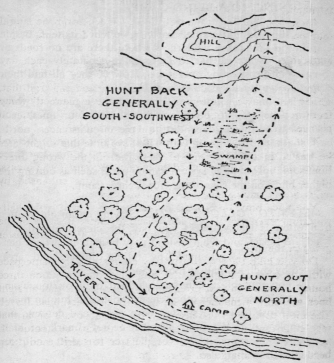

HILL

HUNT BACK
GENERALLY
SOUTH-SOUTHWEST

SWAMP

RIVER

HUNT OUT
GENERALLY
NORTH

CAMP

Finding Your Way Back to Camp. Camp should, if possible, be located near a broadside, such as a river. When returning to camp, camper should bear to one side of his destination so that when he reaches the broadside, he knows which way to turn.

definite side. So from the very beginning in starting back, you don't proceed due south at all. Instead, because the going is somewhat more open that way, you choose to bear slightly east of due south. Then, after traveling for the same safe four hours, you can swing west with the assurance that the fire lane lies broadside a short way off in that direction.

RETURNING TO A BLIND CAMP

Now suppose that a small party has pitched its tents beside a spring in flat, dense wilderness where there are no roads or landmarks. Everyone has to leave camp separately each day to carry on prospecting operations. How do they all find their respective ways back each evening?

The reasonable solution will be to make a mark at which to aim. One way to do this is by blazing four lines, each perhaps a mile long depending on the circumstances, north, east, south, and west from camp. To save time that might later be wasted in following any of these radii in the wrong direction, some informative system can be used, such as cutting the higher blaze on the side of the trees nearer camp.

WAYS TO FOLLOW BLAZES. Staying on an old spotted trail often is tricky unless you pay the closest attention to what are blazes and what instead may be patches where bark has peeled, abrasions made by falling timber, and areas gnawed by such animals as moose and bear.

The apparent blaze can be examined both by touch and sight for flatness and for other characteristics of human manufacture. Most trails are spotted both going and coming, and one simple way to determine whether or not a mark is a blaze is to check the opposite side of the tree to see if a chip has been cut out of that, also.

When one is traveling by the dimness of night, the surest way to authenticate a blaze is by feeling it. One tell-tale clue is the little flap sometimes left at the bottom of the spot where the edge of the ax or knife has driven into the bark but not entirely disengaged it.

If a trail seems to have stopped, the safest procedure is to mark where you are at the moment. Not losing track of that place, return as directly as possible to the last blaze of which you're sure. Then, by looking down the blazed trail in the direction from which you have come, you can usually line up how it should and probably does continue. By figuring where any trail would most reasonably have gone, you will be able, in most cases, to find where it actually does go.

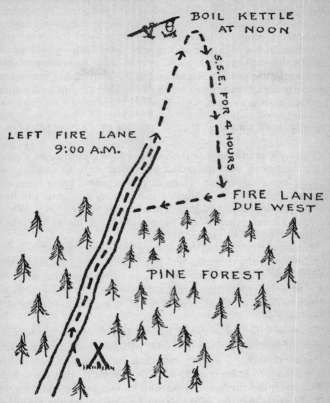

Picking Up Trail Going Away. Roughly parallel lines indicate fire lane running north-south. Dotted line shows route of camper from and back to camp in a day's hike. Fire lane can be reached most easily by aiming at it from one side.

HOW TO STAY ON A TRAIL

One soon discovers that although it is easy to stray from the ordinary bush trail, getting back on such a course can be difficult in the extreme. The important factor, once you find you've gone wrong, is not to lose the new starting point. Often some landmark, such as an oddly shaped tree, is nearby, which you can use as a pivot while methodically searching in widening circles.

If there is no such signpost, a safer way to hunt will be in straight lines from and back to the new beginning point, breaking limbs, cutting blazes, and making any other necessary marks by which to return, all the time checking to make sure the back trail is evident.

USING EYES AND EARS TO BEST ADVANTAGE

To stay lost in comparatively well-settled country one would really, although perhaps subsconsciously, have to work at it. Hiking in a straight line in any direction would bring him out. This he could do even without a compass by continuing to line up two objects ahead of him. These might be two trees. When he had almost reached the nearer of these, he would select another sight in line farther ahead.

Sounds will often lead one toward habitation. So will smoke. A bare knoll or safely climbed tree may reveal a house. Walls and fences generally lead somewhere. Although this may be only to a long-deserted farm, the deep ruts of some ancient path will then, in all likelihood, wind toward a more recently traveled way.

Anyone who finds himself stranded in the blanched wildernesses of North America in winter will, in some respects, have a better chance of getting out than he would in any other season. Two of these reasons arise from the fact that the colder it becomes, the farther it is possible to see and to hear. Either phenomenon may be of the utmost value to anyone stranded or lost.

It often is difficult, especially to newcomers to primitive regions, to determine from what direction a sound is coming. This ability you can develop with practice. In the meantime, one way to get a bearing, when the noise is prolonged enough, is to turn the head until it seems loudest. Holding a hand over one ear may help. Closing the eyes also reduces distractions for some individuals. If you have an opportunity, of course, stand in an open place as far as possible from any broad reflecting surfaces, such as cliffs.

COMMON-SENSE PRECAUTIONS

NOTIFYING OTHERS OF YOUR WHEREABOUTS

An extremely simple precaution that would save thousands of hours of needless effort, anxiety, and agony every season is for everyone to make his plans known every time he is about to head into the wilds! If no responsible individual is present to whom to entrust this information, you can do worse than to note it briefly in a dated message and to leave that in some safe and prominent place.

Even when you park an automobile beside the highway with the idea of perhaps fishing for an hour, it would take you only a moment to jot down that information and to wedge the paper, in a sealed envelope if desired, securely beneath a windshield wiper. No one would be apt to disturb it unless you failed to return for a disproportionate length of time, and there are numerous reasons why anyone might somehow be delayed and in need of help.

Any group functioning in the remoter places will do well to agree beforehand on definite procedure to be used in any apparent emergency. Unless the individuals have been going together into the brush for a long time, they may choose to commit this plan to paper so each can carry a copy. Sensible courses of action will depend largely upon terrain, climate, circumstances, and upon the experience and capabilities of those involved.

When a human being afoot first realizes he is not sure of his whereabouts, he is ordinarily not so far out of the way that he cannot be located—or, if need be, cannot relocate himself —within a safe time.

The trouble very often develops when a lost man keeps blundering along, usually to his own detriment and to the increasing confusion of searchers. Too many times he walks entirely out of an area.

When someone is lost, if there is one essential any more important than another, it is common sense, this to be exercised not only by the individual in difficulty, but by his companions as well. The following true episode is illustrative.

A sportsman was late one evening in making his way out of a rough patch of woodland about one mile square. His friends started driving around and around the road that bounded the area, blowing the horn more and more frantically every few minutes. The hunter started out in one direction, corrected his line, changed it again, began hastening still another way, and finally became so confused and exhausted that he was not able to get out until daylight.

FOLLOWING ROADS

Although such a precaution would seem so elemental as not to merit mentioning, if one is really lost, no road should be spurned just because it may not seem to be the right road.

Yet even in Alaska Highway country—a wilderness as large as all Europe west of prewar Russia, and inhabited at the time of its building by scarcely enough people to fill the Rose Bowl —trackers saw where lost men, trying to find their way, had crossed this engineering epic two and three times. On each occasion they'd deliberately left the wilderness road to blunder back into the bush, where they could easily travel in a straight line for as many weeks as they could keep going before coming across another man-made thoroughfare of any description.

Chapter 8

SKILLS WITH WOODSMAN'S TOOLS

ONE doesn't need to be a lumberjack in order to acquire enough know-how in the use and care of axes, hatchets, saws, and knives to handle these tools effectively when undertaking such common tasks as felling, chopping, and sawing timber.

Even the greenest tenderfoot can fell his first trees in a given direction if he will follow the simple principles set forth here. Wind, incline, weight, and surrounding objects must, of course, be taken into consideration.

A small safety notch is first made to minimize any possibility of the butt's kicking back or the trunk's splitting. Below this on the opposite side, where the tree is to fall, a wide notch is cut. When this indentation is about three-fifths through, a few strokes at the first nick should send the tree crashing.

The two notches are so placed that they form a natural hinge. This hinge controls the direction of the fall and lessens the chance that the butt may thrust backward. However, one should have his eye on a safe place and should hurry there when the moment comes for the call of "Timber-r-r!"

It is even easier to drop a tree by using a saw. The principles remain the same. Make the same brief initial cut. Follow it with a deep slit opposite and below; then deepen the first incision.

An ax, or perhaps a wooden wedge cut on the spot, may have to be driven into one gash or the other to free the saw. Too, you often can topple a heavy tree that is pretty much on balance and come closer to pinpointing its fall by using a wedge in the higher cut.

AXES

The ax is an almost indispensable tool for woodsmen, many of whom rate it even above matches as the most valuable item to have along in the bush. It may be, however, a very dangerous instrument in the hands of a novice.

The ax is not really needed in the average warm weather camp. It is not necessary, either, on summer backpacking trips. It is, rather, the tool for heavy work, for getting in large wood for fires, for building big shelters, and for cutting out timber that may fall across horse trails and canoe streams.

HOW HEAVY AN AX?

The ax with a 2½ - or perhaps a 3-pound head is big enough for most outdoorsmen. Heavier axes bite deeper and therefore, in the hands of an expert, do faster work. That is why lumberjacks, frontiersmen, and others who grow up in ax country and who use these mobile wedges regularly, pick a heavy model. These, besides being tiring in the hands of a tyro, require a lot of skill and are, therefore, more potentially dangerous.

Double-bitted axes are very tricky in the hands of all but experienced and careful men. In addition, they cannot be used easily as hammers, for which purpose, although it is not to be recommended, the outdoorsman is sometimes apt to find himself employing it a dozen times a day.

The handiest ax for packing, although not for any great amount of work, is the Hudson Bay model, with a narrow butt and a face of normal width. Sometimes an occasional craftsman uses one of these painstakingly on a log cabin, but such an individual is usually a perfectionist who has more of the qualities of the cabinet maker than of the carpenter. This model, because of its narrow poll through which the handle is attached, does not hold up too well in all cases.

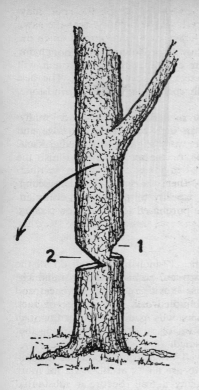

Controlling Direction of Timber Fall. Tree should fall in the direction of the arrow if a small notch is made at position 1, a larger notch at position 2, and a few additional strokes made at the first notch.

But for ordinary outdoor requirements, where weight is a factor but you still want an ax, a Hudson Bay with a 1½-pound head and a 24-inch handle will do a lot of work. The Hudson Bay ax, incidentally, is a convenient one to tie behind your saddle.

Outdoorsmen who use an ax very much probably will be most satisfied with an ordinary single-bit ax with about a 2½-pound head. A handle or helve about 26 to 28 inches long is generally enough, although some may find they can swing the 36-inch handle more naturally. In any event, if you adopt one length of handle and use it exclusively, you will come to do better and safer work.

SHARPENING AN AX

The edge on the ax you buy is probably sharp enough for the average two-weeks-a-year camper. The good axman will probably want to thin this edge for keener cutting. The best tool for this, and for rough sharpening as well, is a grindstone, kept wet during use.

In the woods a 12-inch or so flat file does a good job. To sharpen an ax, start about an inch back from its edge and carry that out straight. Taper very slightly to the edge itself. Do not overdo this, however, or the ax will bind. Finish the job with a sharpening stone.

It is false economy to look for ax bargains. This is especially true since well-balanced, expertly tempered, and conscientiously forged brands may be purchased for a very few dollars.

HATCHET

The light 1-pound ax with a 12-inch handle will do all the work necessary in many camps and on backpacking trails. The average outdoorsman can use it with more effectiveness and greater safety than a long-handled ax. As a matter of fact, some of the more skilled backwoods axmen often turn to such a hatchet, smoothing a pole or log so skillfully with one that you'd suppose it had been planed.

Such a hand ax works well in securing wood for a small campfire, when you bother to use an ax at all. It's a lot more useful than a knife for blazing a trail. Secure a substantial sheath for it, but don't ordinarily carry it on your belt. This is both inconvenient and uncomfortable. Stow it, instead, in a rucksack or saddle pocket.

AXMANSHIP

A whole book could be written on the subject of axmanship. The best axmen almost all picked up the art as boys on the farm or in the woods, but with practice and care, anyone can learn well enough for all the usual outdoor chores. Incidentally, experienced golfers find the desirable free and easy swing to an exact point almost second nature.

The main thing is to be careful. You can ruin an outdoor

trip in a hurry with just one stroke that lands a fraction of an inch from the place it should go. The best general precaution is to anticipate the worst and to be so placed that even if it does occur, no one will be hurt. Too, a sharp ax is safer than a dull one in that it is not so likely to bounce off the wood.

Be prepared, though, to have the ax glance off a knot, and have your feet and legs where they will not be hit. Instead of relying on a perfect swing, take the time to clear away any shrubs and branches that might catch the blade. Don't take the risk of steadying a billet with hand or foot.

Avoid, too, the common practice of leaning a stick against a log and half chopping and half breaking it in two. A lot of head injuries from flying wood have resulted from this all too prevalent habit. When you're felling a dead tree for firewood or for a cabin, watch out that another tree doesn't break off the top and send it crashing back toward you. In other words, there are a great many possible misadventures. The more of these you can foresee and protect yourself against, the less will be the possibility of an injury.

When you stop to think of it, axes are far less dangerous than such a very common substance as glass. Any shortcomings do not lie in the ax but rather in the individual. Use this wedge with a nice easy swing. Let the gravity fall of the ax do most of the work, and you'll be able to cut all morning without pressing. Keep your eye on the exact spot where you want the edge to strike, and practice until it always does strike there.

REPLACING HANDLES

Ax handles, especially in the hands of beginners, occasionally break. If this should happen, cut off the remaining handle near to the head and try to drive it out the wider end of the slot. If this doesn't work, you'll have to burn it out.

This can be done without injury to the tempered metal. Just wet a small area of ground. Then shove the ax blade into this damp soil all the way to the eye. Kindle a fire directly over the head. The heat and flames should so char the wood that it can be driven or broken out easily.

The driving on of a new handle should be accomplished by blows on the end of the upraised handle, not on the head itself. Finally, tighten the ax with a wooden wedge. Cut off any portions of the wedge and handle that protrude beyond the head.

If you have salvaged a metal wedge from the old combination, use this to tighten the head further.

Incidentally, do not paint or varnish ax handles, as this causes your hands to blister.

PRESERVING THE TEMPER OF THE BLADE

Woodsmen may be seen on frosty mornings, warming axes in their hands. Another trick is to keep your ax in your shelter. An ax left out during a really frigid night may shiver to fragments at the first stroke. Incidentally, care must be taken not to bend a saw that has become brittle with frost.

Heat, whether from fire or from a too vigorously turned grindstone endangers the temper of steel. A well-tempered blade is something to cherish. Some lumberjacks will not leave an ax in green wood on the theory that this may draw the precious temper.

SOME ESSENTIALS

Chop at an acute angle to the grain. The ax, hitting at a right angle to the grain, will hardly bite at all.

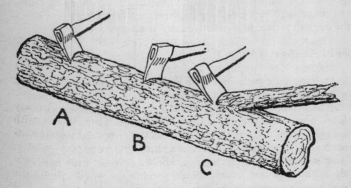

Axmanship Fundamentals. Always chop at an acute angle to the grain, as in *A*. An ax, hitting the grain at a right angle, as in *B*, will hardly bite at all. The way to chop limbs off a trunk is upward, the way they grow, as in *C*.

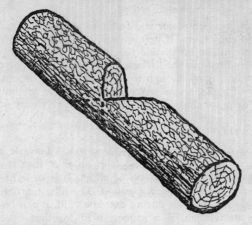

Chopping a Fallen Log in Two. Two V-
shaped notches, started on opposite sides
of the log, will do the job nicely.

The way to chop limbs off a trunk is upward, the way they
grow.

Start each of the pair of side notches needed to chop a fallen
log in two as wide apart as the log itself. Two such V's, joining
at the stick's center, will sever it most economically.

As for squaring a log, methods vary with workmen. An easy
way, however, is to walk along the top and score a side with
an easy swing of the ax. That is, make naturally slanting cuts
several inches apart to the same approximate depth. This latter
may be indicated by a guide line. The chips are then hewn out
by walking back the other way and cutting parallel along the
real or imaginary guide line.

You can spend as much time as you want from then on in
slicing off a shaving here and there until, with sufficient patience and skill, the surface becomes as smooth as if it were
planed.

SAW

It is usually much easier and faster to saw all but small logs than it is to chop them. If you are using a wood-burning stove, such a tool will be invaluable for working available fuel into the right lengths to fit the firebox. Even when you're bivouacking in weather nippy enough to require the companionship of an overnight blaze, a saw will make the task of accumulating enough fodder for that campfire a comparatively easy one.

SWEDE SAW

The long slim blade of the Swede saw is a favorite of outdoorsmen in the cold climates. It is so thin that it speeds through wood with a minimum of effort. It is so light that it can be easily handled in any position. The long, narrow blade is so flexible that, except during extreme cold, it can be coiled to the circumference of a saucer, held together by a cord wound and tied among its teeth, and wrapped with a piece of canvas for carrying.

The two-piece, light, tubular handle is easily slid apart and packed. If you want, you can even dispense with this and bend a husky green sapling into place for a frame when necessary. Make a small hole through each end of the sapling, at right angles to the wood, with a knife or nail. Then split each end. The improvised handle can then be attached by inserting the blade in the slits and securing it, through each hole, by wire or whatever else is handy. Carrying two butterfly bolts for this purpose can save time.

The cranky side of a Swede saw is its disposition to twist and bind. Many select the heavier, comparatively rigid crosscut saw for this reason. The crosscut is of particular value in cabin construction for making the straight cuts necessary for window and door openings. Besides being surer and steadier than the temperamental Swede saw, it can be inserted in a wall in the space made by removing one log. The one-man crosscut, on which an additional handle can be slipped, will suffice.

Whatever saw you take into the bush, don't make the mistake some tenderfeet do and carry a blade with the small crosscut or rip teeth used by carpenters. See to it that your saw is designed for cutting rough timber.

SAWHORSE

You will save time with one or two sawhorses if you are going to do much sawing. The simplest sawhorse is two poles driven into the ground to form an X. A chunk of wood jammed between the lower gap in this contrivance will steady it. The X often is wired together in the middle for further support. Two such sawhorses placed conveniently side by side can save a lot of maneuvering and stooping.

KNIVES

For all his mastery of earth and space, man is a weak creature, with inadequate teeth and scarcely any claws. He must rely on tools to perform the simplest functions, and since the earliest man picked up the first sharp-edged stone, the knife has been a primary tool in the wilderness. A man in the outdoors without one is a weakling, while the man with one is the master of a hundred situations. With the right kind of knife he can warm himself, feed himself, shelter himself, clothe himself, and defend himself.

Procuring a knife is a very personal undertaking. Your own preference will guide you, but a few rules apply to all knives. Buy the best you can afford, in a pattern designed for the use you have in mind. Beware of war surplus and import bargains. It's best to stick with a known brand from a dependable dealer.

A hollow-ground blade is not satisfactory on an outdoor knife because its thin edge, shaped in cross section like that of a straight-edge razor, is likely to chip. On the other hand, the blunt, chisel-like bevel found on the exceptionally hard-tempered knives that are advertised to cut through bone and metal will not take a keen enough edge to make them suitable for general wilderness use.

For a general-purpose knife, avoid those with stainless steel blades, as ordinarily they, too, won't take a keen edge. When they are dull, it takes forever and a day to bring them to an even half-decent sharpness on a whetstone. Stainless steel knives made by hand are harder than mass-manufactured products, for a tougher metal can be used that can be handled by die stamping. But usually, if you are going to put out the money for a hand-made knife, you may as well have the very finest high carbon steel.

CARE OF KNIFE AND SHEATH

Your knife should always be thoroughly cleaned and dried after use. Never sheathe a wet blade. As a matter of fact, if you intend to store a knife for a prolonged period, coat it with oil, vaseline, or some other protection, and leave it out of the sheath.

Sporting knives need the same attention as carving knives. It is never advisable to immerse either in water. Wiping and drying the blade is generally sufficient.

All carbon steel blades, which are the best now available, will become stained from meat. Furthermore, a knife left for a very long time in a sheath will become stained from the acids present in all leather. Such discoloration does not harm the blade. It can be removed easily by polishing with a crocus cloth.

Any rust that appears on the blade should be removed before pitting sets in, by rubbing with fine grit emery cloth or steel wool. Then, for a fine finish, polish with crocus cloth, available at most good hardware stores.

As is the case with an ax, a sharp knife is safer to use than a dull one.

Shoe polish or saddle soap should be used on leather handles to keep the leather from drying out. Metal polish will refurbish hilt and butt. Shoe polish or saddle soap should be used on the sheath, as well. Never use oil for this purpose, for this will soften the leather, making it flexible and causing difficulty in sheathing the blade.

HOW TO SHARPEN A KNIFE. W. D. Randall, who, in his Orange Blossom Trail shop in Orlando, Florida, makes by hand the finest knives in the world, recommends the use of two hones, one with a medium or coarse grit for starting the sharpening process and the other with a fine grit for finishing. A single, two-sided pocket carborundum will do, too.

To sharpen a knife, just follow these step-by-step directions:

1. Lubricate the hone with a few drops of saliva.
2. Place the knife diagonally on the hone, at a forty-five-degree angle.
3. Raise the side of the blade away from the surface of the hone, to an angle of about twenty degrees.

4. Keeping the edge of the blade to the surface of the hone, holding both the diagonal position and the twenty-degree angle, sweep the edge across the hone from hilt to point.

5. Turn the blade over and repeat the process.

6. Continue sharpening on alternate sides of the blade, one stroke at a time. Be sure to use even, sweeping strokes, and to maintain the same angle on both sides of the blade throughout each stroke. Lessen the pressure as the edge is restored.

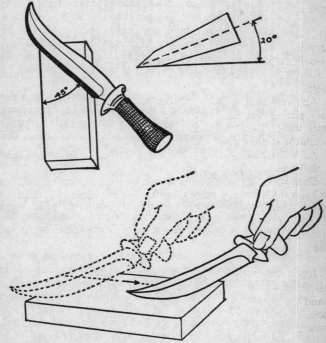

Sharpening a Knife. *Top Left:* Place the knife diagonally on the hone, at a 45° angle. *Top Right:* Raise the side of the blade to an angle of about 20° from the hone's surface. *Bottom:* Keeping the edge of the blade to the surface of the hone, holding both the diagonal position and the 20° angle, sweep the edge across the hone from hilt to point.

7. If a wire edge develops, hone it off by giving the blade a few light sweeps across the fine-grit hone at a high angle of about sixty degrees.

A NEW CONCEPT IN SHARPENING. "If you want a professional edge, and have the time and patience to achieve it," adds Bo Randall, "here's a method of sharpening you may prefer.

"Follow the previous directions, but lay the blade flat and hone it until it is brought to a true razor edge, and light reflection on the cutting edge is no longer discernible. Since such a razor-like edge will not hold up under use, it should be strengthened by a few final sweeps across the hone on each side, with the blade held at a high angle (about 60°). This will leave a minute, edge-holding bevel that can hardly be seen by the naked eye.

"This method will, of course, leave hone marks across the blade bevel. In order to restore a fine finish, it is then necessary to polish the blade by rubbing it with emery cloth, starting with a medium grit, finishing with 600 grit, and following this with crocus cloth to attain the final polish."

THE CROOKED KNIFE

The famous crooked knife is one with a thin, curved blade about six inches long. It is the Indian's and occasionally the backwoodsman's substitute for a plane, drawknife, or spokeshave.

The crooked knife is used for making snowshoe frames, paddles, and thin planks for toboggans. It can be invaluable in the home manufacture of cabin furniture. The worker holds it in his hand, and, drawing it toward him, can easily shave wood to almost any curved or flat surface.

Crooked knives could once be had from many of the Hudson's Bay trading posts in Canada. Now often unheard of in a lot of these, they usually can be secured from Hudson's Bay Company headquarters in Winnipeg, Manitoba. They are made in both right-hand and left-hand models, generally without a handle. You put on your own handle.

Chapter 9

ROPE AND KNOTS
FOR EVERY PURPOSE

KNOTS vary a little in design, depending on their functions. The principles remain the same, however. What is desired in most instances is a knot that will not let go, but which, at the same time, can be untied in a hurry.

The easiest way to learn how to tie the various knots is by using real rope in real situations. This is not always practical, of course, and work at odd moments with a small length of cord carried in a pocket will accomplish wonders. So it will not be too unrealistically limp, this cord preferably should be at least an eighth of an inch thick.

A primary step in becoming familiar with knots is learning the names of the different parts of the rope and knots. A rope, for example, has only two parts. The end is the short, free section with which most knots are tied. The standing part is the remainder of the rope.

Knots are made by combining loops, bights, overhands, and underhands. A loop is formed by making the ends of the rope go in opposite directions. A bight, the beginning point of many knots, is made by turning a portion of rope back upon itself. An overhand, or, for that matter, an underhand, knot is formed by passing the end through a loop.

BEST ROPE MATERIALS

Good manila hemp is the old reliable in most wilderness situations. Sisal is less expensive, but it also is weaker and less durable. Cotton is smoother, but when it gets wet and frozen, it's tempting to take an ax to the knots. Nylon is hard and strong, but it is expensive, slippery, and hard to keep tight, inasmuch as it will stretch as much as a fifth of its total length.

There are two primary kinds of rope. Laid rope is composed of hemp, sisal, cotton, or jute fibers. These are twisted into

Steps in Whipping Rope

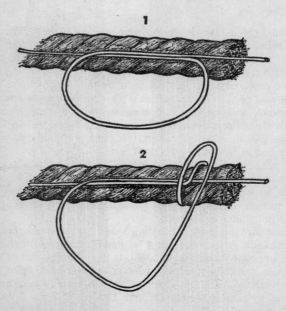

yarn. Two or more yarns are then twisted into strands. Several strands are laid together to make rope.

A soft and flexible braided rope, such as sash cord or clothesline, is manufactured of strands of cotton or other material, woven in a usually complicated pattern.

The solid polyethylene rope, although only slightly stronger than hemp, is favored by some canoeists and boatmen both because it is waterproof and because it floats. In the wilderness, though, where rope usually is put to more than one use, many still select manila, even though it is harder on the hands.

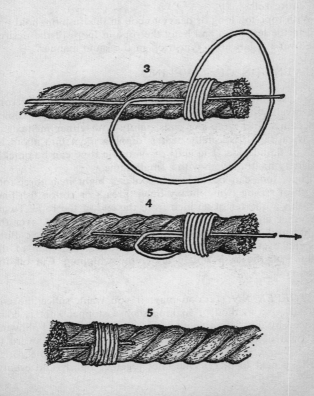

KEEPING ROPE IN WORKING CONDITION

The main enemy of hemp is moisture. This rope should be kept as dry as possible, especially when it is stored. The usual wilderness wettings do not harm it, however, if it is allowed to dry before being loosely coiled and hung in a preferably well ventilated spot, away from woodmice, chipmunks, squirrels, porcupines, and other gnawing rodents.

An easy way to coil rope is by grasping one end in the left hand, bending the upper part of the left arm to vertical and wrapping the rope between thumb and fingers and elbow until all is coiled. Finish off with two snug half hitches (see description under "Two Half Hitches" later in this chapter) around the entire roll.

With rope too long or heavy to coil in this fashion, hold one end in the left hand and hang the rope in loops of the desired size over the left arm. Finish off in the same manner.

PREVENTION OF RAVELING

Unless you take special precautions, the ends of your rope will ravel. With materials such as hemp and sisal, a functional procedure is to wrap the ends tightly with either medical or electrical tape. Especially neat is dipping them into about an inch of liquid glue. The ends of synthetic rope can be quickly sealed by melting them with a small flame.

Rope, too, can be whipped. Make a bight in a three-foot length of strong twine, heavy linen thread, or cotton fish line. Lay this a quarter of an inch from the end of the rope. Twine the other end of the cord tightly around the rope, over the bight, until the whipping is as wide as the rope is thick. Push the end of the cord down through the exposed loop of the bight. Pull the loop snugly under the whipping. Cut off the loose end.

STOPPER KNOT. You may, if you want, splice the end instead. One method of making such a stopper knot is commenced by untwisting about six inches of the rope. Following the twist of the rope, turn each of the strands downward to make a loop. Now bring each adjacent free end up through the loop next to it. Pull the knot together tightly and evenly.

To give it a finished hardness, put it on the hard ground and roll it for a minute under your boot.

You can reinforce this knot by making several smaller knots, one on top of the other. Or you can finish it off with a crown knot.

Stopper Knot

CROWN KNOT. The crown knot can be used by itself to prevent the end of a rope from raveling, or it can be tied on top of the above stopper knot.

You'll need about six inches of untwisted end. Take the center strand and bring the end down toward you against the main part of the rope between the other two strands, to make a bight.

Then grasp the left strand. Bring it around the bight to the right, between this and the right strand. This will give you a perpendicular bight and a horizontal loop around that bight.

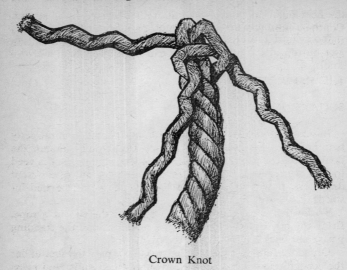

Crown Knot

Take the right strand. Shove it through the bight from right to left without going through the loop. Now each strand is held under one of the others. Pull the strands tight, one by one, to complete the crown knot.

CROWN SPLICE. Most professional of all is the crown splice. Start with a crown knot. Then take one strand and work it down into the main rope by passing it over the nearest rope strand and under the next strand.

Turn the rope a bit and do the same thing with the second loose strand, passing it over the nearest rope strand and under

Crown Splice

the next one. Do the same thing with the third loose strand. Continue until you have made four complete rounds. Now roll the splice under your foot to round and smooth it, and cut the ends off flush.

THE HANDIEST KNOTS

SQUARE KNOT

Basically important is the square knot that, when improperly tied, becomes the disreputable granny knot which commits the double fault of jamming and slipping. The square knot is used to join two ends of the same size. If the ends are of different diameters, it will slip, and the sheet bend should be tied instead.

To tie the square knot, make a bight in the end of a rope. Bring the other end up through the bight, around the standing parts, and back down through the bight.

Or, more familiarly, cross the two ends, pass the first under the second, reverse the directions of the two ends, and cross the first over the second and down through the bight thus formed.

Square Knot

To untie when the rope or cord is stiff enough, grasp the standing parts on each end of the knot. Move the hands together, forcing the loops apart. When the material is soft, it is loosened by tugging one end so as to turn the knot over, whereupon it will easily slip off the end you pulled.

SURGEON'S KNOT

Surgeon's Knot

This is the same as the square knot, except that in making it by the second method described above, the two ends are given an extra twist around each other at the start. It is used by doctors to prevent the first turn of the knot from slipping. It also is handy in doing up bundles.

SHEET BEND

For joining two ends of rope, particularly when they are wet or frozen or of different sizes or materials, no knot is more efficient than the sheet bend. It never slips, is simple to tie, doesn't take much rope, and can be quickly unknotted.

Make a bight in the larger rope. As with the square knot, bring the end of the other rope up through the bight and

Sheet Bend

around the standing parts. Now pass the end of this rope under itself where it comes up through the bight, in such a way that, when tightened, it is held against the outside of the bight.

TWO HALF HITCHES

One is always finding uses for the very simple two half hitches, a particularly useful knot for fastening a rope to a ring, hook, tree, or rail. The only disadvantage to this knot is its tendency to jam under heavy strain. This can be complicated by the useless habit some have of making more than a pair of half hitches.

To make a half hitch, pass the rope around a tree, bring the end back around the standing part, and then down through the loop this formed. The other half hitch is formed by bringing the end again around the standing part and down through its own loop. Tighten.

Two Half Hitches

Clove Hitch

CLOVE HITCH

The clove hitch, which is merely a pair of half hitches made in opposite directions, is handy for fastening a rope so it will stay up around a tree trunk. It will remain secure, even on a slippery tent pole, inasmuch as the rope pulls against itself. It has the further advantage of not jamming.

Loop the rope end around the tree. Bring it over itself and take it around the tree again at a slant. Finally, slip the end under this last loop, bringing it out in a direction opposite to that of the standing part. Pressure on either end of the rope will not tighten it.

BOWLINE

The quickly tied and untied bowline, which has raised and lowered tens of thousands of individuals to safety, provides a loop that will neither tighten nor slip. This knot, which will not jam, also is an excellent way to tie the end of a slippery synthetic picket or mooring rope.

Make a small loop in the standing part of a rope. Bring the end up through it, leaving a working loop of the desired size.

Bowline

Now pass the end around the standing part of the rope and back down through the small loop.

A practical way to tie the same type of knot by feel alone, if, for instance, you want to picket a horse by a foreleg at night, is first to make a loop near the end of a rope and then to pull the standing part of the rope through it in a second loop, as shown in the drawing, "Tying a Non-Slipping, Non-Jamming Knot by Feel Alone." Hold this second loop in one hand and the rope end in the other. Pass the short end not too snugly below the fetlock just above the hoof. Shove the end into the second loop and, by pulling the second loop back through the first, work the knot into position.

FIGURE-8 KNOT

The self-descriptive and easily untied figure-8 knot, often made in the end of a rope to keep it from raveling or to pre-

Tying a Non-Slipping, Non-Jamming Knot by Feel Alone

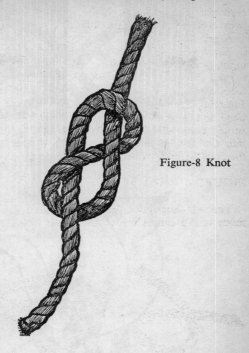

Figure-8 Knot

vent it from slipping through a block, is a good way to fasten a line or leader to a fishhook. This knot should be pulled as tight as possible.

Inasmuch as monofilament slips more than other common materials, its end should not be cut too short. Too, a knot-holding ball can be made on the free end after the knot is tied and trimmed by touching this lightly with a hot match head.

To tie the figure-8 knot, which has the look of the numeral, make a loop by bringing the end across the standing part. Fasten by shoving the end down through the first loop.

HANDCUFF KNOT

In addition to other uses, this knot may be used to help im-mobilize your dog if you ever have to tie him up to get out

Handcuff Knot

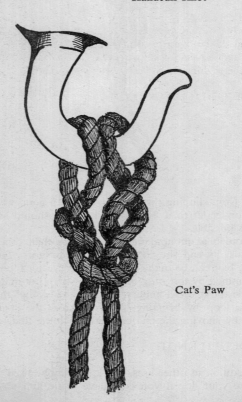

Cat's Paw

porcupine quills. The loops can also be slipped over a man's wrists, tightened, and then secured with a square knot. If you have only fishline, secure the prisoner's thumbs behind his back in the same fashion.

The handcuff knot is very simply made by passing a rope back under itself to make a small loop. Make a second loop in similar fashion and lay it over the first. You'll now have four vertical parts in a row. Pull the second of these down through the first loop and the third up through the second loop.

CAT'S PAW

The cat's paw affords a simple way of attaching a rope to a hook. Just turn a rope back beside itself to form a bight. Lift the end of the bight back on the bight to make two eyes. Pick up an eye in each hand and give each a complete turn outward from the middle. Loop both eyes over the hook.

TIMBER HITCH

Timber Hitch

Although the timber hitch is neither a permanent knot nor secure when left slack, it is a useful knot for hauling cabin logs. To lift a log with it, as from a pole tripod, take a half hitch around the end to be first hoisted. Incidentally, the timber hitch is less liable to slip if old rope is used.

To make it, pass the end of the rope around a log. Make a half hitch around the standing part. Then take two or more turns under and around the loop thus formed. Draw tight and maintain a steady pressure.

SHEEPSHANK

A sheepshank, a practical way to shorten rope that is in use, is very simply made by the above principles. Just lay

Sheepshank

three loops atop one another. Pull one side of the middle loop down through the first loop, and the other side of this center loop up through the third loop. Adjust to your liking and then tighten by pulling on the standing parts.

HITCHING TIE

This is a handy knot for tying a pack or saddle animal or a boat painter. The rope is passed around the tree or other object, and then a simple overhand knot is tied around it with the free end, only the doubled rope is pulled in a bight through the loop instead of the end itself. The free end is then used to anchor the knot by being shoved down through the bight, so the hitch cannot become accidentally untied. When this running end is pulled out of the bight and jerked, it will loosen the rope without a lot of working and fumbling.

Hitching Tie

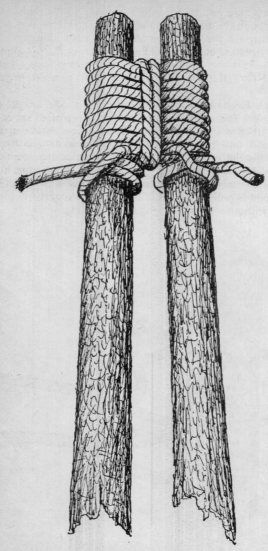

Lashing Shear Legs

LASHING SHEAR LEGS

When two poles are to be joined to support the ridgepole of a shelter, lay them side by side on the ground, wrap a short rope near their tops several times, and then tie this off with a square knot.

A sturdier job can be done, as when more of a weight is to be supported, by first placing a block between the tops of the two poles to hold them a short distance apart. Make a clove hitch around one pole. Take a half dozen turns around the two poles, laying these close to one another but not crossing them. Then remove the block and take several very tight turns around the lashings between the poles. Finish off with a clove hitch on the second pole.

Chapter 10

THE KNACK
OF MANAGING
PACK ANIMALS

THROUGHOUT the mountains and foothills of western North America, from the dusty mesquite of Mexico to the Arctic Circle, almost all unspoiled wilderness is at least two or three days' travel from the railroad or the nearest auto or wagon road. Outdoorsmen have to pack their outfits and supplies into these regions, and although planes are taking over to a certain extent these days, the most common method of transport still is with pack animals.

A large pack mule will freight more than a horse unless it happens not to be in the mood. Pound for pound, so will a burro. But among the disadvantages to be encountered with both mules and burros is that it is almost impossible to make many of them ford rivers, or even fair-sized creeks, or to traverse really boggy country. The result is that their use is confined almost exclusively to desert and high, dry regions.

For general carrying, the more amenable pack horse is commonly used. How much one can pack day after day depends on a combination of facts and imponderables having to do with terrain, weather, feed, equipment, type of load, skill of the human packers, and the temperament and aptitude of the individual animal.

An average grass-fed horse, to generalize, will pack from

about 140 to 180 pounds for weeks at a time along the steep trails to be expected in high country. This minimum can, many times, be increased. To load a horse beyond its limit for very long, however, makes for all kinds of trouble, including a sore back. This limiting figure, whatever it may be where you are going, will indicate the number of pack animals needed to handle a particular outfit.

Pack horses and mules can be expected to travel from five to twenty-five miles a day in western mountains, again depending on such factors as country, trails, and weather. Along fairly decent going, the usual pack train can average about fifteen miles a day, starting about 10 A.M., and stopping about 4 P.M. Burros are much slower. However, the location of good grazing is what generally dictates the selection of the camping sites and, thereby, the duration of each day's travel.

Most of the really fine mountain country in the United States lies within the forest reserves, where luring horse trails wind along nearly every valley and across passes. Throughout much of these western spaces, plenty of grazing exists. It is necessary that camps be chosen where there is good feed. Otherwise, the animals, even though hobbled when turned loose at night, will stray for miles in search of fodder.

When there is ample grass, it is possible, even in wilder regions, to take a pack train through almost any country where steep cliffs, peaks, very heavy timber, and downfall do not bar the way. Almost all the forests except on the thick southern slopes of the mountains are open enough to ride through anywhere. Even where you do not see a good trail, your animal often will recognize one, especially if it is in familiar terrain.

TRAVELING BY PACK TRAIN

The prospective rider who has not previously journeyed with a pack train should understand certain details about the horse and his load, and some of the procedures of traveling and camping. These differ somewhat in various localities and among different outfits. Basically, though, they're much the same in that they are hitched to the proposition that keeping the horses in good condition is the primary essential.

You're already in the wilderness, say. The party is going to break camp and travel on this day. At the first quickening of dawn, the wrangler starts out to find and drive in the animals which were turned loose the afternoon before to feed. Most of them, probably, have hobbles strapping their front legs together. The bells buckled around the necks of the leaders and recalcitrants will clang, bong, and peal the melody of their whereabouts.

Nevertheless, the horses may be feeding anywhere from a few yards to five miles from camp, although the experienced wrangler usually keeps an ear open. If, before dark, they start to drift too far, he'll often edge around and whoop them back. His own horse, if he can manage it, is staked nearby in a lush patch of grass at the end of a picket rope.

Trouble comes when the animals are not all out of the same bunch. Then they may be scattered in several groups. It can take a good half of the morning before the wrangler has located them all. Every once in a while delays of this kind must be expected. If a particular knothead becomes too much of a nuisance, though, it may be tied short to a tree all one night so it will keep so busy eating the next night that it won't have time to wander.

When the wrangler drives the horses into camp, everyone on hand, except possibly the cook, turns out to catch them, tie them up, and saddle them.

In the meantime, the cook has served breakfast. He then sees to it that everyone gets his lunch, in many cases put up the night before. After washing and drying the dishes, he packs the kitchen and the food panniers, making sure that what he needs for the next meal is where he can get at it first. He may then turn to with the others to roll up the tents, so that when the wrangler gets back with the horses, everything will be ready to be packed on them.

CARRYING CONTAINERS

PANNIERS. There is no standard size for panniers. Most of them, the best ones, measure, on the outside, about twenty-two inches long, fifteen inches high, and nine inches wide from front to back. Packers in country where it matters prefer the bottom angled back so the pannier will not stick out too much on the animal and bump into trees. One six inches wide is functional.

Pannier. Dimensions shown are those of the best panniers. The lash ropes that secure the pannier on the sawbuck saddle fit into the notches on the front edges.

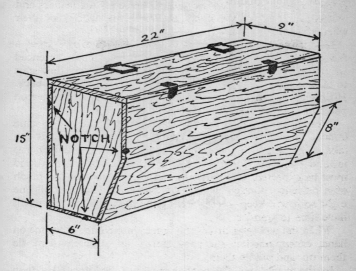

The top, bottom, and sides can be made of ⅜- or ½-inch waterproof plywood, and the ends of ⅞-inch pine or spruce. To prevent mice and chipmunks from getting at the contents, the pannier can be lined with metal or with copper screening. Notches on the front edges are made for the lash ropes that secure the pannier on the sawbuck saddle. Hinges and fasteners can be either metal or leather.

Various camp outfitters sell panniers, or "kyacks" as they are also called, made of fiberboard and plywood. You also can build them yourself, as most bushmen do. Some are made of the heaviest canvas. Especially picturesque, although not so practical as the wooden varieties, are those made of tough, untanned cowhide laced together with the hair outside.

SADDLEBAGS. An outfitter often will assign one pack horse to each outdoorsman for carrying his personal outfit. Camera equipment, however, usually is stored on the riding horse. So are binoculars.

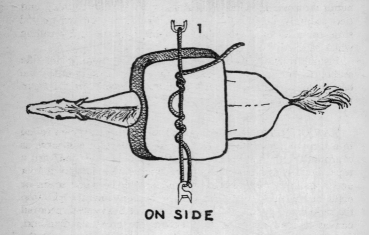

ON SIDE

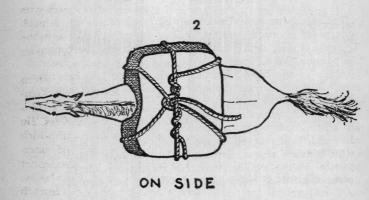

ON SIDE

Steps in Tying the Crosstree Diamond

Saddlebags are handy for this purpose in open country. If you're sidling around through trees, anything breakable is better wrapped in your extra shirt or other such clothing and tied securely behind the pommel. Watch it, too, when you stop, for a lot of cayuses have a habit of occasionally rolling when saddled.

Fishing rods can be a problem. Some stow them in stiff rifle scabbards slung from the side of the riding saddle. Often the best idea is to have a stout aluminum or fiber case for them and to trust their packing to the outfitter.

TARPAULIN. Sleeping bag and air mattress may be rolled in a tarpaulin about eight feet square which later will serve as a ground cloth, small tent, or shelter fabric, and tied with a rope. Such a bundle will measure about three feet by a foot and a half. Flat rather than round, it will be some seven or eight inches thick. It can, therefore, be conveniently laid atop the saddle and panniers. The pack cover of heavy waterproofed canvas, spread over the load before the crosstree diamond, one-man diamond, or other hitch is thrown, will protect the equipment from rain and from snagging in the brush.

If you're on your own, be sure that the ax in its sheath goes where it will be both safe and readily accessible. On a pack horse, it generally can be shoved under the lashings with the handle angling backwards and with the sheath strapped over a rope as an additional precaution against loss.

Many outfitters will furnish you with two panniers in which to carry extra clothing and other items for personal use. Generally speaking, you should place the most often used articles at the top. Shirts and such can be used to wrap breakables. Tie possessions such as binoculars and spotting scopes, with which dampness can raise hob, securely within slightly inflated waterproofs. The oilskin variety used to be popular, but now lighter and far tighter plastic containers are cheaper and not so bulky.

Equal weights must, as nearly as possible, be placed in each pannier so the two will balance on the animal. Many outfitters carry a small bathroom scale for this purpose. The panniers should be within two or three pounds of each other. Desirable maximum weights vary. Fifty pounds is sometimes the limit.

Immediately after breakfast, then, each rider packs his two panniers and bundles up his bedroll. He makes sure that he has everything on his person that he'll want during that day. He checks to see if his camera and extra clothing are ready to secure on his riding saddle.

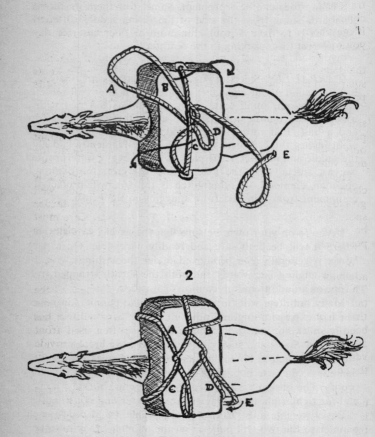

Steps in Tying the One-Man Diamond

PACKING LOADS ON HORSES

Two experienced men working together will pack a horse in about ten minutes when everything is at hand. From this, you can figure approximately how long it will take to get on the trail after the animals arrive. Every outdoorsman in horse country should learn how to pack. You never can tell when it may be necessary for you to lend a hand. Besides, one day you may want to get away on such a trip by yourself.

Anyone can learn to throw the necessary lashes and hitches, the diamond and one or two of the often ample simpler knots such as the squaw, in two or three lessons if he'll do a little practicing with a piece of string during spare moments.

Both saddling and packing are done from the near, or left, side of the animal. When packing, it saves time to work in pairs, but the off-side man goes about his task as an assistant only, taking care of the tasks that can't be handled from the near side.

The first thing to make sure of is that the animal's back is clean. A curry comb and a brush will help keep him well groomed and fit, especially if you are gentle with him at tender spots, such as where bones lie close to the surface. Care must be taken, too, that the saddle blanket is likewise as clean as possible.

SADDLE BLANKET. This good woolen blanket, or other adequate pad, goes on initially. It must be smooth and soft. Throw it on too close to the neck and then slide it toward the tail so the hair will lie right. It should extend at least some three inches beyond where the saddle is to rest. When it has been smoothed into place, put a finger under its center front and back and lift it slightly from the backbone so as to provide ventilation, and to prevent the load from pressing unduly on the spine. The saddle goes on next.

SADDLING PACK HORSES. Some latigos (the long strap used to secure the cinch) have buckles. The trick with these is to make certain that all reasonable slack is taken up between the ring and the cinch, or the tongue of the buckle may slide loose and cause the load to slip.

More commonly, the off-side packer will hand you the cinch under the belly. Shove the latigo through the cinch and then

Steps in Tying the Squaw Hitch

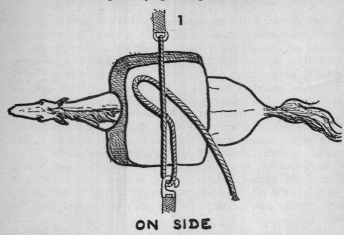

ON SIDE

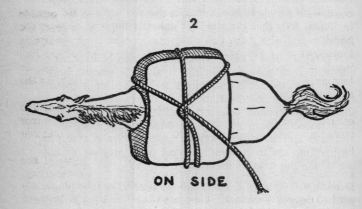

ON SIDE

3

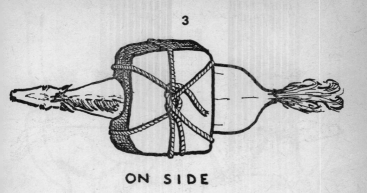

ON SIDE

continue it up through the ring on the saddle from the outside in. Depending on the length of the latigo and the size of the horse, repeat this until you have made at least two complete loops, one over the other. Although the saddle should be forward, the cinch must not be too close to the front legs, or friction will cause a sore. If the saddle has a rear cinch, do the same with that.

Now let the animal stand awhile, going on to saddle the others, if you have a string. A lot of horses, mules, and burros tense up at this stage and often take enormous breaths that will make for slack when they let it out.

When you come back, shove the left hand between the animal and the cinch ring to keep the hide from wrinkling. Draw up on the latigo until it is so tight that you can barely get two fingers between the leather and the animal. Secure with two half hitches to the saddle ring—in from the top on the left-hand side, out from the back, around to the front and across to the right, then in from the right back, out in the front, and down inside the loop made by the crossover. Tuck any remainder out of the way.

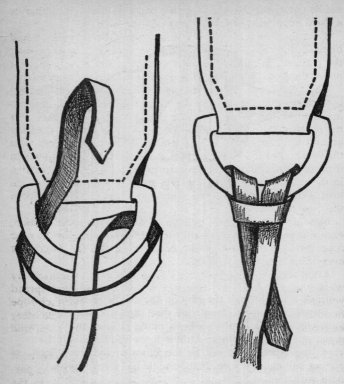

First Step in Cinching   Second Step in Cinching

The rear cinch, which is fastened the same way, should go just behind the middle of the animal, but should not be as tight as the front cinch, lest it interfere with breathing.

SLINGING ON THE LOAD. Some panniers are made with leather loops or sling straps. When the panniers are smooth, a sling rope must be used to attach them to the pack saddle. This is an easy matter, however.

Take the light sling rope and, still standing on the near side, toss one end of it over the animal's back just ahead of the saddle. At about the middle of the rope, tie two half hitches or a clove hitch on the forward fork of the saddle.

Take the free end of the rope on your side and make a half hitch on the rear fork, leaving a large enough loop to go over the pannier. Bring the free end of the rope back and shove it under the loop. The same thing is done on the opposite side.

The off-side packer gets his pannier into place first, because, with this routine, it is easier to remove this last when unpacking alone. Lift it well up into the forks. Hold it in position with the palm of the right hand. With the left hand adjust the loop around the lower side of the pannier. Pull up the slacks with the free end of the rope and take a turn around the loop where it passes across the middle of the pannier. Now tie a bowline in the end of the rope so this will reach the top center of the load. Flip the loop over the animal so it can be reached from the near side.

Now sling on the near pannier in exactly the same fashion, except that no bowline is tied. Instead, slip the end of the near rope through the loop of the bowline on the far line, draw everything tight, and tie it off.

After the panniers have thus been slung and secured, lay what you are going to across or between them, and spread your pack cover into place. Then, with a strong half-inch rope braided to the ring of a canvas pack cinch, which, at its other extremity, has something such as a large wooden hook, bind down the entire load.

One of the hitches shown in the illustrations can be used for this purpose. This should be made as tight as possible, particularly as the tension will be on the pack and not on the animal. Get purchase when you have to by bracing a foot against the animal's side.

SADDLING TO RIDE

Often the sportsman and his guide will start out right after breakfast on their own horses. Many times they'll arrive at the next camp after the train has pulled in, to find the shelters already pitched and the cook sour-faced, maybe, because someone has made a jocose remark about the mulligan that is simmering. On some occasions, too, the sportsman will travel with the pack train, out in front where he can spot game and keep out of the dust. In either event, as soon as he has had enough experience, he should see to the saddling of his own horse.

ADJUSTMENT OF GIRTH RINGS AND STIRRUPS. The natural tendency when saddling, especially with the heavier western jobs, is to heave the girth rings and stirrups too high. This causes them to bang noisily against such tender spots as leg joints and ribs. A lot of resultant shying and sidestepping can be avoided by swinging these just high enough to land easily on your mount's back, where they'll slide down smoothly.

Or, place the right stirrup and the cinch or breeching across the seat of the saddle. Then, gripping the horn with the left hand and the back center of the saddle with the right hand, swing the saddle just high enough so you can settle it easily on the blanket. Go around and straighten up, at the same time taking down the stirrup and cinch or breeching.

The same fundamentals that apply to readying the animal for the pack saddle apply when it comes to saddling for riding.

The knees are not used in western riding as they are in the east. With the western saddle, therefore, the stirrups should be long enough so you will clear the seat by about two inches when standing in them. You'll then be able to rely on balance and on the grip of your thighs, employing your partly tensed knees and ankles as springs to absorb any roughness that otherwise would be jarring or jolting. There is a tremendous difference in horses in this respect. Without exaggeration, some actually trot more smoothly than others walk.

MOUNTING AND RIDING. A smooth and sure way of getting into the western saddle is to take the lines in the left hand, stand to the left of the head of the animal, facing the tail, secure a firm grip on the bridle cheek with the left hand, put the left foot lightly in the stirrup, grab the horn securely with the right hand, and then swing aboard in one fluid motion while using the horn as a pivot. This natural arc is spoiled, as you can readily understand, by the awkward, if common, habit of grasping the back of the saddle with the right hand.

In any event, when you're ready to get on, particularly if you and the animal are strangers, the main thing is to be in control. Horses differ. With a very few, you'll have to rein the head around, forcing the animal into a turn if it insists on moving ahead before you're ready. Others begin to fret and sometimes to pitch if you're heavy on the bit. Mostly, a firm but light hold on the lines will be sufficient.

Unless you want to be bequeathed the deadest old plug in the remuda the next day, don't, like a lot of dudes, clamber into the saddle and then yell for someone to hand you the dingblasted reins.

Slippery Hitch. This knot is used to tie the lead rope of a pack animal to any projection on the animal ahead.

Keep the lines low ordinarily, although, if a knothead is inclined to pitch, you may want to curb that impulse by holding its head high. Don't fall into the practice, very common among dudes, of knotting the ends of the reins together as soon as you climb on a strange horse. Then, if anything goes wrong, or even if you get off for some reason, you're apt to find yourself plumb afoot.

The times when you want to ride reinless, twist them a couple of times around the horn and perhaps top off with a single half hitch. Then, if anything goes amuck, the lines will soon be dangling, to halt the animal if it's been broken to ground rein, or to impede it long enough for you to have a chance to ease around and catch it.

HITTING THE TRAIL

When the outfit is ready to hit the trail, the lead rope of all but the front animal is tied to the tail, pack, or to a rope loop fastened for that purpose around the rear fork of the pack saddle of the horse ahead. The knot used is one that can be instantly jerked free if something goes wrong. The wrangler holds the lead of the foremost animal and rides off.

Or, with the horses turned loose, the wrangler starts ahead, and the cook closes in behind. Occasionally a horse bolts or strays out of line, and the rear man urges him back. This he does slowly and quietly, so as not to excite the string. Some days may be full of all kinds of trouble: spooked horses, turning packs, and snagged or bogged-down animals. Little distance then will be covered. On other days, you may traverse as much as a rousing thirty miles. The thing is to try to keep the pack train moving, all the time watching for slipping loads that will necessitate repacking on the spot.

The wrangler is the man to say where the next camp shall be made. He is responsible for the horses, and he must stop where feed is good, where there's water, and where he can hold the animals reasonably close.

MAKING CAMP

Everyone generally turns to when camp is reached, catching the animals and tying them well apart. Preferably the lead ropes should be secured at least waist high and short enough so the animals can't step over them or become entangled in nearby brush.

Knots are loosened and panniers eased to the ground in pairs, in such a way that their markings can easily be identified. Ropes are coiled and laid together in one place. Pack covers are folded and stacked, or, if the weather is foul, spread protectively over the gear.

Saddles, which probably have been selected to fit certain animals and identified by names or numbers, are lined up over a convenient log or upside-down on the ground. Blankets are spread out, down side up, over their respective saddles to dry. If rain is falling or threatening, all these may be stacked in piles beneath the waterproof pack covers.

Finally, after perhaps some grooming, hobbles and bells should be strapped on and the halters removed so the animals will not accidentally get their feet in them. These halters, with their attached lead ropes, should be hung in one place, away from little forest folk who would gnaw them for their salt.

PACK HORSE TRIPS FOR TWO

There is no reason why two individuals reasonably accustomed to handling horses, to camping in the wilderness, and to traveling with a map, should not take an extended pack horse trip by themselves. It means a lot of work, for if you fish persistently during the day, you will have cooking, tackle, repairs, and odd jobs to take care of sometimes late into the night. Horse wrangling, too, frequently will interfere.

Two outdoorsmen can rent—or often even more cheaply, buy—four horses (two horses for riding and two pack horses) and live the life for months at a time. One pack horse will be able to carry all the outfit needed. The other, if you plan carefully, will have no trouble in handling enough food for a couple of campers for a month. As for taking care of your own horses, lone trappers and prospectors often travel with six or seven.

Or, to a lesser extent, you can do the same thing with mules. In many ways most easily of all, you can pack your gear on one or more burros and hike where you want to go.

Chapter 11

HANDLING CANOES
ON WATER AND LAND

A CANOE will carry more than a half-dozen husky pack animals. Its capacity will vary with the size and design of the hull, but even a sixteen-footer can take up to a thousand pounds. Such a craft, with a width of at least thirty-three inches and a depth of at least a foot, will accommodate two men, an adequate camping outfit, and two weeks' provisions very nicely, at the same time not floating too deeply in the water.

Northeastern America embraces some of the finest canoe country in the world. Maine, adjoining portions of Canada, and the Adirondacks in New York afford opportunities for long and short cruises through interesting silences. There are many small eastern rivers that gurgle and tinkle across lowlands into the Atlantic or Mississippi, traversing regions where one can usually camp freely, and all providing good fishing.

The most superb canoe stronghold of all lies in northern Minnesota and in northern and western Ontario and Quebec. In these latter regions there is a practically unspoiled wilderness with almost as much water as land, and such myriads of small lakes and connecting rivers that it is literally possible on nearly any given day to paddle your little craft toward any point of the compass.

All this land has been Indian canoe country for hundreds of generations. Wherever there is an obstacle to water travel, you usually will find a trail or an easy way through or around. Portages they are called, and in the North you sometimes see where they are worn a foot deep in the soil and where the very rocks have been polished by thousands of moccasins.

The only really practical craft for the sportsman who travels such waters is the canoe. This can be easily portaged—around rapids, past thunderous falls, and between lakes—on one man's shoulders, if need be. In it wild animals can be noiselessly approached. Because the canoe is made to be handled with the occupants facing forward, it is the only satisfactory craft for running the usual rapids and for ascending swift streams. It can be poled. It can be lined. You can wade it, too, handling it where waters momentarily deepen by swimming with one hand on the stern.

Today the aluminum alloy canoes are superior to other types in almost every way, although it is often desirable to subdue the glare with a deadgrass shade of paint, and to include the available rubber gunwale guards for both stern and bow paddlers in the interest of silence.

CANOE UPKEEP

In fresh water particularly, aluminum canoes require a minimum of upkeep. An occasional washing will keep bottom fouling from interfering with the craft's speed. Although the metal dents easily, like a good boxer it rolls with the blow and is not easily cut. Minor dents can be tapped out with a rubber or nylon mallet, the spot being backed with a rounded block of metal or hardwood. Begin by striking around the outer edges, gradually working toward the middle.

With an aluminum craft, you should include one of the special kits containing patches, sealing compound, and rivets. Minor punctures can usually be temporarily repaired with cold solder, marine glue, or even a strip of ordinary waterproof adhesive tape from your medicine kit. Permanent patches of aluminum need not be unsightly.

With a canvas canoe, pack along one of the waterproof glues, some heavy canvas, a can of copper rivets, some white lead, and maybe an old spoon and brush. You also can do pretty well in a pinch by using spruce pitch, melted along with a candle stub, in which to soak and cement on a strip of fabric requisitioned from the flap of a duffle bag.

SPEED, STABILITY, AND MANEUVERABILITY

In canoe country an 18-footer is a practical length for two outdoorsmen. A 16-footer often is excellent for one man.

Besides adding to stability, length has the advantages of easier paddling and more speed because of higher buoyancy that lifts the whole craft higher, reducing water resistance. Length can be excessive, however, especially along windy stretches. On the other hand, shortness and the resulting reduced weight are most often advantages only during portaging and storing.

Stability and capacity increase with width. So does the exertion required to paddle and to make speed.

Canoes with round bottoms are faster and hold their course better than crafts with flat bottoms. The former, therefore, are preferable on lakes, although more tippy until you get used to rolling with the craft. On the other hand, a keel can lend maneuverability to a flat-bottomed canoe. So can a heavy load. Shallow draft is another attribute of the flatter bottom. Among the rocks and fast currents of rapids, a canoe of this type will respond much more promptly to the paddle. A deep keel will interfere with this manageability, although a broad, flat keel will not.

When the bottom and keel round up slightly toward stern and bow, the then highly tractable canoe becomes especially fitted for running rapids and for similar tight work. An experienced paddler can practically spin such a craft on its center. A canoe with no real upcurve, in contrast, will hold steady much better in wind on a large body of water. It will also paddle faster and easier and take shallows better.

Low ends will reduce the wind's effect. So will a fairly deep keel, at the same time adding slightly to stability. Such a keel can be dangerous in white water, though, impairing control as the currents hit it in different directions. A flat keel about three-eighths of an inch deep, sometimes known as a shoe, does not affect a canoe's actions, being used mainly as protection in the same way as are rub stripes that may be screwed on parallel to the keel.

The way a canoe is loaded may have even more effect on seaworthiness than its design.

LOADING THE CANOE

A canoe should be loaded only when it is afloat or nearly so. The weight, preferably centered as low as possible, usually is so distributed that when its occupant or occupants step in, the canoe will ride just noticeably deeper at stern than at bow, making it easier to steer. Contrary to considerable opinion, however, a canoe slips through the water most easily when it sits on its waterline, with neither bow nor stern higher. It should always be trimmed, of course, so the side balance is absolutely central.

If you figure to run rapids during the day, crowd the weight as close to the center as possible. Loaded thus, the craft will turn much more quickly.

Then, elbows ever straight and arms swinging naturally from the shoulders, you can control it with a stroke so basic that, in its customary unhurried rhythm, the first descending arc of each full-armed sweep can be largely maintained by gravity. The resulting intervals of relaxation before each forward lurch of the shoulders keep you from seriously tiring, although, toughening as you go, you continue along day after day.

LOADING FOR WET GOING

If you expect rain or rough going, place four light poles or a few spruce boughs in the bottom before loading to keep articles slightly above any water that may come aboard. This will then run harmlessly to where the stern paddler can bail it out from time to time. It's also sometimes a good idea in such exigencies to make sure that what's at the base of the load is either something that will not be damaged by soaking, or that it is in waterproof containers.

Another good angle, in some water, is to lay a light tarp amidships and to stow all but the heaviest articles in this. Finish by drawing the canvas up around the thus enclosed outfit and lashing it as securely closed as possible. The ax can be shoved within easy reach under these lashings and the strap of its sheath buckled over one or more as an extra safety measure.

Do not tie or otherwise attach this bundle to the canoe.

Anything particularly cumbersome and heavy, like bags of canned goods (their contents identified by scratches in case the labels are soaked off), should be laid by itself, directly on the bottom of the craft, with the tarp-wrapped essentials packed atop them. Then, if you happen to have a wreck, the latter will float, and you'll have an excellent chance of recovering them intact and dry.

This is particularly true if the highly buoyant sleeping bags are included within the tarp. The canoe can be loaded much more compactly, in any event, if the larger of these are so folded before being rolled that they can be wedged from side to side instead of being stowed lengthwise.

LIFE PRESERVERS

Sleeping robes have an additional use that it may be well to keep in mind. Those with down and similar fillers make good life preservers to grab in an emergency, especially if there is a stout strap or thong on them which you can grasp in a hurry.

A lot of bushmen keep their sleeping bags handy for this reason, often using them for a seat or for a pad on which to kneel while paddling. In a small canoe, however, an inexpensive life preserver cushion filled with fresh kapok will serve the same purpose a lot more conveniently.

Too, warm, practical, comfortable jackets, coats, and vests are now available which serve like other outdoor clothing but which have the additional advantage of acting as life preservers. Their buoyancy can save your life.

There are two basic types of such clothing which contain the usual pockets and, in numerous instances, duplicate conventional outer jackets. The inflatables depend on a small carbon dioxide cartridge which will instantly inflate an inner air chamber. The unsinkables generally employ sheets of polyvinyl foam concealed among various outer and inner fabrics.

EVERYTHING IN ITS PLACE

Anything you want to get during the day, such as lunch or a boiling kettle, tuck conveniently into a side space. Camera and fishing tackle also should be accessible. Tents and waterproofs should be on the outside of rolls and packs in case you have to make camp in a downpour. If you figure you are going to need your down jacket, wedge it up under the bow or stern deck where it can easily be reached.

The first individual across a portage should bring an ax, in case any cutting has to be done. The fellow whose job it is to tote the canoe should go over a strange carry with a pack first to become familiar with it. When he takes the canoe, another packer should go along with him, if possible.

If two canoeists can reduce their duffle to just three packs, each of which they can carry without undue effort, the work of portaging will be greatly simplified. They'll then have to make but two trips. Each will take a pack on the first. On the second, one will bring a pack and help the other, where he can, with the canoe.

Whether you adopt these methods of packing and handling your outfit, or have the fun of devising a routine of your own, adhere to a system. Have a place for everything and everything in its place. It means less delay, labor, and confusion in traveling and in camp, too, and you'll have more time to devote to the wilderness about you.

Such a system also takes most of the drudgery out of portaging. It can even make a carry something to look forward to as a break in the monotony of paddling, an opportunity to stretch the legs, and in chilly weather, a chance to get some welcome exercise. As for any discomforts, you'll soon forget them at the next glittering challenge of open water.

PORTAGING

It is not nearly so difficult to take a canoe over a portage as anyone who has not tried it might imagine, especially as the load balances itself on the shoulders and presses straight down.

Almost invariably the experienced canoeist uses his two paddles to form the carrying yoke. These are lashed with something such as heavy line between the center thwart and front seat, blades to the former and handles to the latter. The part of the upper portion of the blade which is about three inches wide should come just in front of the thwart. The distance between the two blades should be such that they will lie comfortably on the shoulders when the back of the neck is resting slightly against the thwart.

A well-made canoe should nearly balance on the center thwart, being just a trifle heavier towards the stern. Then, when your head and shoulders are in place, and, reaching a little ahead, you grasp each gunwale and pull down slightly to balance the boat, its bow will ride about six feet above the ground. This clearance will enable you to choose your footing and to steer the craft past trees and other obstacles.

HOISTING THE CANOE

There are several ways to get a canoe up on your shoulders. Until you get the knack, any of these can strain you, especially when you're still soft from city living. Better get an experienced canoeman to coach you, and don't attempt anything beyond your strength.

The easiest and safest method is to turn the canoe over. While your companion raises the bow at arms' length above his head, step under, place your head between the paddles and the back of your neck against the thwart, and lift. If you are alone, lift the bow and lean it against a tree or rock while you get underneath.

For a carry of more than fifty yards or so, some padding for the shoulders will be desirable. Many simply put on their jackets. Incidentally, keep your eyes open for a tree crotch or boulder that will hold the bow and let you step out from under for a rest.

USES OF THE TUMP LINE

The almost universal method of portaging grub and equipment across a carry is with a tump line, packsack, or combination of the two. The tump line consists of a broad band of thick, soft leather, about three inches wide and fifteen inches long. Canvas sometimes is used instead. To each end of this head piece is attached something such as a rope or rawhide thong, perhaps ten feet long. Tapering straps are so employed, too, their length being adjustable by buckles.

These two extremities are secured to the bundle to be packed, in such a way that, at the proper height above the bundle the headband forms a loop. This usually goes over the forehead at about the natural hairline, while the bundle rests against the middle of the back, just over the hips. The weight is thus supported by the head, the neck muscles, and the spinal column. It is steadied by pressure on the shoulders, back, and hips.

The sportsman will find the tump line a vexing way of packing until he develops strength and endurance in his neck muscles. He should never attempt it, except experimentally, on his first wilderness journey. But if he is to continue taking canoe vacations year after year, he should learn to use this flexible accessory, for with it a greater weight can be packed than in any other manner.

The base to which the tump line is attached often consists of a roll of bedding or a sack of flour. This rests low down, almost on top of the hips. When it is in place, other bundles, such as flour sacks, duffle bags, and loose articles of almost any kind, are piled on top.

Reaching in some instances above the top of the packer's head, these go more or less between the two lines stretching up from the base bundle to the headpiece. The packer keeps everything in place by bending slightly forward. It's not so difficult to balance the load as one might expect. Depending on the individual's strength and experience, regular loads may weigh up to 200 pounds or more.

The tump line is at its best for short distances on plainly marked portages. Its advantages are too often offset when you have to pick your way over rough ground, for the head is bent downward in such a way that you cannot turn it without swinging your whole body. You cannot even easily see what lies ahead.

The tump line's chief value lies in the fact that, with it, more can be taken over the portage in one trip. Only one tump line per man is needed. It is simply untied from one load and hitched to the next.

PACKSACK FOR PORTAGING

The other form of pack that is most commonly used by experienced voyageurs is the packsack, variously known by such names as the Duluth, Maine, Woods, Poirier, and Northwestern. Basically, it is simply a canvas pack or sack, approximately fifteen to twenty inches wide and twenty-five to thirty inches long, opening at the top. Shoulder straps extend from a central point at the top to the two bottom corners.

Many outfitters make it up in a reinforced boxlike bag of waterproofed duck, about eighteen by twenty-six by eight inches. Extra pockets are sometimes sewed on the outside and in the flap that covers the square top opening. In addition, provision often is made for attaching an optional tump line to buckles or D-rings on the outer edges of the sack near the top.

Camp duffle and grub are stowed inside the sack up to its capacity in weight and bulk, soft materials nearest the back and lighter goods at the bottom. One packsack commonly carries all eating and cooking utensils, as well as victuals to be used at the next meal. On arrival at the new camp, this is deposited near the site for the fire so the cook can get busy pronto.

Blankets can be folded and packed inside a sack, and so can the tent or shelter cloth. But, commonly, these are rolled and the bundle balanced on top of a fully loaded packsack, where it is easily carried. Rations and other essentials are frequently packed in waterproof duffle bags, about nine by twenty-four inches, which are supplied by most camp outfitters. These also can be conveniently balanced atop the pack.

As the shoulder straps may, at times, have to bear a considerable weight, they should be broad where they go over the shoulders. It also is a good thing to pad them there with sheepskin to which the fleece is still attached. The tump line may be used to take some of the heft off the shoulder straps. In fact, employing the support in this manner is the easiest way to get the hang of using it alone.

PACK BASKET

A good pack for those kitchen goods is the old-fashioned pack basket, so popular in northern New York and Maine. Strong and resilient, it protects the breakable and crushable objects from being jammed together, and at the same time rides easily on the back. In camp, you can hang it in a shady place, along with perishables that need coolness and ventilation. The bedroll perches so easily on top of one that the two combined make a load that's light enough for almost anyone.

OTHER PACKS

Many other types of packs can be used for carrying fairly heavy loads short distances. Steer clear of those which have the shoulder straps attached far apart to the top of the pack. These will be slipping down on your arms continually. Shoulder straps should start very close together from the top of the pack, even from a single large D-ring. Those of thick, oil-tanned leather are far superior to webbing.

The Bergans type of frame rucksack and the Alaskan pack board are excellent. Even though the former cannot very well have bags piled atop it, one is convenient for packing valuables like camera and binoculars that have been safely tied within partially inflated plastic bags, and indispensables, such as fishline, hooks, and flies. You can stow this under your seat, buckling or snapping one strap fast if you want. If it'll float, and a sealer cloth at the open end may be enough to assure this, the better procedure may be to leave it free. Either way, you can get at it in a hurry, if need be.

Probably the only reason why the especially adaptable pack board has not become widely popular among canoeists is because it has not yet reached the northeastern canoe country. It certainly is the best way to pack hard and unwieldy objects, particularly outboard motors. Instead, these last are often wrapped in some impervious cover and then in a tent, and packed with the tump line.

Cans of gas or oil are often tied one to each end of an eight-foot pole, and the pole then balanced over one shoulder in coolie fashion. Loose articles, such as rods and axes, are carried by hand. It is not uncommon to note a bucket, filled with almost anything, also so borne.

OUTBOARD MOTORS

Canoes are available with square sterns to which motors can be attached. Or an outboard can be secured, with the help of a bracket, to the side of a regular canoe.

The motor, in any event, should be a small one, although the broader and longer the craft, the larger the outboard that can be utilized safely. But the point is, a real canoe is designed for paddling speed. An outboard that will propel it at that speed is capable of bringing out the best in the canoe's design. Added power, as well as being possibly dangerous, is largely wasted in that it merely churns up the water. Too, the smaller motors are economical besides being lightweight, a quality appreciated on portages.

PADDLING

CHOOSING A PADDLE

Canoe manufacturers, particularly the veterans in the business, are the best sources for paddles. Paddles sold by motor boat dealers are generally made to be carried for emergency use on outboard motor boats. Paddles made of ash, maple, and spruce are the staunchest. Be sure to buy a spare, too. Select a medium-wide rather than a very wide blade. The paddle for stern use should reach from the ground to your nose; for bow paddling, to your chin.

BEST PADDLING POSITION

Most experienced canoeists paddle from a kneeling position, on one knee or both, sitting on the thwart or a seat only for resting and for wider vision in white water. The stability of the canoe depends on keeping the weight low. Too, by staying most of the time in the bottom of the craft, you will be able to put more power into your strokes and still finish the day less tired than if you had paddled from a sitting position.

Unless the canoe is especially packed or heavily loaded, the usual stern position lifts the bow too high out of the water when you're traveling alone. There are two remedies. Shift your position to the next thwart forward. Or put a rock or other weight in the bow. With an empty canoe, without a weight in the bow, paddle from near amidships.

STEERING

When paddling alone for the first time, learn as soon as possible how to maintain a straight course without changing sides almost every stroke. Begin on whichever side seems easiest for you. Reach well ahead to start your stroke. Then angle the blade slightly in drawing it back. The inside edge should lead, with just enough angle to offset the ordinary tendency of the bow to be shoved to the opposite side from which you're paddling. If necessary, give the paddle even more of a twist before completing the stroke. All this you will be able to determine for yourself by easy experimentation.

Another way to keep straight is to conclude each stroke with an outward push of the blade. Again, personal experimenting is the key. If you overdo the final lunge and the bow is pulled too far to the side opposite your stroke, another stroke or two, with the blade held straight, will get you back on course. Actually, it's all easier to do than to describe.

When you have mastered this technique from one side, it's a simple matter to shift sides. You'll want to do this occasionally, anyway, if only to rest your muscles.

Get in the habit of leaning well forward. The arms may be kept straight effectively, although some bend the upper arm a little. Short, rather rapid strokes are more effective than long, slow ones when you are trying to cover distance. Short, choppy strokes are not only less tiring, but they maintain the canoe's momentum better, particularly if you're paddling against current or wind.

With two canoeists, the more experienced paddler should be in the stern where his strokes will offset those of the man in the bow. Paddling on opposite sides will pretty much keep the canoe on a straight course, although it still will be up to the bow man to steer. Whenever the man in the bow wants to shift paddling sides, the man in the stern should follow suit. With the bow paddler maintaining even, regular strokes, the stern paddler often will find himself taking advantage of the momentum by finishing his strokes with the paddle held as a rudder. This way, with the blade at right angles to the current, it will be easy to urge the stern smoothly either right or left.

LINING THROUGH RAPIDS

Where fast water is encountered, a hundred feet or so of half-inch rope should be included in the outfit, to be used as a tracking line as well as for the various other uses for which rope may be required. Polyethylene line is better than manila or nylon, in that it does not stretch and is unaffected by water.

Rapids that are either too rough or too shallow to be safely navigated are often traversed by tracking. Different canoeists have their own methods. One way is to attach one end of the rope to the bow and the other end to a middle thwart on the land side, thus distributing the strain. Then one man tows the canoe. The other man, walking the bank with a pole, keeps the craft clear. In shallow water, however, it is frequently necessary to wade and to guide the canoe by hand.

Two ropes are sometimes used, one attached to the bow and the other to the stern. By varying their length, it is possible to angle the canoe in the current in such a way that it can be both steered and towed.

POLING

Poling often beats paddling, especially along shallow streams and in sloughs. Such softwoods as fir, spruce, and tamarack are best when you have to cut them on the spot. Standing deadwood will pay off in toughness and lightness. The pole should be some twelve to fourteen feet long, at least an inch thick at the top, and about twice that at the butt.

MAKING A POLE

Get off the bark and smooth down the knots. If possible, attach a soft-iron point, available from dealers. If such a shoe is not at hand, round the end and then harden it in the fringes of an open fire for a half-hour or so to prevent splitting and fraying.

In logging country, maple, hickory, and ash pickpoles are available. Although heavier than softwoods, they are tougher and will come in very handy in a canoe, under proper circumstances. Incidentally, treat them like ax handles and never paint or varnish them, or they'll blister your hands. Such a pole can be rubbed with boiled linseed oil. Even this is not necessary, however, as using it will give it a really genuine hand-rubbed finish.

Along many small, rocky streams, canoeists proceed more often with poles than paddles, especially in the dry season. With the canoe trimmed as for paddling, one or two men can thus take it, either upstream or downstream, many places otherwise inaccessible except by laborious lining. The technique is not difficult. A couple of afternoons with canoe and pole will usually teach you the fundamentals. After that, it's merely a matter of practice.

Any canoe will do, especially one with broad beam and flat bottom. Round-bottom canoes and the small, narrow varieties are less stable. Ordinary shoeing makes little difference, but a pronounced keel will make it difficult to set a canoe over sideways in a hurry.

If you're alone, stand comfortably in the stern with one leg braced against the stern thwart or seat. Poling can be done from either side, and it is customary to shift at will, either to take advantage of terrain or to rest. Grasp the middle of the pole, with the master hand higher. Set the butt firmly in the stream bed. Then push lightly and evenly, swinging into the pole with arm, shoulders, and entire body. As the canoe advances, climb the pole hand over hand, continuing the even thrust until you reach the top.

Then, going into a slight crouch, give the pole one final shove, continuing to make this smooth and steady so that you won't push the canoe out from under you, as beginners often do.

STEERING AND STOPPING

Now walk your hands back down the pole, and, with a sudden upward flip, lift the pole from the water. Some canoeists try to steer by dragging the pole back through the water, but this cuts down on the momentum. Steering can be controlled instead by the direction of the pushing itself. Get another bite with the pole and repeat, never losing momentum. As you gain experience, you'll find that this continued momentum is easier to achieve if you take every advantage of the water, seeking backwaters and eddies where the current is comparatively still.

Snubbing becomes an important technique for slowing or stopping forward motion when coming downstream. The technique, which will come naturally to those with good balance, is simple. Merely reach ahead while the canoe is moving and set the pole as firmly as possible at a point opposite the center of the canoe, as close to the gunwale as possible. With feet braced and knees flexed, lean into it. This will stop a slow-moving canoe.

At higher speeds, as in white water, you may have to snub the craft several times before you can bring it to a standstill. Then come in to shore, shove the canoe around a rock or other obstruction, or merely hesitate long enough to plot a course ahead.

Chapter 12

MAKING SHELTERS
WITH WHAT'S
AT HAND

A FALLEN tree often is at hand under whose roots a browse bed can be laid so as to benefit from a crackling night blaze. It is not unusual, either, to come upon a dry indentation in a stream bank that can be speedily roofed with brush and cheered by a campfire in front.

No ceiling is more pleasant, under favorable conditions, than the open sky. The only refinements one wants on such nights, if indeed he desires any, are a mattress of evergreen boughs, a long hardwood fire, and maybe a log behind him to reflect warmth on those portions not turned toward the friendly blaze.

On other occasions—when there is storm or cold, or when the situation is such that every reasonable effort should be directed at conserving the utmost energy, as when one is lost —the time and effort required for throwing up a bivouac may well be repaid severalfold.

Under circumstances when it may be desirable or even necessary to remain in one area, you may as well enjoy the best available shelter. This will be especially true if food is in short supply, for then you may expect strength to be conserved in direct proportion to your ability to remain comfortably and warmly relaxed.

CAVES

These temporary shelters today are distinguished by the same qualities that would have made them desirable during the Stone Age. You want some place dry, protected from the wind, safe, and preferably small enough to be easily heated. Such natural bivouacs, in the form of shallow caves, are happened upon everywhere in the wildernesses of North America.

EVERGREEN BIVOUACS

No one should have much difficulty in finding sanctuary in softwood country, for no ax is necessary and, in fact, you can get along very well without even a knife.

A heavy grove of big evergreens itself affords considerable shelter. How many times during a sudden shower have you kept dry by lingering under a spruce or pine, and on how many occasions in snow country have you avoided deep going by keeping as much as possible to tall, thick stands of conifers? There usually is sufficient small growth in such forests to break off and angle in lean-to form against a protective log or trunk.

On those occasions when you find yourself among low fir and spruce, few things are simpler than to make a niche by stripping a few lower branches from a well-situated tree. These boughs, augmented by others from nearby trees, will rapidly floor and thatch the shelter. Such a nook is especially easy to heat with the abundance of fuel almost always available in such terrain.

If a blizzard is scuffing or rain dripping and some easily handled bark such as that from birch trees is available, you'll probably want to insert a few sheets at least overhead. For bedding, a soft mass of additional boughs sandwiched between such waterproofing bark can furnish surprising comfort, even when the rest of the wilderness is restless with wet and cold.

SNOW SHELTERS

Snow can make the task of bivouacking even easier. Suppose you're traveling along a wilderness river. There may be boulders along the shore between which snow walls can be heaped and over them several young evergreens spread. Among the driftwood likely at hand, there's apt to be some large, dry snags which, when a fire is kindled against them, will themselves burn with the help of enough occasional small fuel to keep them going.

Another way to get by is to tunnel into sufficiently deep snow, taking care to do this at right angles to the wind, so there will be less chance of the opening's being choked by drift.

When snow lies heavy, still another procedure is to open a crude hole from the top down. Such a trench often can be made by stamping. It may be in the shape of a rough triangle with the wider end, roofed and floored with evergreen, large enough to sit or curl up in, with the narrower part reflecting a small fire.

PRECAUTION AGAINST DRIFTS

Naturally, one should avoid making a snow camp where there may be danger from rapidly forming drifts, from over-hang, or from slides.

If in open country, beware of making a snow shelter on the side of a slope that is protected from the wind. Taking such a precaution is exactly opposite from what you would do in the forest, but in open terrain such lees gather drifts that can bury and suffocate one.

Keeping dry is particularly important under such conditions, inasmuch as clothing that becomes damp or frozen quickly loses its qualities of insulation. Instead of sitting or lying in direct contact with snow, you will find it safer to have some protective material between. This may be an oilskin game-bag, section of plastic, mitts, boughs, or any handy bark.

SNOW HOUSE

An easy way to go about constructing a snow house in very cold weather, as you may have found out for yourself, is to heap snow in a mound slightly larger than the shelter desired. Pack down the final surface. If the weather is well below freezing and if water is at hand, throw that over the pile so

Snow House. Dotted lines indicate ventilation hole.

a glaze of ice will be formed. Otherwise, let the mound harden as well as it will in the air for a half-hour or so.

Then burrow into the pile at right angles to the wind. Keep scooping out snow until as thin a shell as seems practical remains. Build a small blaze within. Any water will be blotted up by the remaining snow. Finally, drag out embers and ashes, poke a ventilation hole through the dome, and allow the shelter to ice.

A very small fire within such a snow house, augmented by body heat, will keep the temperature surprisingly comfortable. The tendency, in fact, probably will be toward overheating. Extremely important in any event will be the maintenance of good ventilation.

LEAN-TOS ARE EASY

The lean-to put up for temporary occupancy in the wilderness will be essentially a simple frame on which is leaned, hung, lashed, pinned, woven, or otherwise affixed such covering as may be available.

One way to go about building such a shelter is by driving two forked sticks into the ground about seven feet apart and laying a pole between the two crotches. All you have to do then is make a tentlike enclosure by angling long evergreen boughs from ridgepole to ground along each side. Then close at least one end, possibly by laying several small firs against it.

More complicated frames are easily enough assembled, particularly when the joints are fastened, perhaps by lashing them with fine but tough spruce roots, or with wiry birch or willow withes. Natural forks can be used instead, of course. So can braces. Although a knife will simplify the task, not even that is necessary.

The skeleton can then be draped, laced, or otherwise covered with green branches, moss, bark, grass, reeds, leafy vines, or other such wilderness materials.

There are a few basic principles in building such a shelter, but these are self-evident. When thatching a roof, as you may do with bark, start at the eaves and lay the bottom of each succeeding layer across the top of the thickness beneath, so any water will tend to run unimpeded off the edge. If you happen to build a roof with a double pitch, you can waterproof it further by bending bark over the ridge and fastening or weighing it down on each slant.

When thatching the walls, commence at the bottom, as in all shingling, and work up, layer by layer, with each higher series covering the top of the one immediately below. Water then will be more apt to run down the outside of the structure instead of into it.

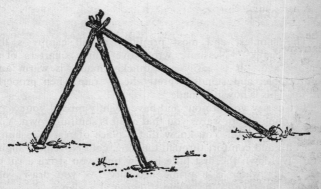

Lean-to Frame

Elaborate Lean-to Frame

The most satisfactory way to describe some of the more common types of lean-tos is by means of the accompanying self-explanatory illustrations. From these even a greenhorn can readily figure out the most practical way to use whatever wilderness materials happen to be near at hand.

If you've something such as a tarpaulin to stretch over a pole framework, your work will be considerably lessened. This will be true if only because the roof can thus be quickly rendered waterproof. A large rectangle of plastic, folded and carried in a shirt pocket, is not a bad thing to take along at all times in the wilderness, if only for possible emergency use as a rainy day cover.

INDIAN CAMP

"The simplest and most primitive of all camps is the 'Indian camp,'" Nessmuk wrote over three quarters of a century ago. "It is easily and quickly made, is warm and comfortable, and stands a pretty heavy rain when properly put up. This is how it is made.

"Let us say you are out and have slightly missed your way. The coming gloom warns you that night is shutting down. You are no tenderfoot. You know that a place of rest is essential to health and comfort through the long, cold November night. You dive down the first little hollow until you strike a rill of water, for water is a prime necessity. As you draw your hatchet you take in the whole situation at a glance.

"The little stream is gurgling downward in a half-choked frozen way. There is a huge soddened hemlock lying across it. One clip of the hatchet shows it will peel. There is plenty of smaller timber standing around—long, slim poles, with a tuft of foliage on top. Five minutes suffices to drop one of these, cut a twelve-foot pole from it, sharpen the pole at each end, jam one end into the ground and the other into the rough bark of a scraggly hemlock, and there is your ridgepole.

"Now go—with your hatchet—for the bushiest and most promising young hemlocks within reach. Drop them and draw them to camp rapidly. Next, you need a fire. There are fifty hard, resinous limbs sticking up from the prone hemlock; lop off a few of these and split the largest into match timber; reduce the splinters to shavings, scrape the wet leaves from your prospective fireplace, and strike a match on the balloon part of your trousers. If you are a woodsman you will strike but one.

"Feed the fire slowly at first; it will gain fast. When you have a blaze ten feet high, look at your watch. It is 6 P.M. You don't want to turn in before 10 o'clock, and you have four hours to kill before bedtime. Now, tackle the old hemlock. Take off every dry limb, and then peel the bark and bring it to camp. You will find this takes an hour or more.

"Next, strip every limb from your young hemlocks, and shingle them onto your ridgepole. This will make a sort of bear den, very well calculated to give you a comfortable night's rest. The bright fire soon will dry the ground that is to be your bed, and you will have plenty of time to drop another small hemlock and make a bed of browse a foot thick. You do it.

"Then you make your pillow. . . . It is half a yard of muslin, sewed up as a bag, and filled with moss or hemlock browse. You can empty it and put it in your pocket, where it takes up about as much room as a handkerchief. You will have other little muslin bags—an' you be wise. One holds a couple of ounces of good tea; another, sugar; another is kept to put your loose duffle in: money, match safe, pocketknife. You have a pat of butter and a bit of pork, with a liberal slice of brown bread, and before turning in, you make a cup of tea, broil a slice of pork, and indulge in a lunch.

"Ten o'clock comes. The time has not passed tediously. You are warm, dry and well-fed. Your old friends, the owls, come near the fire light and salute you with their strange wild notes; a distant fox sets up for himself with his odd, barking cry, and you turn in. Not ready to sleep just yet.

Starting an Overnight Shelter in Evergreen Country

"But you drop off, and it is two bells in the morning watch when you waken with a sense of chill and darkness. The fire has burned low, and snow is falling. The owls have left, and a deep silence broods over the cold, still forest. You rouse the fire, and, as the bright light shines to the furthest recesses of your forest den, get out the little pipe, and reduce a bit of navy plug to its lowest denomination. The smoke curls lazily upward; the fire makes you warm and drowsy, and again you lie down—to again waken with a sense of chilliness—to find the fire burned low and daylight breaking. You have slept better than you would in your own room at home. You have slept in an 'Indian camp.'

"You also have learned the difference between such a simple shelter and an open-air bivouac under a tree or beside an old log."

BUILDING A HUT

It may be expedient to build an emergency shelter so substantial that its walls can be additionally insulated by heaping sod or earth against them. If these walls are leaned in slightly from the bottom, gravity will tend to hold such reinforcements more firmly.

The roof also can be rendered warmer by covering it with several inches of vegetation, topped by enough dirt, or preferably by more substantial sod, to keep everything in place. An animal skin, some contrivance of woven vines, or perhaps an available fabric may be hung over an opening to serve as a door.

An open stone fireplace can be made in the center of the dirt floor of such a shelter. Although a chimney hole will have to be cut in the roof for ventilation, this vent may be kept covered when the fire is entirely out. It should not be covered otherwise because of the threat of carbon monoxide poisoning.

DOOR AND THE WIND

When the wind is a problem, the opening of a temporary shelter usually is located on the side away from it. In open snow country where blocking drifts may form in that lee, however, the entrance is best built crosswise to the wind. This also is the most satisfactory compromise when you are camped where air currents alternate back and forth, as in canyons and along mountain streams.

If you are building a structure that may be used for several days or longer, do not be governed too much in this matter by the direction in which any breezes may be blowing at the moment. In such a case it will be wise to look around for natural signs, such as deadfall and leaning trees, which will indicate the quarter of the prevailing wind.

DITCHING FOR DRAINAGE

You may want to ditch the wilderness shelter so as to conduct away water that, depending on the terrain, might otherwise soak the floor. Any such drain should be placed so it also will catch any moisture running down the walls.

A channel several inches wide and deep may be made with a sharp stick in lieu of a handier tool. If this furrow is in the way of foot traffic, as it may be at the front, or if the ground is such that it will crumble easily, the drain's usefulness may be maintained by filling it loosely with small stones.

If your shelter is on a slope, water will, of course, have to be shunted only from the upper sides. If you are camped on sand or in forest so carpeted with vegetation that water sinks into it almost immediately, no ditching at all may be necessary.

BROWSE BED

There are many wilderness materials on which it is pleasant to sleep. If you want, you can make a rectangular enclosure by securing with stakes four poles in the shape you wish the bed to be. This pen you can fill with aromatic pine needles, dry moss, leaves, ferns, or sweet marsh hay. The result, however, will not be the famous browse bed about which many have heard.

You can simplify the matter and toss a few armfuls of evergreen boughs beneath a pine tree, after first having prepared the ground by kicking flat any hummocks and by scooping out hip and shoulder holes. The result still will not be the renowned browse bed. The construction of that requires a great deal more systematic effort.

You'll need, first of all, a probably surprising quantity of the softest available boughs. Among the best for the purpose are the small young branches of the heavily needled balsam, but fir and even spruce will do nearly as well. These boughs can, in the absence of knife and ax, be stripped off by hand. They can be easily carried if laid, one by one, over a long stick which has an upward angling fork at its bottom. Interlocking needles will hold the light, although bulky, load in place.

The operation is commenced by placing a thick layer of resilient green boughs at the head of the bed. These you lay with their underneaths upward. They are placed, in other words, opposite from the way they grow. The butts are kept well covered and pointing toward the bottom of the bed. The browse bed is thatched in this manner with row after row of boughs until it is a foot or more thick. It then is reinforced and leveled by the poking in of soft young evergreen tips wherever an opening can be found.

The first night on such a bed is a sleep-lulling, aromatic pleasure that everyone should experience at least once. The second night will be a bit bumpy. After the third night, one will feel inclined to attempt renovations with a load of fresh boughs.

DOME SHELTERS

Even if no wood large enough for the ordinary lean-to is available, you still can make a very comfortable structure from growth as slight as willow.

The thing to do first is to obtain a quantity of the longest wands you can find. You then can, after examining them, scratch on the ground a rough outline of the house. This, at most, should not ordinarily be much wider than the average length of the material.

The base of such a structure may be oval. It may be rectangular, in which case the final shelter may well resemble a barrel split lengthwise. Whatever the general shape, in other words, you will find it advantageous structurally to employ rounded sides and roof.

One way to commence is by securing the larger end of one wand in the ground on the outline scratched there, which, for

Dome Shelter

purposes of illustration, may be assumed to be a circle. Opposite the first wand on the round line, set the bigger end of the second switch. You then can draw the two tops together and tie them with roots, string, vines, rawhide, or any convenient material.

Similarly set and bend another two wands so that, above the center of the circle, they cross the first arch at right angles. At this apex lash all four together. The curve of the dome roof, now defined, will govern the size of the other arches.

A few inches away, or perhaps as much as a foot, if your covering is to be canvas or light skins, you may make a slightly lower arch parallel to the first. This you may cross at right angles with a similar arch. This crisscrossing operation may be continued in this fashion except to allow for an entrance. Tie each of the numerous joints until the frame is sufficiently sturdy.

There need be no particular methodicalness, however, for functional variations are as numerous as materials and situations. If additional supports are needed later, they may be added as necessary.

You may weave moss or grass through the final basketlike framework in lieu of anything better, perhaps laying on a second coat which can be both secured and insulated with a thick plastering of mud and snow.

The shelters described in this chapter, rough as they may be, are nothing to be ashamed of. "A comfortable house was once made here almost entirely of such materials as Nature furnished," an old woodsman, Henry David Thoreau, noted more than a century ago. "Most men are needlessly poor all their lives because they think they must have a house as their neighbors have. Consider how slight a shelter is absolutely necessary."

Chapter 13

FINDING SAFE
DRINKING WATER

A HEALTHY human can get along entirely without food for a month or two under favorable conditions. Anyone would do well to stay alive for much more than a week without water.

Fortunately, there needn't often be a shortage of drinking water, especially when you understand how to locate some of the more unusual sources now recognized by only a few. The more common problem lies in making sure that water is fit for human use. Understanding a minimum of fundamentals, this you also can solve with reassuring certainty, for it is only the most basic common sense never to take the slightest unnecessary risk with doubtful water.

Anyone usually can get along awhile longer without a drink. Just moistening your lips with water one drop of which is contaminated can, on the other hand, so sicken you that, if nothing worse, you'll become too weak to travel.

WHEN IS WATER SAFE TO DRINK?

How can you tell, then, if water is pure? Short of laboratory tests, you can't. Even when a mountain rill bubbles through sheer mountain fastnesses, the putrefying carcass of a winter-killed animal may be lying a few yards upstream.

The folklore that any water a dog will drink is pure enough for his master is unfortunately as baseless as it is charming, as even the fondest master must testify upon recalling a few of the potions his pet has assimilated with impunity. The more reasonable assumption that anything your horse will drink is safe for humans is likewise at fault. Pollution may be entirely odorless, whereas a horse's basis for rejection or acceptance is familiarity of smell.

The fact that natives may assert a water source is pure may mean, instead, that either they have built up a certain degree of immunity or that, because of familiarity, they cannot believe that water is tainted. A domestic water supply used by the inhabitants and guests of a Montana ranch for some twenty years was found to have been infecting not only present but previous owners with tularemia. The germs of this, incidentally, can be carried to water by pets such as dogs, and by domestic animals such as pigs, even though they themselves may seem perfectly healthy.

Even the loneliest wild stream can be infected with this so-called rabbit fever by such wild animals as muskrat and beaver. Yet taking a chance with drinking water in a well-settled community is, in one sense, a lot less dangerous than laying yourself open to a small fraction of similar risk in wilderness where medical help may be hours and perhaps days away. The safest principle in any event is to assume all water is impure until it has been proved otherwise, positively and recently.

PURIFYING WATER

BOILING

Water can be rid of germs by boiling. The exact time required to do this depends on altitude, the nature of any given impurity, and several other factors. Altogether, these are so elastic that although a shorter time often will suffice, a sage general rule is to boil questionable water at least five minutes.

If there is any reasonable doubt that water may be contaminated, it would be hard for even the most hurried and harried not to agree that it should be purified before human use, although such a process may be expected to take both time and trouble. A great deal more inconvenience and delay can result from just using any water indiscriminately.

This does not apply only to water that is actually drunk. It is equally applicable to any water, a drop of which may enter the human body, examples being water in which the toothbrush is dipped, water in which food utensils are washed, and water used in cooking except when kept at a high enough temperature for a sufficient time to insure purity.

Boiled water, as everyone knows, tastes flat because air has been driven from it by heat. Air, and therefore taste, can be restored by pouring the cooled water back and forth between two utensils or by shaking it in a partially filled jar or canteen. Or, if one is in a hurry and has salt, it is common practice to add a pinch of that.

CHEMICAL PURIFICATION

One can purchase at most sporting goods and drug stores for about forty cents a small two-ounce bottle containing one hundred halazone tablets. Since their purifying action depends upon the release at the proper time of chlorine gas, these should be fresh. The container should be kept tightly closed in a dark, dry place.

No purification of water by chemical means is as dependable as boiling, but two halazone tablets will ordinarily make a quart of water safe for human consumption in half an hour. If the water is muddy or particularly questionable, it is good insurance to double at least the amount of halazone and probably the time, as well.

Care should be taken with all chemical purifiers to disinfect all points of human contact with the container. This is to insure that, once the water is sterilized, it will not be easily reinfected. If a jar or canteen is being used together with halazone, replace the cover loosely and wait two or three minutes so the tablets can dissolve. Then shake the contents thoroughly, allowing some of the fluid to spill out over the top and lip of the holder. Tighten the cover then and leave it that way for the desired time before using any of the liquid.

CHLORIDE OF LIME. Chlorine in some form is regarded as the most dependable disinfectant for drinking water in temperate climates. When introduced in proper quantities, it destroys existing organisms. For as long as enough remains in the water it prevents recurring contamination. It is better to err moderately on the side of overdosage, if at all, for waters of varying chemical and physical composition react differently to equal quantities of a given disinfectant.

Emergency chlorination of drinking water may be accomplished in three steps: (1) dissolving one heaping tablespoon of chloride of lime in eight quarts of water; (2) adding one part of this solution to one hundred parts of the water to be disinfected; and (3) waiting at least thirty minutes before using.

The stock solution should be kept tightly corked, preferably in a cool, dark place. Even then it should be renewed frequently.

IODINE AS A GERMICIDE. Tincture of iodine can be used as an emergency water purifier. A drop of this fresh antiseptic, mixed thoroughly with one quart of water in the same manner as halazone, will generally make the water fit for human consumption in thirty minutes. Both the amount and the time may be doubled if this precaution seems warranted.

IODINE WATER PURIFICATION TABLETS. Chlorine-releasing compounds cannot be relied upon in semitropical and tropical areas. Neither there nor anywhere else, incidentally, does the addition of liquor to water or ice rid either of the latter of germs. Water in these aforesaid regions should be boiled or when this is not feasible treated with iodine water purification tablets. Containing the active ingredient tetraglycine hydroperiodide, these have been adopted as standard for the armed services of the United States.

The tablets have been proved effective against all common water-borne bacteria as well as the cysts of Endamoeba histolytica and the cercariae of schistosomiasis. Manufactured as Globaline by WTS Pharmaceuticals, Division of Wallace & Tiernan, Inc., in Rochester, New York, fifty water purification tablets are packaged in a glass bottle with a wax-sealed cap. Added to water, each tablet frees eight milligrams of iodine which acts as a purification factor. Each tablet will purify one quart of clear water.

These tablets, too, must be kept dry. The bottle therefore should be recapped tightly after being opened. Directions for use are: (1) add one tablet to a quart of clear water in container with cap, two tablets, if not clear; (2) replace cap loosely and wait five minutes; (3) shake well, allowing a little water to leak out and disinfect the screw threads before tightening container cap.

RECOGNIZING POISONOUS WATER HOLES

A few water holes, as in the southwestern deserts of this continent, contain dissolved poisons such as arsenic. One is usually able to recognize such a water hole easily, partly because bones of unwary animals may be scattered about, but mainly because green vegetation will be conspicuously absent. The safest general rule, therefore, is to avoid any water holes around which green plants are not thriving.

If, in the section where you may be traveling, there is hard water to which you are not accustomed, severe digestive upsets may result if, while getting used to it, you sip more than small amounts at any one time. Boiling may be of some help, inasmuch as when magnesia and lime carbonates are held in solution by carbon dioxide, these hardening agents can be partially solidified by the driving off of the gas by heat.

HOW TO MAKE A FILTER

Water can be cleared by filtration, although this process will neither materially affect any dissolved minerals, nor will it assure purity. Water is polluted by animal and mineral matter, rather than by discoloring vegetable substances such as grass roots and dead leaves. The first two cannot be removed with any sureness by ordinary filtering.

The function of the makeshift filter is to clear water by straining solid materials from it. You may be canoeing up near the Yukon border on the Sikanni River, for example, which is so muddy that some rivermen save time and effort by lugging kegs of drinking water with them. Filtration will serve instead, however.

A wilderness filter can generally be made without too much trouble, particularly in sand, by scooping a hole a few feet from the source of supply and using what water seeps into it.

HOW TO SWEETEN WATER

One evening you may make camp in a swamp or by a pond which has an unpleasant odor. It will be handy in such a contingency to know how to sweeten and purify water in a single operation.

This can usually be accomplished by dropping several bits of charred hardwood from the campfire into the boiling pot. Fifteen or twenty minutes of simmering will usually do the job. You then can skim away most of the foreign matter, and then either strain the water as by pouring it through a clean cloth, or, if you've plenty of time and utensils, merely allow it to settle.

WHERE TO FIND WATER

One is always learning from nature, and not the least of these gifts is the increasing ability to determine with little, if any, conscious effort where water lies in a wilderness area. Several principles serve to aid one in this respect. These everyone knows already: that water runs downhill, that it grooves the ground while so doing, and finally, that it encourages vegetation, and particularly some types of vegetation.

It is not uncommon in high country to find water near the tops of mountains, perhaps indicated by a comparatively lush area, or, sometimes, by a thread of green unraveling down a slope. Perhaps, too, a glacier or permanent snowbank may furnish refreshment.

Water also is prone to lie near the base of hills, where it can be distinguished many times in distant ravines and canyons by the density of growth. The main problem, as a matter of fact, often becomes less the discovery of water than the finding of a sufficiently gradual descent to it.

When country is flat and open, long meandering tangles of alder and willow tell their familiar story.

FOLLOWING GAME TRAILS

Game trails very often indicate the presence of water, usually a reliable indication being a marked increase and a progressive deepening and widening. If you want water, what you will do, of course, is follow them. However, in the North such trails commonly mean only that muskeg lies ahead.

LOCATING FRESH WATER ON A SEACOAST

One often successful procedure for locating drinking water on an ocean beach is to wait until low tide and then dig below the high-water mark. There generally will be some object such as a shell available that either can be used as a scoop or lashed to a length of driftwood to provide a shovel. Fresh water, if there is any, will remain atop salt water because it is lighter. The hole for that reason should not be deepened beneath the first signs of seepage, at least not until a reasonable water supply is assured.

WATER IN THE DESERT

Water seeks the lowest levels available, and on the desert these may be underground. If there seems to be no particular direction in which you should travel and you can see hills, head toward them, for the likeliest place to locate water will be at their base.

Perhaps you'll come across the thin shallow bed of a stream. Even though it is dry, water may lie beneath the surface. Hunt for a low place in the cut and dig. The same procedure may be followed in the case of dry lake bottoms. The presence of any water soon will be indicated by damp sand.

Game trails in desert country usually lead to water. Follow them downhill, if the land so slopes that you can do this with certainty. Otherwise, scout until you can make sure in which direction the paths have become more frequented, and this will be the way to go.

If you happen upon a palm, water is undoubtedly at hand, generally within several feet of the base of the tree. Reed grass is also a sound sign that moisture is near.

SIMPLE SOLAR STILL. The same piece of plastic which may be folded and carried in a shirt pocket for use as a shelter can save you from dying of thirst in the desert or on the open sea.

In the desert, with a plastic sheet six feet square, up to three pints of water a day can be extracted from a bowl-shaped hole some twenty inches deep and forty inches across. Place a cup, can, upturned hat, or other receptacle in the center of the cavity. Anchor the plastic all the way around the top of the hole with stones or dirt. Set something such as a rock in the center of the sheet so the plastic will sag in a point directly over the container.

Heat from the sun will cause moisture in the desert ground to condense on the underneath of the plastic and to drip into the receptacle. You'll get even more fluid if you help matters along by cutting cacti and other water-holding desert plants into pieces and dropping them under the plastic. Even contaminated water can be purified if poured into the hole and allowed to vaporize and drip in the heat.

Sea water in the bottom of a boat can be vaporized and condensed in pure potable form by the same method.

MOISTURE FROM CACTI. Discovering water in vegetation is most spectacular in desert regions. There the various cacti are able to thrive because of an ability to store fluid in the form of thin, watery sap which, in turn, can furnish a human being with an emergency drink.

If you need that juice, cut off sections of cactus and, being continually wary of spines, mash them in a container. You can either drink any resulting fluid on the spot or pour it into a second container. Then repeat the process as often as necessary or expedient. If you have no utensils, just mash the segments of cactus one by one and suck the pulp.

Some of the larger cacti, such as the barrel cactus, which looks about like what might be expected from the name, will provide their own utensils. The top can be sliced off, the soft interior crushed to a pulp, and the watery sap either scooped out with the cupped hand or drunk from a hole tapped in the side.

RAIN WATER

When up against it for water, it is sometimes possible to find rain that has accumulated in the large leaves of plants and trees, or that has been trapped in natural basins such as are frequent in rocky terrain.

SNOW

Clean snow may be eaten any time one is thirsty. The only precaution that ever need be taken is to treat it like ice cream and not put down too much at once when you're overheated or chilled.

Snow, after all, is, in flake form, the purest of distilled water obtainable from the atmosphere. Its only drawback is that a considerable amount is required to equal a glass of water. One soon learns to break off sections of crust when this is available. Heavy granular snow from former storms is usually better still. Most concentrated, of course, is ice itself.

One finds out about low water content very quickly when melting snow in the noon tea pail. Particular care has to be taken first of all not to burn the pot, the best procedure being to melt snow in small quantities until the bottom of the utensil is safely covered with several inches of water. Secondly, the container must be filled with more snow and refilled again— and possibly again—if anything like a capacity amount of liquid is desired.

This nuisance is compensated for by the fact that snowfall makes water readily available throughout the wilderness. All one has to do is scoop up clean handfuls while walking along, a valuable convenience inasmuch as one requires a lot more water in cold weather than he'd ordinarily expect, the kidneys then having to take over much of the process of elimination otherwise accomplished by the sweat glands.

ICE

The winter water supply of many an Arctic establishment consists of what is adjudged to be a sufficient number of blocks of laboriously procured ice. The task of melting these is sufficiently inconvenient, however, that when it is feasible, most prefer to chop or chisel water holes in lake or stream ice. Such holes may be kept covered to discourage their refreezing.

As far as purity is concerned, ice and the water obtained from melting ice differ in no respect from the water originally frozen. Although heat kills germs, cold very definitely does not.

FRESH WATER FROM SALT WATER ICE. "The soundest reasoning leads to the wrongest conclusions when the premises are false," as Dr. Vilhjalmur Stefansson, famed Arctic explorer, pointed out. "There are few things considered more certain than that the ocean is salt, and there is no inference more logical (although no inference is ever really logical) than that the ice of salt water must also be salt."

It so happens, noted Stefansson, that sea ice becomes fresh during the period intervening between its formation and the end of the first summer thereafter.

If, during freezing weather, you are ever in a position where there is no source of water other than salt water, catch small amounts of the available brine and allow ice to form in it. The slush and any remaining liquid should then be removed. The ice will be fresh enough to use in an emergency.

Ocean ice loses its salt so rapidly that ice one year old is nearly fresh. Ice formed two or more years before cannot be distinguished, as far as taste goes, from river ice, unless waves have been breaking over it recently or spray has been dousing it. Melted hollows, otherwise, will usually be found to contain ample fresh water.

SALT WATER POISONING

One characteristic of salt water making it unfit for use as drinking water is its cathartic property. When there is a scarcity of fresh drinking water, every effort usually should be made to discourage anyone's drinking salt water. This will not only give rise to tormenting thirst, in part by diminishing moisture already in the body, but it will progressively weaken one, cause actual poisoning, and, if continued without relief, inflict eventual madness.

SALT INTAKE IN HOT WEATHER

There is a time, however, when the drinking of some salt water is to be recommended. On hot days when the normal supply of salt in the human body is depleted by perspiration, and when no amount of fresh liquids seems to sate one's thirst, what the system often needs is salt. This can be supplied by making every cup of drinking water from one-fifth to two-fifths seawater, or by adding a salt tablet or one-fourth teaspoon of table salt to each cup of fresh water.

THINGS TO AVOID WHEN THIRSTY

When one becomes extremely thirsty, any liquid is a temptation. If you should ever be in such a plight, be sure to warn any companions against drinking alcoholic beverages, which, aside from other possibly dangerous effects, will only further dehydrate the body.

Medicines, it will be realized, cannot be substituted for drinking water, either. Most compass fluids are poisonous antifreeze. Body wastes contain harmful byproducts and, at best, will only increase thirst. Smoking, incidentally, is dehydrating and heightens the need for fluid.

Sluggishness of the digestive system is a natural consequence of going without normal amounts of water and food. This condition need not cause concern, as it will adjust itself when regular eating and drinking habits are resumed. One very definitely should not take any laxatives under such conditions, as such medication depletes the system of moisture already in it.

When inadequate water supplies are replenished eventually, it will be inadvisable to drink a great deal at once. If the satisfaction is extended over several hours, the body will utilize the intake to the fullest instead of sluicing it through the system and dissipating a considerable amount wastefully in rapid elimination. Even when there is suddenly all the water you possibly can want, drinking it too rapidly and in too large amounts will cause nausea.

CONSERVING BODY MOISTURE

If you have ample water at the moment, but may have little or none later, the soundest procedure will be to drink as much as you reasonably can before quitting the source of supply. In dry country, it will be a good idea to drink a lot while at and just before leaving a water hole. Carrying something such as a button or small clean pebble in the mouth will help to decrease the sensation of thirst.

An often unbelievable amount of water is lost through the pores of the skin, and the rate of perspiration is markedly increased both by heat and by exertion. The need of water intake can be lessened, therefore, by keeping as quiet as possible and as comfortably cool as you can.

If in arid wilderness without sufficient water and obliged to depend on your own resources to get out, your best chance will be to stay as relaxed and cool as possible during the hot hours. Traveling can be done during the respite of dawn and dusk, and, particularly across open sands, at night.

If on flat, shelterless desert, you always can scoop out a narrow pit in which to lie while the sun is blazing down. The utmost shade will be secured if this trench extends east and west. Two or three feet of depth can result in a difference of as much as a hundred degrees in temperature between its shadowy bottom and ground level. Before you take to such a refuge, though, you may want to leave some sign of your presence in case someone passes by. Weighting a shirt over one of the excavated piles may serve.

Chapter 14

WHAT THE COOK NEEDS TO WORK WITH

WHEN an experienced outdoorsman merely wants to get water boiling and to toast a sandwich or two, he builds a small fire in the easiest way he can, depending on what fuel is nearby. Then he gets a green stick several feet long. This stick he shoves into the ground so one end extends over the heat. He may adjust its height by propping it up with a rock, chunk of wood, or forked stick. If the ground is hard, he may weigh down the lower end with a billet or stone.

The pail he hangs by its bail at the end of the stick. The surface of the stick is generally rough enough so the handle won't slide. Also, branches usually are trimmed from it in such a way that a few projections remain. If necessary, of course, a notch can very easily be cut. Incidentally, a practical pail often is only a large tin can with two opposite holes punched just below its rim to accommodate a makeshift wire handle.

A larger meal often is prepared with the help of additional angled green poles. However, the round fire generally is not too convenient for cooking purposes. One answer is to arrange a number of such small fires of varying intensities, just as you use the different burners on a city range.

Boiling Water in a Hurry

But the problem becomes supporting the various cooking utensils in the easiest way. As usual, solutions are numerous. One handy method that will do away with a lot of teetering and tipping is to scoop, scrape, or stamp a trench. This may be about six inches wide and deep and perhaps two feet long. Running this trench in the same direction as the wind will assure a better draft. Get a good fire going in this trench, perhaps by raking it there after it starts blazing well. Then kettle, frypan, and pots can be steadied across it. Such a fire, however, probably won't be successful if the wind is quiet or the fuel is none too ardent.

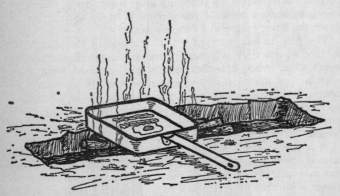

Trench Fire for Cooking

The answer then may be the more usual above-ground fire, but one that's some eight inches wide and four or five feet long. This fire may be contained by two fairly dry logs some four to six inches in diameter, laid either parallel or at a slight angle to each other, with the open end toward the wind. If these logs are raised an inch or two by stones or billets, air will be able to circulate advantageously beneath them. Fuel this fire preferably with long split hardwood, and, if possible, let it burn down either to a hot bed of coals or to a steady blaze which does not flame up more than a foot.

Meanwhile, cut two substantial forked green poles. Drive these upright into the ground at each end of the fire so a green crosspiece laid between the crotches will extend the length of the fire along the center. Make pothooks for each kettle by cutting handle-holding notches in forked green sticks that can be inverted over this crosspiece. Or carry several pot-hooks made by bending short lengths of coat-hanger wire into S shapes.

A convenient variation of this technique is to use two green poles, one on either side of the fire, instead of the somewhat seasoned logs. Take pains to raise these evenly above the ground, perhaps notching the supporting billets if that's what you're using. Such green poles will take a long time to burn through. Just set your cooking utensils across them.

Cooking Fire between Two Logs

Cooking a Full Meal

GRATES AND IRONS

A substantial wire grid, available from dealers in camp equipment, will provide a convenient base on which to set pots and pans above a wood fire and over which to broil fish and meat. Some of these have folding legs which, stuck in the forest floor, will hold kettle and frypan above the heat.

These sharp extremities, however, can be somewhat of a menace when one is on the move. Some remove them for this reason, and also partly to save weight. The grid can as handily be laid across rocks or billets. In a stony and often in a treacherously soft spot, this has to be done, anyway.

A similar arrangement, less bulky to pack, is two iron rods about one-half inch in diameter and four feet long, or flat or angle irons of similar stiffness. Support them above your fire with rocks or logs at each end, and have them just far enough apart so the smallest kettle will not slip down between them. If transportation is no problem, a sheet of metal to lay across these will give you much of the convenience of a stove.

STOVES

In spite of all that can be said for an open fire, there are times when a stove either is necessary or is at least indicated by common sense.

CAMP STOVES

The most popular camp stove today is one that uses gasoline for fuel under its one, two, or three burners. In many cases, the gasoline stove solves the cooking problem admirably, especially when it comes to boiling and frying. A separate oven can be used for baking.

This type of stove is ideal and often a must for public camping grounds. It is good for the places where wood is no longer to be had and where space is limited. It is excellent for those automobile tourists who like to cook their own meals beside the road, both for the pleasure of eating outdoors and for the very real economies thus afforded. When you take off into the remote wilderness, it can be left with your motor vehicle.

Such a cooking fire can be lighted immediately. The even and easily regulated heat will allow the refugee from the city range to put out good meals with a minimum of effort and guesswork. Such a stove is fine, too, for travelers in those areas where nonresidents are prohibited from lighting an open fire except when accompanied by a resident or by a licensed guide.

Gasoline stoves are inexpensive, easily and compactly packed, and durable. They can be used, if desired, atop a handy metal stand that supports them at normal stove height and, when not in use, folds into a small bundle that is easily stowed in the car or boat.

PRIMUS STOVES

The one-burner primus stove often is the answer for winter sports enthusiasts, fishermen and mountaineers who climb beyond the tree line, and even motorists who like to heat water or cook very small meals inside their cars. These light, efficient little heaters may be obtained in units burning alcohol, kerosene, gasoline, canned gas, and similar compact fuels.

For example, there is a 2½-pound combination selling for about fifteen dollars, which includes one 3½-pint casserole, one 2½-pint casserole, one lid pan, one upper and lower wind guard, a potholder, a strap, and a gasoline stove. All these nest into a space 8¼ inches in diameter and 4¾ inches high.

Lightweight, leakproof, aluminum fuel bottles also are inexpensively available. The big, catalog-issuing camp equipment dealers stock a functional variety of these units and combinations.

WOOD-BURNING STOVES

Whenever a stove is to be used where firewood is available, a sheet-metal model burning this fuel has decided advantages. You'll seldom see one today in city stores, and they're unfamiliar to campers with little experience. But along the receding frontiers in whose forests you still encounter oldtimers, these wood-burning models usually are the only portable stoves ever considered.

Such a stove generally weighs a little more than the gasoline stove. Although available in folding types, it is generally bulkier. But there is no fuel to transport, and the sheet-metal stove is not difficult to carry, even over a portage or on a pack horse.

You can cook on it in the rain. With a little care, it will safely warm closed tents. Many sourdoughs, as a matter of fact, have no other stove, not even in their home cabins. It is easy to dry clothing around it. Broiling and toasting over an open pot hole can be a comparative pleasure.

It is particularly handy for river trips in the large outboard motor boats that travel the broad and often sluggish streams on the roof of this continent. There, odds and ends of driftwood quickly afford concentrated heat, protected from the ravenous winds often howling along such shores. By providing a shallow box filled with sand, you can even cook afloat.

If the stove you select has an oven, baking and toasting will be possible. If it is without an oven, a folding reflector baker or a separate collapsible oven can be used.

OVENS

REFLECTOR BAKER

Light and compact varieties of the reflector baker, which our pioneer ancestors used for baking in front of open fireplaces, are still invaluable outdoor equipment. The modern articles are made of brightly reflecting metals such as aluminum. They fold flat for easier carrying. Because they operate on the principle of reflecting heat to all parts of the food being cooked, maintenance of their efficiency depends on their being kept reasonably clean and bright.

These portable ovens provide the simplest and most convenient means of baking and roasting with an open fire. Not only breads and biscuits, but fish and meat as well, come out hot and appetizing. Just stand the reflector before a blazing fire or hot stove. Regulate the temperature by moving the contraption toward or away from the heat. Food is placed in a pan on the center shelf of the reflector oven and occasionally turned end for end so the baking will be more uniform.

THE DUTCH OVEN

A Dutch oven is the one and only. It's not that this old-fashioned oven of cast iron doesn't have its disadvantages. It's awkward and heavy to carry unless you're traveling by pack train, boat, or motor vehicle. Furthermore, although it holds the heat, it will rust if not kept well greased. Other varieties, such as those made of aluminum, are both lighter and easier to keep clean. But they're for city stoves, if anywhere. They won't even come close to getting the job done over outdoor fires.

What you need for cooking food in the farther places is a heavy, thick, cast-iron pot with a similarly rugged top, lipped to hold a ruddy bed of coals. If your dealer doesn't have one, write the Lodge Manufacturing Company in South Pittsburg, Tennessee. A satisfactory model for use with small parties is twelve inches in diameter, four inches deep, and seventeen pounds in weight. Models are available also in diameters of 8, 10, 14, and 16 inches.

The Dutch oven you get should have squat legs, both to keep the bottom safely above the otherwise scorching ardor of hot embers and to anchor the contraption levelly. It will need a convenient handle by which the hot top can be lifted and an easily manipulated bail by which the entire contrivance can be moved.

Both these jobs can be performed with the help of a forked stick cut on the spot. When shifting the coal-heaped lid, though, a second stick held in the other hand will help to balance it. You'll also need a shovel. One of the husky, folding models available at surplus stores is convenient to carry. Dutch ovens are used both above and below ground.

Oldtimers season their Dutch ovens, when they first buy them, by boiling grease in them. Otherwise, they'll tell you, the cast iron, which is porous, will make food stick. This is a sound precaution when you buy heavy iron frypans, too.

CLAY OVENS

If the chances are that you'll be in one place long enough to merit the effort, you may elect to make an oven in a clay slope or bank. One way to commence this is by hammering a sharpened pole, about as thick as your forearm, straight down into the bank about three feet back from the edge.

Then, a foot or so down the side of the bank, far enough to allow a sturdy ceiling, scoop out the size oven you want. A usual procedure is to shape it like a beehive, with a narrow entrance. Dig as far back as the pole. Then pull this out to form the chimney. You can give the interior a hard coating by smoothing and resmoothing it with wet hands. A small blaze may then be kindled within to harden this lining.

It is very possible that you will be able to find an old burrow to serve as the basis for such a contrivance. Or, at the other extreme, construct a rough form of arched green sticks and daub the wet clay in thick layers over this. The successive layers may be allowed to dry in the sun, or the drying of each succeeding layer can be quickened by small fires lit within.

Baking in such clay ovens is simplicity itself. The oven is preheated by a fire kindled within. Fire and ashes are then scraped out. The food is laid within on stones, leaves, or whatever may be handy. Both flue and front openings are tightly closed. One then goes about his business. The meal will cook without further attention.

GRIDDLE

A griddle will clear the way for the quick serving of bacon, eggs, and flapjacks in quantity. One of these plates can be laid across a couple of logs between which a cooking fire has largely burned to coals. Matter of fact, such a griddle can also be used as a substitute stove top to keep utensils steady and free of soot. Magnesium griddles are the lightest available. Unless you plan to wrap it in papers, it's a good idea to buy a protective traveling cover so as to keep the rest of the outfit clean.

FOIL

Aluminum foil cookery is the modern version of enclosing food for cooking by bundling it in moist leaves, clay, or dripping green seaweed. This modern method also encourages food to retain its juices and to warm evenly. Therein, as a matter of fact, lie the shortcomings. Meat wrapped in foil, for example, is steamed rather than broiled or roasted. The deliciously crisp brownness is missing. There are ways around, of course. But these largely erase the virtues of simplicity.

A fish can be cooked directly on the coals if it is first wrapped in oiled foil, and in the case of small catches, you can impart a certain charred touch by toasting it unwrapped beforehand on a forked stick. With large fish, you can help along the taste by cooking sliced tomatoes, diced onion, bacon, and the like in the foil along with the fish.

Then there are the vegetables and such whose taste this variety of cooking does not seriously impair. The major drawback to any large amount of foil cookery, from the vacationist's viewpoint, is that its nature is more that of an occasional novelty. It does not really lend itself to serious cookery. Once in a while it's fun. But in the long run it saves no time or energy.

More importantly for go-light woodsmen or extended trips, it also saves no weight. This is not to say that aluminum foil does not have innumerable admirable outdoor uses. But it does not fit in with the real wilderness.

NESTED COOKING UTENSILS

You'll need cooking and eating paraphernalia. Pots, pans, dishes, and tableware from home often will do.

For the lone outdoorsman, the practical minimum is two small kettles with covers and with bails by which they can be hung over a fire, a frypan preferably with a folding handle, a tablespoon and usually a light fork, and a paper cup for cool liquids. The frypan will serve as a plate; the cup as a bowl.

One's pocket or sheath knife can be used whenever necessary.

Two nesting aluminum kettles, the larger holding about 1½ quarts, are available from dealers in camping goods. Weighing less than two pounds, they add no appreciable bulk to a pack, inasmuch as food and other essentials can be packed within them. Even when there are two or three individuals in the party, this same outfit can suffice, along with a plate, cup, spoon, and fork for each individual.

Good for wilderness use is a small nested cooking and eating kit made of a light, tough aluminum compound. Anyone who has ever burned himself on aluminum, however, will agree that the nested cups, and preferably the plates as well, may well be of stainless steel. The frypan, too, should be stainless steel.

A good nested outfit of this sort can last a lifetime, and often does, without replacements or changes. As a matter of fact, many of the components are so handy that even when you're in the city, one or another of them can still be used almost daily. However, some flimsy and highly impractical sets are on the market. Buy your nested outfit, if you get one, from the best established and most reliable sporting goods dealer with whom you can get in touch. Cost will still be surprisingly low.

KEEPING UTENSILS CLEAN

Light fabric holders available for the pots and frypan permit their being cleanly packed, when camp is moved frequently, without a whole lot of work scouring off the black every time. Actually, a certain amount of this exterior blackness makes for faster and more even cooking. You also can secure a fabric knife, fork, and spoon roll that can be handily hung to a tree or tent when you set up camp.

When you get home, spots and discolorations on aluminum ware can be removed by using a solution made by dissolving a tablespoon of cream of tartar in a pint of water.

A durable set of nested aluminum measuring spoons takes up very little space and can be handy in both the cooking and eating areas. There is no need to take a regular measuring cup. Just mark accurate proportions plainly on one of your drinking cups.

MIXING SURFACE

Simplest and handiest thing to take along for mixing and working purposes is a thin sheet of plastic. This can be easily washed, quickly refolded, and conveniently carried from one place to another with a minimum of bother. Bark may also be used, but at best it's a nuisance. Waxed paper or foil is an answer for motorized campers.

As a matter of fact, one of the most convenient things for each individual to carry when hiking, camping, skiing, fishing, or otherwise enjoying himself outdoors is a thin sheet of light-weight plastic, perhaps five feet by seven feet. This will quickly fold into bandanna handkerchief size, small enough for the pocket of a sport shirt. It can be drawn over the head and shoulders as a protection against wind and rain, laid atop the lower boughs of a tree as a storm shelter, spread on the ground as a dining cloth, and used as a clean waterproof wrapping for a string of sleek, bright trout.

COOK'S KNIFE

A knife is needed constantly afield for many purposes. For example, the camp cook will require one for slicing bread and meat, paring vegetables, and for a dozen other chores. Any fair-sized knife will do for such duties. Unless you're traveling particularly light, however, it is better to have a special one for kitchen work. This blade is almost sure to get such rough treatment that it would take a lot of work to keep it sharp enough for other jobs. Aside from that, a kitchen knife both performs better and holds up more satisfactorily if not given the fine edge desirable for pocket and sporting knives.

One reason for this is that meat is carved and bread sliced more easily with what actually is a sawing motion. A coarse edge made by sweeping the blade forward a few times against a carborundum diagonally from heel to tip, first on one side and then on the other, actually resembles saw teeth. This most functional edge can be renewed quickly by the same process.

A small butcher knife, particularly one of those stocked by specialists in outdoor equipment, goes well with most canoe and pack train outfits. Have a sheath for it, and keep it in the bundle with the knives, forks, and spoons. See Chapter 8 for care of knives and sheaths.

CLEANING CARBORUNDUMS

Carborundums are used so often in the wilderness that it's little wonder that these abrasive stones become more and more clotted with grime, thus progressively losing their effectiveness. To restore the cutting ability of your dirt-clogged carborundum, just put the stone in a good bed of coals until it is red hot. Then it will be all right again.

PAILS

Plenty of water is wanted at most campsites, and sources of supply are often some distance away. Collapsible and folding canvas or rubberized buckets are procurable and are handy for most kinds of camping. For other types of outdoor living, where transportation is little problem, two galvanized pails will be cleaner and more convenient. Breakables can be packed in them during traveling.

Chapter 15

STOCKING A PANTRY
IN THE WILDS

WHEN your appetite is sharpened by the healthy sort of outdoor living for which mankind was made, the mealtimes can include some of the best moments of any vacation—if you take along foods that keep well, cook readily, and are easy to handle.

Now is not too soon to get started on your provisioning for that next trip back of beyond, for, done right, it's going to take some time. It's best to take foods you like and know how to prepare. Experimenting at home and on weekend journeys is the soundest way to find out how much of each item you're going to need to keep going under full power.

Your meals should be satisfying as well as sustaining. As the Hudson's Bay Company, with nearly three centuries in the remotest and most primitive reaches of this continent, says, "There is usually little object in traveling tough just for the sake of being tough."

Rough it, sure, if you want to prove to yourself the actually very important fact that you can rough it. One day, it's true, anyone at all might be thrown entirely upon his own resources and forced to get along as best he can with a minimum of comforts.

But so far as preference goes, roughing it is a developmental stage. Once you've successfully tested your ability to take it, a whole lot of doubts and inhibitions disappear. You eventually realize that the real challenge lies in smoothing it. You come to appreciate that making it easy on yourself takes a lot more experience and ingenuity than bulling it through the tough way.

"Nothing is more important on a camping trip than the grub," Colonel Townsend Whelen pointed out. "Most of us go camping to have a good time. If the food is poor, unwholesome, or not what we crave, we have a continual grouch. If it is excellent and there is plenty of it, everything is rosy. Good food even makes up for rain and hard beds. Good fellowship is at its best around good meals.

"Unless you are lucky enough to have a professional cook booked for your party, it will pay you to study the commissary problem in advance. Exercise in the open air doubles the appetite and adds sauce to plain food. In quantity, quality, selection, and in preparation, this food should be good, wholesome, the kind you like, and attractively served."

Far from the humdrum concerns of man-made civilization, it is possible as nowhere else to appreciate the simple pleasures of life—browning frypan bread, steaming coffee, and bacon sputtering over apple-red coals. The crackle of a campfire takes on unexpected coziness, and even the smallest shelter all at once seems as snug and satisfying as a mansion.

BASIC GRUBSTAKES

The standard foods taken by experienced outdoorsmen on trips into the farther places, and which in general form the basis of most grubstakes, include: all-purpose flour, triple-action baking powder, baking soda, a packet of dry yeast if sourdough breadstuffs are to be made, sugar, compact cereals such as quick-cooking rice and oatmeal, cornmeal, side bacon (which has nearly triple the calories of back bacon), salt pork, oleomargarine, salt, macaroni and such, powdered milk and eggs, and dehydrated fruits and vegetables. All these are practically free of water.

Some of the more nutritious spreads, such as honey, jam, and peanut butter, work in well. So does cheese. Practical beverages are concentrated tea powder or tea itself, one of the instant coffees, malted milk, and chocolate. Bouillon solids and dry soup mixes, although short on nourishment, are often welcome because of the easy variety they afford. Seasonings such as powdered celery and onion, pepper, and a favorite spice or two may be desirable.

The old Three B days are gone, not that steady diets of beans, bacon, and bannock ever had much glamor in real life after the first couple of days.

IMPROVED DEHYDRATED FOODS

Such words as pemmican, jerky, parched corn, buccan, and pinole are reminders that dehydrated foods were important along the trails of this country even during flintlock days. The basic formula has not changed. It is to remove as much moisture from the edible portion of the particular food as may be practicable. Drying by sun and wind often extracted no more than three-fourths of this water. Modern processes sometimes leave less than 1 per cent.

Old-time outdoorsmen did not have much affection for most of the commercially dried foods, with the exception of a few such as peas, beans, and the fruits. There has been a tremendous improvement in dehydrated foods since the time of the Korean crisis. Most of the new dessicated foods are simple and speedy to prepare temptingly, usually requiring only water, heat, and a whit of discriminate seasoning. Few now require lengthy presoaking. Most take no more than ten to twenty or so minutes to prepare.

Freeze-drying has been called the greatest innovation in the food field since the invention of the tin can. The way the new method works is similar to how clothes dry in freezing weather. Many a subzero day in the Far North, you'll see lines outside log cabins filled with wash which immediately freezes stiff. Although the cold continues, the clothes still dry, because of water's unique property of being able to change from a solid to a vapor without melting.

Carefully trimmed and readied foods, some of them already cooked, are frozen. They are then put into a vacuum chamber in precisely controlled heat, where their moisture is gently vaporized away. That is, the ice crystals disperse without ever melting to a liquid, in a phenomenon known in physics as sublimation. Generally, some 98 per cent of the original moisture in foodstuffs is floated away in this fashion.

The food at this stage, even with nearly all the water removed, looks amazingly like the original, particularly in size and shape. As might be anticipated, however, its surface resembles that of a cellulose sponge. It is about as thirsty. So it will be prevented from drinking the moisture in the air, the food is hurried into airtight plastic, foil, and other containers. Thus protected, it can be stored for months without refrigeration and without deterioration, until reconstituted in camp by the addition of a specified amount of liquid obtained on the spot. There is another boon. Foods packed in this manner have no odors to attract hungry animals.

FREEZE-DRIED MEATS. One of the greatest breakthroughs afforded by freeze-drying is its more convenient way of preserving meat. You now can travel a couple of weeks away from the nearest supply point and each night, farther and farther back of beyond, sit down to tender juicy beefsteaks. Pork chops, hamburgers, sliced beef, and other such meats are available, too.

The first time you ever do it in the wilderness, it's quite an event when you open, say, a foil packet and look at the light, porous steaks that tilt the scales at perhaps one-fourth of their original weight. You mix a small package of accompanying seasoning with cold water and pour it into the handy packet, which does away with need for an extra dish—a boon in wilderness cookery.

As the meat's cells refill with fluid, the hemoglobin, which was still present in the dried steak, reunites with water to form fresh blood that starts to turn the water pink. In fifteen minutes the steaks, now full-bodied and red, are ready for the frypan. After a couple or so minutes' cooking on each side, they're tender and startlingly delicious.

Although it's not necessary, many like to spread margarine liberally on both sides of such reconstituted meat before consigning it to the heat, both for flavor and to help prevent the added moisture from boiling away. In any event, plenty of fat will add to the flavor, as in the processing all the natural fat that can be removed is trimmed away. So is all bone and waste. What's left is all meat, which, if the brand is good, was the choicest available to begin with.

FREEZE-DRIED VEGETABLES. Although freeze-drying does not always conserve much bulk, some of its greatest successes in this connection have been achieved with vegetables, whose reconstituted natural flavor and color are now a far cry from what used to be available in dehydrated vegetables.

It now is possible to pack enough carrots into a two-ounce package to furnish sixteen servings when water is added. Vegetables with higher water content furnish even more dramatic savings. Cabbage, to give one example, is some nine-tenths water, which explains why eighty pounds of what was fresh cabbage fits into a can about the size of a flat can of tuna, weight two and one-half pounds.

LIMITATIONS OF DEHYDRATED FOODS. There are disadvantages to consider. Even with the savings afforded by lower transportation costs and fewer storage problems, freeze-dried foods remain generally expensive for outdoorsmen. Because many of the products, including the meats, retain much of their original size and are liable to crush or chip, the packaging is still often bulky.

Flavors, although greatly superior to those of other dried foods, are still not always equal to those of the fresh product, although that may sometimes mean you'll like them better. Some processors tend toward complicated, multicourse repasts, whereas the camper is most interested in a meal he can prepare with one pot and one frypan.

But when you're back in the wilderness, sitting down to a feast fit for the home table, and hungry enough to enjoy it, the above shortcomings seem meager indeed. This is especially true because these days you can easily backpack as much food as, in the old years, would have bent the spine of a good-sized pack horse.

Try the dehydrated products first. It is most satisfactory to do this food by food. But sampling two or three items from any one company will, in practice, pretty well establish your liking for the entire line. Do this testing before you leave home. Tastes differ. A major error is to load up with dehydrated meals for the entire trip, especially with some of those dried by older methods, without everyone's doing considerable sampling beforehand. This is especially true when there is little to save but time.

Ordinarily, you'll be heading out for fun and relaxation, and the enjoyment of the meals is going to be a determining factor. Unless weight, space, and perhaps temperatures are basic considerations, dehydrated foods, despite their continuing improvements, are still most satisfactorily used to supplement, rather than replace, regular victuals.

MAXIMUM WEIGHT OF PROVISIONS

Available transportation will, of course, be the limiting factor in provisioning. A pack horse can balance from 140 to 180 pounds or so a day over mountain trails while feeding off the country. Burros under the same circumstances are good for from 70 to 100 pounds, depending on the animal. A canoe should not be loaded so deeply that it will have less than five inches of freeboard, depending on the water. This should be increased to at least six inches for windy lakes.

A husky man fresh out of the cement jungles can, without particular difficulty, shoulder about 75 pounds at a stretch over short portages, and he can take his time in making several such trips. He should not usually pack more than 35 pounds, of which 20 pounds may reasonably be food, when hiking day after day for pleasure over high country.

HOW MUCH OF EACH?

No one can give you more than an idea of the quantities of various items to take. Detailed grub lists as such are ordinarily of little value, for they seldom suit anyone but the compiler. It all depends on the number of meals you expect to make of each food, how many are to be in the party, and how much of each particular nutriment it will take to make a satisfying portion for each individual concerned.

To determine quantities, experiment at home. If you want oatmeal every morning, for example, find out just how much rolled oats are needed to make the breakfast you will eat in the woods. Just as a suggestion, take at least double the amount of sugar and sweets you would use at home, for your desire for them will be out of all proportion to what you want in the city.

Here's a yardstick you may find valuable. Generally speaking, the total weight of reasonably water-free foods should not be less than two and one-quarter pounds per adult per day. This does not include fresh vegetables and fruits. The figuring necessary will take time. But it will pay off in satisfaction, and it's fun!

FOODS FOR ENERGY

Fat is, in calories, the most concentrated food. It also is the hardest to come by when living off the wilderness. Butter, oleomargarine, lard, and cooking oils have double and triple the amount of calories that even such a quick-energy food as honey contains. If you plan to augment your meals with fish and other wild foods, for instance, the staples you carry should include a large proportion of edible fats.

Other concentrated foods that have figured conspicuously in rations where space and weight have been stringently restricted include dried, shelled nuts, peanut butter, chocolate, dried whole milk, and malted milk tablets. If you want a bulky starch, rice is one that cooks up appetizingly with nearly everything.

CALORIE REQUIREMENTS

You can, if weight and space are at extreme premium, use a calorie chart as a basis for figuring how to go about packing the most nourishment with the least trouble. In brief, you're burning up a certain amount of energy every moment. Energy not supplied directly by a sufficiency of food is taken from the body's carbohydrates, fats, and proteins.

Even during a relaxing sleep in the most comfortable of eiderdowns, the human body consumes heat units (or calories) at the rate of approximately ten calories a day per pound of body weight. In other words, for people weighing 160 pounds, the minimum number of calories used each day is 1,600. These basic requirements diminish but slightly, as a matter of fact, even when an individual is starving.

The more you move around and the more energy you expend in keeping warm, the more calories are burned up. Even lying in a sleeping bag and reading will increase your basic caloric needs about 25 per cent. The city man who gets very little exercise consumes on the average 50 per cent more than his minimum requirements. To maintain his weight, therefore, a 160-pound individual requires about 2,400 calories daily.

It is reasonable to generalize, therefore, that a fit, healthy man enjoying a robust outdoor life can require twenty calories of food a day per pound of body weight and perhaps more, depending on his activity and on the climate. Cold weather, for example, compels the system to put out more and more heat to keep itself warm. The same 160-pound city man bivouacking in the north woods can very easily take in 3,200 or 4,000 or more calories a day and still trim down lean and hard.

HOW TO PACK

Dry foods such as flour, cereal, beans, salt, and sugar may be packed in small, waterproof sacks which are available in a variety of types and sizes from most camp outfitters. You can make them, too. Each should be plainly labeled. Repackage dry foods whenever this can be done advantageously, cutting out and enclosing any special directions. Unless you've plenty of room, foods such as corn flakes should be compressed into as small a space as possible.

Available inexpensively from a number of outdoor outfitters, small plastic bags are excellent for packing all dry mixes suggested in this book. These bags can be readily sealed by a hot iron. If you want to reuse them, close them instead with one of the adhesive cellulose tapes.

Lightweight unbreakable plastic bottles and flasks of a wide variety of styles and shapes are on the market. These are good for carrying cooking oil and other inert liquids.

Both regular and high-density polyethylene containers are suitable for use with vanilla extracts. However, they have not proved satisfactory with other extracts because the aldehydes and esters in these latter cause a softening of the polyethylene. Such extracts, therefore, are better left in their original glass containers which may be wrapped in tape for safety.

Although high-density polyethylenes have been found suitable for use with spices, the essential oils present in significant quantities in black pepper, nutmeg, mace, and the like attack regular containers of this sort.

Dried meats may be wrapped in wax paper or aluminum

foil. Lard, margarine, and such travel well in tightly closed tins such as half-pound and pound tobacco cans. Powdered eggs and milk keep better in snugly closed receptacles, as do all beverages in powder form.

SELECTING AND STORING PERISHABLES

Fabric sacks can be used for carrying oranges, potatoes, onions, and apples when you have room for these. Choose oranges heavy for their size. Smoother, thinner skins usually indicate more juice. If possible, try a few potatoes before outfitting to make sure they're what you want. Pass up any with wastefully deep eyes. Size and color do not affect either onions' flavor or quality. Any with wet necks should be avoided. The very hard, long-keeping varieties are stronger than the Bermuda and Spanish types. With apples, good color usually signifies full flavor.

Cabbage and head lettuce will keep fresh for several weeks if wrapped in waxed paper and then in several layers of ordinary brown paper. Select heads that are heavy for their size. Avoid cabbage with worm holes and lettuce with discoloration or soft rot.

USING NATURE'S REFRIGERATION

Foods can be kept cool by placing them in a pail that is partly submerged in a shady portion of a lake, brook, or spring. Small amounts of fresh meat will keep for several days this way in hot weather if air is allowed to reach it. Cooked meat, broth, mulligan, greens, and the like will keep better if covered individually. Several yards of inexpensive cheesecloth tucked in the outfit will protect such food when flies become pestiferous.

You also can knock a couple of bottom strips out of a wooden box so that water will circulate through it. Weight down the bottom of the box with several large flat stones, and on these place a few perishables. If there is danger from slightly rising water, put these in containers that will float safely. It is usually a good idea to have a partially screened top, which can be held in place by another stone.

For fixed camps where refrigeration is a problem, capillary action may be harnessed to help solve food-keeping difficulties. Start by building a wooden frame in the general size and shape of an orange crate. Make one side a hinged door, using bits of leather or canvas for the hinges, if you want. Put in several shelves of slats or poultry wire, making them as open as possible so as to encourage circulation. Then screen the box to assure its being flyproof.

Tack burlap over the contraption, lapping this generously at the door and leaving the top and bottom both long and loose. Place a large pan of water on the top of this food container. Immerse the top burlap ends in the water. Capillarity will keep the burlap saturated. If the box is set or suspended in a breezy spot, evaporation will do the cooling.

AVOIDING SPOILAGE FROM FREEZING

Some foods will spoil if allowed to freeze. Days these can be wrapped in bedding. Nights they can be stowed near the reflected warmth of a fire. When traveling with a small outfit and sleeping out in temperatures of 60° and more below freezing, more than one individual has kept a few canned goods, which otherwise would burst from the cold, snuggled safely out of the way at the foot of his sleeping bag.

When food does freeze, it preferably should not be thawed until it is to be used. Fresh meat and fish keep well frozen. So do cheese and eggs, although their flavors are impaired. The taste and texture of such fruits as oranges are best preserved by letting them defrost in cold water.

Frozen potatoes, which take on the aspect of marble, should be dipped in boiling water and their skins scraped off. Then drop them singly into boiling water that is kept bubbling. Cold weather increases a potato's sugar content, so you may find the resulting flavor especially appealing.

CANNED FOODS

Canned goods are usually ruled out except on trips where transportation is of little worry. Otherwise, their weight and bulk can quickly add up to prohibitive proportions. If you cannot expect to produce fresh meat or fish, however, you may care to pack along a few of the canned meats. Canned tomatoes also go particularly well in the woods if you can manage them.

Canned butter, although expensive, remains sweet and fresh, but now there is nutritious oleomargarine whose taste, for all practical purposes, soon becomes practically indistinguishable from butter and which stays good for months at ordinary temperatures.

HEATING CANNED VEGETABLES

The most economical way to heat canned vegetables is to puncture the top of the can slightly, as with a small nail, and then to place the container in a deep pan of water. This should not cover the tin, which should be left in the hot water only the brief time necessary to heat the contents thoroughly. It will then give no trouble in opening. Incidentally, if a tenderfoot ever tries to heat that unopened can of soup or beans by dropping it in the campfire, either rake it out in a hurry or stand a long way back.

Nutriment that you may as well capitalize on to the fullest, especially after packing it for miles, is wasted by emptying commercially canned vegetables into a pan for heating. But if you do this, simply warm them before using. Boiling destroys much of their food value.

Don't throw away any of the juice in the can. Containing both vitamins and minerals, it can be profitably used in sauces, gravies, and soups. Seasoned if you want, it also makes a tasty beverage, especially in the bush.

LABELING, STORING, AND INSPECTING CANS

If there are any cans without distinguishing markings except for paper labels, and if there is a reasonable chance your outfit may become wet, scratch the identity of the contents on an end of each tin. Otherwise, you might have to pick what you want from a perfectly blank array.

The cleanest and safest place to keep the contents of an open can, incidentally, is in that can. Cover this, perhaps with one of several elastic-rimmed little plastic fabrics bought for the purpose, and store away from squirrels and their like in as cool a place as possible. With acid foods such as tomatoes, however, a metallic although harmless taste may insinuate itself because of the acids' eating into the iron of the opened can, so these may as well be shifted to a non-metallic container. Unopened canned goods preferably should be kept at moderate temperature.

Inspect all cans before buying them for an outdoor trip. Do this again before opening them. Such common-places of wilderness travel as denting, rusting, and freezing all can cause trouble. One test is to press each end of the can. Neither end should bulge, nor should it snap back unless the can has been been sprung or unless the contents have been frozen sufficiently to exert pressure against the ends, although not enough to break the seal. Ordinarily, both ends should either be flat, or they should curve slightly inward. Seams should be tight and clean, with no evidence of any leakage.

When you open a can, watch out for spurting liquid and for any off colors or odors. All are danger signals. Cans should be clean and smooth inside, with very little corrosion. If the metal of a meat product can has merely turned dark inside, though, this is only a harmless reaction with the sulphur in the meat.

Whenever there are any signs of spoilage, the wise thing to do is to discard all contents without testing, burying or burning them to protect wildlife. It's important enough to repeat: do not even touch your tongue to the product. Although you may expel any spoiled food at once, then thoroughly rinse your mouth, that one taste may be sufficient to cause an extremely severe digestive upset, if not worse.

Tops should always be well cleaned before any canned foods are opened. For one thing, the metal often picks up poisonous insecticides sprayed in stores.

CAN OPENER

The small roller type of can opener is the easiest to pack and to use. Just stow it, for example, inside the nested cups. The usual attempt to open a can with an ax or hatchet is wasteful at best, while performing the chore with a knife makes cut hands a distinct possibility, to say nothing of the damage done to a good blade. To avoid metal slivers, begin opening the can beyond the side seam, and unless you need the top off all the way, stop before reaching this seam.

Instead of puncturing the camp's evaporated milk can on top and plugging, taping, or sealing the holes with congealed milk, try making these small openings on opposite sides just below the rim. Then you can close them with a wide elastic band.

WILDERNESS PANTRY TIPS

SALT

Add cornstarch or a few grains of rice to salt in shakers to keep it dry for easy pouring. A few grains of salt added to cooked foods, such as stewed apricots, will enhance the sweetening of the sugar content. On the other hand, it is sometimes possible in cooking emergencies to hide the taste of excess salt by adding a small amount of vinegar or sugar.

Away from the table, salt can be invaluable as a preservative. The salt draws water from the fish or other food to be preserved by the process of osmosis, forming a brine that prevents or retards the growth of micro-organisms.

SWEETENINGS

There are several so-called sugar substitutes, one tiny pellet of which will sweeten a cup of coffee to the same degree as would a teaspoon of white sugar. Don't use them under ordinary wilderness conditions unless for dietetic reasons. The minute pills furnish the taste, certainly, but they add no fuel to the body.

The various natural sweets, such as sugar, are among our most readily assimilated energy foods. Granulated white sugar provides roundly 1,750 calories per pound. An equal amount of brown sugar contains 1,670 calories. The same amount of pure maple sugar has 1,580 calories. A pound of honey has 1,400 calories. Good jams average some 1,260 calories per pound, jellies slightly less. In comparison, one pound of fresh lean beef runs about 630 calories. In other words, it would be a mistake to try to save weight in this department.

WILD FOODS

These days you can dine about as easily and well in the wilderness as in the city. Matter of fact, you're apt to find yourself eating considerably better at times. There may be the drawback of not being able to pick up the numerous frozen specialties featured in modern markets. This disadvantage is more than offset by all the fresh foods that are at hand, free for the taking.

Whenever you learn how to recognize and use a reasonable number of these, you're sort of like the old prospector who kneels on a lode of silver while he pans gold and platinum from a creek. Whatever your epicurean whim of the moment, you can satisfy it. See Chapters 17, 18, and 19.

COOKING WITH FAT

Oleomargarine, largely because it keeps so well, is recommended for general wilderness use. To cut hard margarine or butter cleanly, use a knife that has been heated in hot water.

To protect yourself from popping hot fat, stop the spattering by sprinkling a bit of flour into the frypan. If the grease catches fire, throw a handful of flour on it or extinguish the flames by covering the burning fat and shutting out the air.

The camp shortening pail, which may be some handy container such as a friction-top can, can be kept replenished by pouring in surplus bacon fat.

THE BEAN FAMILY

Dry beans, peas, and lentils are oldtime dehydrated foods that remain favorites in many a wilderness camp. See Chapter 16.

JAMS

An outdoor trip makes jams and marmalades more enjoyable. Some campers are bothered by the white crystals that often form in these foods. Looking like mold, such crystals tend to spread through the mixture once the first of them have appeared. Actually, they're the result of sugar's combining. Although they do nothing for texture and appearance, they are not at all harmful.

YEAST

It is a good idea, when using sourdough breadstuffs, to carry a recently dated package of dry yeast in case something happens to the sourdough starter. It's true enough that a fresh starter can be made on the spot by mixing a cup apiece of flour and water in a scalded jar, covering it loosely, and stowing it in a warm place to sour. If the first results are not satisfactory, you can always try again with a new mixture. But the addition of yeast to these sourings will eliminate guesswork. The details are in Chapter 16.

HOW TO STRETCH VINEGAR

Here's a pioneer stratagem to stretch supplies of sometimes hard-to-pack vinegar. When half of the vinegar is used, dilute the remainder with an equal amount of water. Then restore its authority by adding a cup of sugar (brown sugar, if you have it). The sugar will ferment and supplant the missing acid.

CHEESE

Cheese is one of the most versatile and delectable of outdoor foods. It may be relished in its natural state or added to everything from soups and salads to sauces to make all sorts of delicious combinations. More than one outdoorsman has enjoyed it at breakfast with scrambled eggs, at lunch in a sandwich melted over the noonday tea fire, and at night with baked macaroni and tomato. Preferences vary. A sharp, aged cheddar keeps well, as does Edam and Gouda. Provolone is probably the best choice in high country.

If heat makes the cheese rubbery, a solution is to wrap it well and to revive it in a cool stream. If you are going to spend a month or more away from civilization, sew one-week portions in cheesecloth and immerse them in melted wax. You can keep mold off cheese harmlessly to a large extent by wiping the cheese with a clean cloth soaked either in baking powder solution or in vinegar.

MILK

Whether or not you use powdered milk and eggs will depend to a large extent on your preferences and your location. As far as nutrition goes, both compare favorably with the fresh products. Taste preference is mostly a matter of familiarity. In other words, nothing is the matter with either variety, and you can become satisfied with each.

POWDERED MILK

Powdered milk is especially handy in cold weather, if only because the quality of evaporated milk is impaired by freezing, which may cause it to spoil entirely by bursting the can. Besides, evaporated milk is still three-fourths water. Condensed milk is one-fourth water and nearly one-half sugar. Depending on the product, one pound of whole milk powder makes one gallon of liquid whole milk.

Whole milk powder is sometimes a little difficult to mix with water, but there are several ways to get around this. When you open the container, stir the powder and lightly take up the needed amount without packing it down in any way. Even measures are best obtained by leveling off the top of the cup or spoon with the straight edge of a knife. Place the powder on top of the water with which it is to mix. Then stir with a spoon until smooth. The mixing can be speeded somewhat by having the water slightly warm. You can also shake the water and powder together in a tightly closed jar which will subsequently serve as a pitcher.

Better spray dryers have improved the quality of dehydrated milk. The quick hydrating quality of skim milk powders, however, is the result of a second drying step which gives the particles a porous, spongelike fluffiness that thirty years of research were required to achieve.

Dried skim milk has all the nourishment of fresh skim milk. It has the calcium, phosphorus, iron and other minerals, the B vitamins, natural sugar, and the protein that make liquid skim milk such an important food. Powdered whole milk has all these, plus the fat and Vitamin A found in the cream of whole milk. Adding two tablespoons of butter or margarine to a cup of reconstituted skim milk make this equal in food value to a cup of whole milk. And it's often a lot easier to mix.

You can even use dried skim milk to make a whipped topping for desserts. Mix ½ cup of the milk powder with ½ cup of the coldest water available. Beat for 3-4 minutes until soft peaks form. Then add 2 tablespoons lemon juice, fresh or reconstituted, and beat about the same length of time until the mixture is stiff. Fold in ¼ cup sugar. About 3 cups of topping will result. Serve while you're still ahead.

Powdered milk, mixed dry with flour, makes a valuable addition to biscuits and other breadstuffs. Mornings when you're in a hurry to get away exploring or fishing, milk powder can be mixed directly with cereals such as oatmeal, then cooked as indicated on the package.

Containers holding any of the dry milk products should be kept tightly closed, as the powder attracts moisture and becomes lumpy if long exposed to the air. It also picks up odors unless care is taken.

EVAPORATED MILK

Many settle for evaporated milk, which is homogenized whole milk concentrated to double strength by evaporating part of the water. By using equal parts of evaporated milk and water, you can utilize evaporated milk as you would any other fluid whole milk. The lumps in evaporated milk are formed by solids settling during storage and are harmless. Cans of evaporated milk can be turned or shaken at frequent intervals during an outdoor trip to prevent such lumping.

EGGS

POWDERED EGGS

An egg is 11 per cent waste unless you're going to bake the shells and then pulverize them, as many bushmen do to increase the calcium content of their dogs' feed. Water constitutes 74 per cent of the remaining yolk and white.

Yet dried whole egg has virtually the same food value, includes no waste whatsoever, and is only 5 per cent water. More efficient processing equipment and methods have improved the quality of dried eggs.

Varying somewhat with the brands, a pound of dessicated eggs is the equivalent of some five dozen fresh eggs. One level tablespoon of the yellow powder, beaten with two tablespoons of water until smoothly blended, equals one hen's egg, again depending on the individual product. Also, you don't have to bother cushioning powdered eggs, as you would fresh, with crumpled newspaper in the more stable types of their own cartons, nor arranging them with the large ends up so as to keep the yolks centered.

The flavor of egg powder cooked by itself is not like that of fresh eggs. Most individuals in the United States are accustomed to the latter. Their natural taste reaction, therefore, is that the former is inferior. With different taste habits, as many have witnessed in Europe and elsewhere, this taste prejudice also works the other way around.

In any event, scrambled eggs prepared from the powder come to taste mighty good in the hinterlands. If you haven't prepared these before, dissolve powdered eggs, possibly with some powdered milk, in lukewarm water to make the quantity equivalent to the fresh eggs you might ordinarily use. Add salt, pepper, and any other seasoning, together with a chunk of butter or margarine. A little flour may be stirred in for thickening. Scrambling all these with ham or bacon gives the dish added flavor.

WHOLE EGGS

Never wash whole eggs until you're ready to use them. However, eggs with clean shells do keep better, so any soiled spots should be wiped off with a damp cloth. Regular washing, though, will remove the natural protective film which aids in keeping out bacteria and odors. Matter of fact, oiling the shells will help the eggs to retain carbon dioxide which, in turn, will serve to retard chemical and physical changes in the albumin and yolk. Such oiling also cuts down moisture losses.

DESSERTS

The dehydrated fruits such as raisins, apricots, currants, apples, prunes, peaches, dates, pears, and figs give everyone plenty of choice. Numerous prepared dessert mixes of one sort and another also afford a wide selection. Find out by experimentation which ones you like before you take to the woods. Especially delicious and nutritious in the wilderness? That dense, heavy fruitcake that ordinarily seems a little too rich for city consumption.

SPICES AND FLAVORINGS

Everyone has his own ideas on these, which is as it should be. Nearly everybody wants a little pepper. Small containers of powdered celery (not celery salt), onions, and garlic pack a lot of possibilities. Paprika and powdered parsley combine taste and eye appeal. Then there are nutmeg, cinnamon, and their ilk.

Small containers of thyme and rosemary afford occasional taste variations with fowl and red meats respectively. Like the rest, they cost only a few cents and occupy little room.

Among the flavorings that seem to taste particularly good in the woods are vanilla, banana, and the peppermint which really touches up chocolate. There also are lemon and other pure fruit juice powders, crystals, etc. Suit yourself.

BEVERAGES

CAMP COFFEE

One favorite way to make camp coffee is to put a rather coarse grind into fresh cold water, using two level tablespoons for every cup of water. Amounts can be varied, of course, for a stronger or weaker brew. Hang or set this over the fire. Watch it carefully. As soon as it boils up once, lift it to a warm sanctuary to take on body for five minutes. Then settle the grounds, if you want, with a couple of tablespoons of cold water and start pouring.

Unless you have decided preferences to the contrary, powdered instant coffee is far preferable to the ground article for general camp use except, perhaps, for those first cups in the morning. It is more economical in weight and bulk, cheaper, longer-lasting, and both quicker and easier to prepare. It can be made to individual order and without waste.

If you'd like to pocket several enjoyable pickups before going on a hike or for a day's fishing, you can ready a number of these in a jiffy beforehand. For each, mix one teaspoon of your favorite instant coffee with an equal amount of sugar. Roll securely in foil. Dissolved pleasantly in the mouth, each will provide the same amount of stimulation and energy as would a similarly based cup of black coffee.

B'ILING THE KITTLE

The northern woodsman, particularly the Canadian, must sip his steaming cup of tea at noon, and contemplate its swiftly seething surface colors, even if he has nothing to eat. This is almost a religion up under the aurora borealis, and it's called "b'iling the kittle."

Only a temporary fire is needed, a mere handful of dry wood that will flare up briefly and as quickly fall to ashes, a few feathers of which invariably seem to swirl up to float unheeded in the dark brew. Get the water bubbling. Drop in a roughly measured teaspoon of tea for every cup of water and set immediately from the heat in a safe place. Five minutes of steeping is sufficient.

Tea is something many prefer to carry in the usual form, if only for the pleasant rite of tossing a handful of palm-measured leaves into the bubbling kettle. There is powdered tea on the market, however, that mixes immediately with water, and which tastes a lot closer to regular tea than any of the powdered coffees taste like regularly brewed coffee. This tea can't reasonably be spoiled by improper making, although probably some camp cook, by trying to make enough for everyone at once, can still somehow manage to boil it.

MISCELLANEOUS DRINKS

Fruit juices are particular treats in the bush. Lemon, for example, is also sometimes welcome with fresh rainbow trout. A number of concentrated fruit juices are now available, both dried and liquid.

Bouillon cubes and powders make hot drinks that taste good around a campfire. A lot of times they're more appreciated than either tea or coffee. They also are useful for flavoring broths, soups, gravies, and stews. Other worthwhile beverage concentrates include cocoa, malted milk, and chocolate.

CHOCOLATE. Hot chocolate and cocoa in particular have a way of easing those last few steps between fire and bed. As for chocolate bars, these are one of the best known and liked energy foods.

It's a common thing on extended wilderness trips to find a whitish appearance in such chocolate. This does not indicate spoilage, but is due to cocoa butter which has separated out. At a temperature no more than 85°, the cocoa butter in ordinary chocolate melts and comes to the surface. It whitens upon hardening. Only the appearance of the chocolate is affected.

CHECKLIST FOR PROVISIONS

What you take on your wilderness trip is pretty much a personal matter. The main thing is not to drive off and leave some wanted item behind. Here are two ways to avoid that disaster:

Unless you live where there's plenty of room, make a checklist with a separate column for each group of essentials. One column will be for dry foods, a second for perishables, another for eating materials such as dishes and tableware, and so on.

Tape or glue this list on a heavy piece of cardboard, if that is what you have to settle for. Use it during preparations, of course, but also have it at hand when you pack for the start. At that decisive moment, recheck items one by one as a preventive measure against going off and forgetting some indispensable.

Those who have ample space can take advantage of the visual technique of building little piles. Place cooking utensils in one group, dining paraphernalia in a second, foods in another, etc. When a certain article is in use at the moment, or needs to be picked up at the store or removed from the refrigerator, a note to that effect, weighed down in the proper heap, will serve as a handy reminder.

Keep a record for future reference. Note, finally, what is left over at the end of the journey. Such intelligence can guide your efforts when you provision for your next sojourn in the silent spaces.

Chapter 16

EATING WELL IN THE WILDS

WILDERNESS living adds its own relish to the plainest outdoor meals. Nevertheless, the outdoorsman need not settle for the elemental in preparing his meals, and there is always a best way to cook even the simplest dishes. As this chapter amply demonstrates, outdoor cooking with limited equipment not only provides great latitude for individual ingenuity, but also is capable of turning out meals to satisfy the most epicurean palate.

"Bacon," a sourdough friend translated, when asked what he meant by saying he'd gorged himself with vast quantities of *tiger*. "That's because it's striped. Sounds nobler when called tiger."

The main trouble that camp cooks experience with bacon arises from their submitting it too soon to too much heat. Not only is the bacon thus burned and toughened, but very often the frypan becomes a mass of leaping flames. Aside from resulting offenses to taste and digestion, this is wasteful, if nothing worse. The nearly 3,000 calories per pound that fat side bacon contains lie largely in its grease, any excess of which should be saved, particularly in the wilderness.

You'll do better to start the bacon in a cold frypan and to fry it slowly over a very few coals raked to one side of the blaze. Move and turn the bacon from time to time. If you like it crisp, keep pouring off the grease. Don't waste any of this, though. It has numerous camp uses.

More satisfactory still is the practice of laying the strips well apart in a pan and baking them evenly to a golden brown in a moderately warm reflector baker.

Slabs of bacon have a tendency to mold. This mold can be wiped off harmlessly with a clean cloth moistened either in vinegar or in a solution of baking soda and water.

EGG DISHES

BOILED EGGS

Get enough water boiling in a pan to cover the eggs by an inch. Place the eggs in the pan with a spoon and let the temperature immediately drop to a simmer, keeping it that way until the eggs are done. With all egg dishes, moderate heat is necessary to avoid toughness. Usual preferences here range between 2½ and 3½ minutes of cooking, depending on how stiff you like the whites. Remove and break open at once. Serve immediately, preferably in heated dishes.

HARD-BOILED EGGS

Get things started the same way as above. Keep the eggs simmering, completely covered, 8-10 minutes. Then remove from the heat and plunge into cold water. If the shells are cracked slightly before the eggs cool, peeling will be easier.

Woodsmen sometimes get their hard-boiled and raw eggs mixed. There's an easy way to tell the difference. If the egg will spin freely, it's cooked. The only egg that will cross you up is a frozen one.

POACHED EGGS

There's a gimmick to this one. Fill a frypan 2 inches deep with water, with roughly a teaspoon of salt for every 4 cups of water. Bring the water to the bubbling point. Then take a spoon and start the water revolving in one direction.

Now slide each egg gently into the water from a saucer. The movement of the liquid will keep the whites from spreading. Dip some of the water over the top. Three minutes of simmering suits most people. Or, once the eggs are in, you may set the water off the heat for five minutes. Try these poached eggs sometimes on a small mound of buttered rice, noodles, spaghetti, macaroni, or potatoes.

SCRAMBLED EGGS

The addition of milk has a tendency to toughen scrambled eggs. Instead, add a tablespoon of cold water for each egg. Mix the eggs and water well with salt and pepper to taste. Heat a tablespoon of fat in a frypan just hot enough to sizzle a drop of water. Pour in the egg mixture and reduce the heat. When the eggs have started to harden, begin stirring them constantly with a fork. Remove while they're still soft and creamy.

FRIED EGGS

Have about half an inch of fat warm, not hot. Break in your eggs. Keeping the heat low so the whites won't become tough and leathery, baste the yolks until they are well filmed. Salt, pepper, and serve on a hot plate.

Or, get a tablespoon of fat just hot enough to sizzle a test drop of water. Break in the eggs. Take the frypan off the heat at once. Baste the eggs with hot fat three or four times.

TOMATOES, ONIONS, AND EGGS

This nourishing and easily digestible dish with a mild and provocatively elusive flavor is unusually good when someone hauls into camp late, especially as its preparation is both simple and swift. Proportions, which are flexible, may be varied in ratio to appetite.

For two late arrivals, brown a couple of diced onions with a little grease in a frypan. When these have cooked to a dark blandness, add a small can of tomatoes. Let these begin to bubble. Then break in 6 eggs. Season with salt and pepper. Keep scrambling over low heat until fairly dry.

POOCH IN A POUCH

Let everyone impale a frankfurter, canned or fresh, on the peeled end of a sharpened green stick. Make some bannock dough, per the instructions later in this chapter. Roll out and cut into narrow, five-inch ribbons. Or so mold a ball of dough between the palms.

Spiral one of these strips around each of the dogs. Press the dough firmly together at each end to hold it in place. Bake over the edge of a small campfire, turning slowly, for about five minutes or until done.

BAKED TOMATOES

Drain the juice from a large can of tomatoes. Use for beverage. Mix with the remaining solid portions: 1 cup cubed toast, 1 teaspoon salt, ½ cup sugar, and 2 tablespoons margarine. Spread this out in a greased pan or baking dish. Sprinkle with bread or bannock crumbs. Bake in a moderate oven or reflector baker 25 minutes.

MACARONI, SPAGHETTI, NOODLES

A quarter-pound of any of these uncooked doubles in volume to about 2 cupfuls cooked and makes an average portion. Cook each such portion in 2 quarts of boiling water seasoned with 2 teaspoons of salt.

Break macaroni into small bits before cooking. Let spaghetti and noodles gradually soften in contact with the boiling water and so adapt themselves to the kettle. Stir occasionally to avoid sticking.

Boil, uncovered, only until the macaroni or other paste is tender but still firm. Test by chewing. The time varies with different pastes, but averages between 8 and 12 minutes. Drain immediately, as by holding the lid over the pan in such a way that just enough of an opening is left to allow the water to run off.

BAKED MACARONI AND CHEESE

Boil half a pound of macaroni in 4 quarts of water with 4 teaspoons of salt, according to the preceding directions. Cut half a pound of cheese into cubes. Open a small can of tomatoes.

Alternate layers of cooked macaroni with cheese in a greased pan or baking dish, seasoning each layer with salt and pepper. Add a tablespoon of solid tomato to each layer. Then pour enough tomato over everything to come within a half inch of the top. Top with sliced onion if you want. Bake in a hot oven or reflector baker until well browned.

CEREAL

Prepare according to the instructions on the package.

A favorite camp cereal of many is oatmeal. The quick-cooking variety saves time. One way is to ready it the night before by adding, if cooking just for yourself, ½ cup oatmeal and ½ teaspoon salt to 2 cups cold water. Plump out overnight ¼ cup of raisins, more or less, to add flavor.

The next morning, hunch far enough out of the sleeping bag to get the fire going, put on the covered pan, and let the contents come to a boil before setting it to one side for a few minutes. Then either pour in evaporated milk straight out of the can, or in colder weather, add a liberal spoonful of margarine or butter, and begin satisfying the inner man.

This is really luxury when deepening cold has condensed, close above the throbbing earth, a twinkling ceiling of ice crystals to which the smoke of your solitary campfire ascends in an unwavering pillar.

MEAT DISHES

STEAKS

Cooking steaks over open embers is unbeatable. A good trick at the start is to get a glowing bed of coals, then to sprinkle on a few chips and shavings. These will flare up enough both to help seal in the juices and to give that flavorsome char relished by so many.

As you're already aware, the grill should be greased beforehand to prevent sticking. A handy one for wilderness use is one of those light-weight campfire grates available from most large outfitters. Removing the folding wire legs will make for easier packing if that's any problem. It's a simple matter to lay such a grid between logs or rocks.

Individual steaks also can be very pleasingly grilled merely by holding them over the heat by means of sturdy forked green sticks.

Pan-broiling, not frying, is excellent, too, especially if the meat is top grade and cut about two inches thick. Salt the meat well before putting it in a really hot, preferably heavy frypan. Quickly sear both sides and then cook with slightly less heat until done to taste. No grease at all is used, and that sputtering from the meat is tipped out. Salt and pepper, if you want, and daub with butter or margarine after cooking. Serve on preheated plates.

Lean meat cooks more quickly than fat meat. Aging also progressively shortens the cooking time. Then there are such factors as size, shape, and the amount of bone. Outdoor fires add another variable. A practical way to test is to prick the steak with a sharpened stick. If red juice wells out, the meat is rare. Pink, medium rare. Colorless, overdone (unless that is the way you want it).

ROASTS

Tender roasts are best cooked rare, unless you object, to take fullest advantage of the natural savor of the meat. If the meat isn't tender, treat it first with one of the unseasoned commercial tenderizers.

Moderately slow oven temperatures give the best results with large roasts. About twelve minutes per pound should do it, to give you an idea. Searing, inasmuch as it keeps in no juices, is unnecessary. If one side of the meat is fatter, placing this uppermost will give you the energy-conserving advantage of some natural basting. Meat should be left uncovered, salted beforehand, if you want, but not floured, and cooked without any addition of water.

The reflector baker does a particularly wonderful job in this department. Turn the roast occasionally to encourage uniform cooking. While you're at it, scrub enough potatoes for the meal. Slice off the ends to allow steam to escape. Rub with shortening or cooking oil. Place in the oven to cook along with the roast.

"BOILED" MEAT

Cut the meat into two-inch cubes. Drop these individually into just enough bubbling water to cover. Do not boil. Don't salt until almost ready to serve. Meat so cooked can best be relished after it has been simmering, covered, only five minutes or so. However, many get the habit of letting it cook an hour or more.

MULLIGAN. Often rice and other vegetables, particularly onions, are cooked along with the meat to make what is called *mulligan.* The addition of any such components, except when included for flavor only, should be so staggered that everything will be done at the same time. Any extra fluid should be heated before it is added.

If you are going to use the meat cold, let it cool in the broth. The Dutch oven will conveniently so "boil" a big solid chunk of meat. Place the meat in the bottom of the oven along with onions, if you have any, perhaps a sliced carrot or two, and 1½ teaspoons salt per pound. Half cover the meat with simmering water. Cook about an hour for every pound, at the end of which time the meat should be tender, but not stringy or mushy.

If you want to use it in cold sandwiches, let it cool in the broth. Then move it to a flat utensil that will hold a little of the broth. Press it into shape with a weighted cover or plate so it later can be more handily sliced.

STEWING

Stew meat, which can be the toughest in the critter, is best browned at the onset with fat, chopped onion, and seasonings in the bottom of the kettle. You then can, if you want, stir in enough flour, first mixed to a paste in cold water, to make a thick, smooth gravy.

For liquid, use any fluid in which vegetables have been cooked or canned, broth from boiled meat, or water. Season to taste, bringing to a bubble, and then place, tightly covered, where it will simmer all morning or all afternoon.

A Dutch oven is a handy receptacle for stew, inasmuch as you can dig a hole, always in a safe place where fire cannot spread, and leave it buried there among hot coals while you spend the day hiking, fishing, or exploring.

BROTH

You sometimes find yourself back of beyond with more good meat than can possibly be brought out. Maybe you'll delay in camp a few days longer. Still, you can scarcely begin to eat it.

On occasions like this, why not really splurge on broth and enjoy all you possibly can? Get the kettle simmering, hang a ladle or cup nearby, and let everyone help himself until the pot is exhausted. Then begin another. The thing to remember is that the liquid will boil down, so don't get it too salty at the start.

Just cut the meat into small pieces so you'll get the most good out of it. All lesser cuts that you haven't time to handle otherwise are fine. Marrow bones, split or sawed, are unequalled. So are bony portions. Add about a cup of water for every half-pound of meat and bone. Cover and simmer, not boil, upwards of four hours.

Incidentally, if you get hungry between meals, the meat itself is wonderful, hot and simmering in melted butter or margarine.

PRESERVING MEAT

If you're camping in one place and have a quantity of fresh meat you'd like to preserve with a minimum of trouble, cut it into forearm-size strips, following the membranous divisions among the muscles as much as possible. Pull off as much of this parchment as you can.

Roll the pieces in a mixture made proportionately of 3 pounds of table salt, 4 tablespoons of allspice, and 5 tablespoons of black pepper. Rubbing this well into the meat, then shaking off any excess, will give the best results.

You can either drape the strips over a wire or similar support, well away from any animals, or suspend them, after first piercing an end of each with a knife, by looping in a string or wire. The treated meat must be kept dry. When traveling, rehang it after reaching your destination.

About one month is needed for it to shrink and to absorb

the seasoning properly, less in dry country and more in damp regions. Sliced thin, it's then really something to chew on raw. Scraped and trimmed some, and soaked overnight, if you want, it also goes well in mulligan. Meat so cured, if kept dry, remains delicious after several decades.

JERKY. The simplest way to preserve meat is by drying it. When this is done most advantageously, it's also one of the most delicious methods. Try some of the beef jerky available in markets if you have any doubts. And note the price. The amount charged for two or three slim, blackened strips of this dehydrated meal often will buy a good steak.

There's nothing complicated about making jerky. Cut lean, red meat into long strips about half an inch thick. Hang these apart from one another in the sun, or, if home, in the attic or some other place where, kept dry, they gradually will lose most of their water content. At the same time, they'll become hard, dry, and, most important of all, both nourishing and tasty.

The strips may first be soaked, if you want, either in brine or sea water. If you are along the seacost, you may care to try the ancient method of boiling down sea water until it becomes extremely salty. While it is still bubbling, immerse a few strips at a time for three minutes apiece. If there is no convenient place to hang this meat, it can be laid across sun-warmed rocks and turned every hour or so. You also can make your own brine by dissolving all the salt possible in boiling water.

After the meat has been allowed to drain, some makers sprinkle it with pepper. In many cases, they also add favorite spices, such as origanum, marjoram, basil, and thyme, for increased flavor. Good? Many ranchers, with plenty of empty space in their freezers, jerk a critter or so a year in this fashion just for their own personal eating.

A common bush technique for jerking meat involves draping the strips, or hanging them by string or wire loops, on a wood framework about four to six feet off the ground. A small, slow, smoky fire of any non-resinous wood is built beneath this rack. The meat is allowed to dry for several days in the sun and wind. It is covered at night and during any rain. The chief use of the fire is to discourage flies and other insects. It should not be hot enough to cook the meat at all.

When jerked, the meat will be hard and more or less black

outside. It will keep almost indefinitely away from damp and flies. This covered wagon staple is best eaten as is. Just bite off a chunk and chew. It also may be cooked in stews. It is very concentrated and nourishing, and a little goes a long way as an emergency ration. Alone, it is not good food for long-continued consumption, as it lacks the necessary fat.

The fat, which would turn rancid, should be trimmed off before the drying operation is commenced. It may then be rendered for use in cooking or in the manufacture of pemmican.

PEMMICAN. Some frightful conglomerations appear on the market from time to time under the name of "pemmican." To make real pemmican, one of the best concentrated foods ever, you begin by pounding up a quantity of jerky.

Then take raw animal fat and cut it into walnut-size hunks. Try these out in a pan in the oven or over a slow fire, never letting the grease boil up. Pour the resulting hot fat over the shredded jerky, mixing the two together until the mixture is about the consistency of ordinary sausage. Finally, pack the pemmican in commercial casings or waterproof bags. Despite some practices, no salt at all should be added. Dried berries? Suit yourself. Their function is as a flavor only.

The ideal proportions of lean and fat in pemmican are, by weight, approximately equal amounts of well-dried lean meat and rendered fat. It takes approximately five pounds of fresh, lean meat to make one pound of jerky suitable for pemmican.

Such genuine pemmican will afford practically every necessary food element with the exception of Vitamin C. The average individual can get along without this vitamin for at least two months, if in good health to begin with. Furthermore, supplementing the pemmican with some fresh food—for example, just several fresh rose hips daily—will supply all the Vitamin C necessary to prevent scurvy over even an extended period.

FISH

Cooking methods for fish may be determined to some extent by their fatness. Plumper varieties such as lake trout, salmon, and whitefish are best for baking, as in a reflector baker or

Dutch oven, and for broiling over the cherry-red coals of a campfire. Their fat content helps keep them from becoming too dry.

Leaner catches such as pike, bass, perch, and Arctic grayling are preferable for poaching and for steaming because they remain firmer. They also can be satisfactorily baked and grilled if frequently basted or if topped with a sauce.

All fish are eminently suitable for frying. As far as that goes, any fish may be satisfyingly cooked by any of the basic methods if allowances are made for the fat content.

The main thing is not to overcook the catch. To keep fish moist and tender, and to bring out its delicate flavor, cook only until the flesh is no longer translucent. Once the fish is easily flaked, it is done. The taste will be enhanced further if the fish is salted, inside and out, as much as an hour in advance of cooking.

A second thing to avoid is soaking any fish before or after it is cleaned.

SPITTED FISH

Sometime when you have a mess of small brook trout or such, let everyone roughly trim and peel his own hardwood wand. Thread a slice of bacon on the wand and broil it over ruddy coals until translucent. Then place the opened and cleaned fish lengthwise over the bacon, fastening the fish by skewering it with sharpened twigs. Cook slowly over glowing embers. Repeat as long as fish and appetites hold out.

Large fish also may be spitted and roasted over hot coals. They have a tendency to roll on the stick, however, and usually must be lashed to it with twine or old fishline. Unless the fish is fat, it will be the better for basting.

GRILLED FISH

The smaller the fish, the hotter the grill should be. If the fish sticks or breaks when you attempt to turn it or to take it up, then odds are you didn't let the grill get hot enough to start with. Too, grease it well at the onset.

Either salt the inside and outside of the fish up to an hour before broiling, or sprinkle the inside with pepper and lemon juice before it goes on the heat. Whole fish may be split or not, depending on your preference and on the size. Even when the fish has a thick skin well cushioned with fat, basting will add to the flavor. When the translucency of the fish has clouded to opaqueness, it is ready to serve.

FISH BAKED IN CLAY

This seals in the flavor, but you need the kind of fine, sticky clay that makes good log-cabin chinking. If it isn't already wet, work it with water until it reaches the consistency of a stiff dough. Then mold it about an inch thick completely over the whole fish. Bury in hot embers until the covered fish resembles a hard, hot brick. Baking will take fifteen minutes per pound of fish. When you break open the shell, such externals as fins and scales will be imbedded in it, leaving a steaming, savory feast.

EELS

This elongated fish outdoes all normal expectations. Fry them skinned, cut into two-inch pieces, salted, and then browned on both sides in the frypan with several tablespoons of margarine or butter.

BREADS

FRYING PAN BREAD

This is the famous bannock of the open places. The basic recipe for one hungry outdoorsman follows. If you want more, increase the ingredients proportionately.

> 1   cup flour
> 1   teaspoon baking powder
> ¼   teaspoon salt

Mix these dry, taking all the time you need to do this thoroughly. Have your hands floured and everything ready to go before you add liquid. If you are going to use the traditional frypan, make sure this is warm and greased.

Working quickly from now on, stir in enough cold water to make a firm dough. Shape this, with as little handling as possible, into a cake about an inch thick. If you like crust, leave a doughnut-like hole in the middle. Dust the loaf lightly with flour, so it will handle more easily.

Prospectors, trappers, and other professional outdoorsmen still widely continue the pioneer practice of mixing bannock in the flour sacks themselves. Just make a small hollow in the flour. Drop the salt and baking powder into this. Then, stirring with the fingers of one hand, add the water gradually until the resulting dough has picked up all the flour it can. Press and pat into shape.

Lay the bannock in the warm frypan. Hold it over the heat until a bottom crust forms, rotating the pan a little so the loaf will shift and not become stuck.

Once the dough has hardened enough to hold together, turn the bannock over. With a bit of practice and enough confidence to flip strongly enough, you can accomplish this easily with a slight swing of the arm and snap of the wrist. Or you can use a spatula, supporting the loaf long enough to invert the frypan over it, and then turning everything together.

With a campfire, however, it is often easier at this stage just to prop the frypan at a steep angle so the bannock will get direct heat on top. When crust has formed all around, you may, if you wish, turn the bannock over and around a few times while it is baking to an appetizing brown.

When is the bannock done? After you've been cooking them awhile, you will be able to tap one and gauge its doneness by the hollowness of the sound. Meanwhile, test by shoving in a straw or sliver. If any dough adheres, the loaf needs more heat. Cooking can be accomplished in about fifteen minutes. If you have other duties around camp, twice that time a bit farther from the heat will allow the frying pan bread to cook more evenly.

BISCUITS

Start with the basic bannock recipe. Work 3 tablespoons of solid shortening per cup of flour into these dry ingredients. Mix thoroughly, perhaps by cutting through the flour and shortening again and again with two dull knives, until the mixture has the consistency of coarse meal.

Then, working quickly, add enough water or milk to make a dough just soft enough to be easily handled. You'll find that ¼ to ⅓ cup of fluid per cup of flour will generally suffice. If the dough becomes too sticky, rapidly scatter on a little more flour. For best results, knead no more than half a minute.

Flatten the dough speedily into a sheet about ¾-inch thick. A cold bottle or can makes an effective rolling pin. Cut square biscuits with a sharp, cold knife or press out round ones with the baking powder tin top held upside down. Dust each with flour.

Place on a lightly greased pan or sheet. Bake in a very hot oven or reflector baker until a rich brown, by which time the biscuits should have risen to about two inches high. These biscuits also can be cooked in a frypan like bannock, in which case you may have to turn each one several times to assure even cooking. Or bake them in a Dutch oven, as suggested later in this chapter. In any event, if you don't care for crust, keep them close together.

SUBSTITUTING SNOW FOR EGGS

In the North, when oldtimers lack eggs for breadstuffs, they often use snow successfully instead. Fresh dry snow is best for this purpose. It is rapidly stirred in just before the breadstuff is put over the heat. It must not be allowed to melt until the cooking is under way, for its function is entirely mechanical.

The air-loaded flakes of snow hold the ingredients apart. Cooked while these are so separated, such breadstuffs come out airy and light. Egg is able to accomplish the same result, as you can appreciate by watching the way an egg rapidly beats into airholding froth whose elasticity heightens its raising and spacing process. Two heaping tablespoons of fresh dry snow will take the place of each egg in the batter.

SOURDOUGH STARTER

The starter can be readied at home. Once you have it, you have commenced growing your own yeast. That's what you actually are using when you bake with sourdough. The sure, simple way to begin is with:

> 2 cups flour
> 2 cups lukewarm water
> 1 yeast cake or package of dry yeast

Mix the flour, lukewarm water, and yeast thoroughly. Then set overnight away from drafts in a warm place. By the next morning, the mixture should be putting forth bubbles and a pleasant yeasty odor. This overall process needn't stop for as long as you're going to be in the wilderness, even though this may be for years.

STORING SOURDOUGH STARTER. For best results, keep the starter in a well-washed and scalded glass or pottery container. Never leave any metal in contact with it. Keep the starter as much as possible in a cool spot. As a matter of fact, if you want to store the starter or a part of it for a period of months, perhaps between trips, just freeze it.

The sourdough starter can be kept fresh and clean by drying, also. If you want to carry it easily and safely, work in enough flour to solidify the sponge into a dry wad. A good place to pack this is in the flour itself. When you're ready, water and warmth will reactivate the yeast plants.

REVIVIFYING SOURDOUGH STARTER. Starters occasionally lose their vigor, particularly in cold weather. Old-timers then sometimes revive them with a tablespoon of unpasteurized cider vinegar. This puts new acetic acid bacteria on the job. A tablespoon or two of raw sour milk or cream, unpasteurized buttermilk, cultured buttermilk, or cultured sour cream will get the lactic acids working again.

A sourdough starter is kept going best by the addition of flour and water only. The starter, unless temporarily frozen or dried, should be so fed about once a week at least. If you are regularly cooking with the starter, this process will take care of itself.

Sourdough starters should never be stored in warm places for very long. Heat-encouraged organisms hurtful to yeast grow at an extremely rapid rate. These soon may gain sufficient control to produce putrefactive changes, the reason for some of the unpleasant smells one occasionally runs across in old starters. Another result is that starters become progressively weaker in dough-fermenting ability.

It is sometimes necessary to begin a new starter. This is a practical reason for including some spare yeast in the camping outfit. Better take recently dated, packaged dry yeast. Stored where reasonably cool, this will keep several months or more.

SOURDOUGH BREAD

If commencing from the beginning, set your starting sponge as already directed. The commercial yeast is used only to get the starter going. From then on, the mixture will grow its own yeast. When doubling a recipe, by the way, you needn't double the starter.

Take your starter. Add enough flour and lukewarm water in equal volumes to make about 3 cups of sponge. Let this stand in a warm location overnight or from 6 to 8 hours, whereupon it should be bubbling and giving off an agreeable yeasty odor.

From here on, the general procedure remains the same. Take out, in this instance, 2 cups of sponge. Place the remainder aside. That's your next starter. No matter what the recipe, at this stage always keep out at least a cup of the basic sourdough.

Mix 4 cups of flour, 2 tablespoons sugar, and 1 teaspoon salt. Make a depression in the center of these dry ingredients. Blend 2 tablespoons liquid shortening and the sponge in the hollow. Then mix everything together. A soft dough should result. If necessary, add either flour or fluid. The latter may be water or milk. Knead for 3 or 4 minutes on any clean, floured surface.

"Keep attacking," goes an old trapper's instructions. "Don't gentle it. That is where most cheechakos make their mistake. Too much pushing and pressing lets the gas escape that's needed to raise the stuff. Just bang the dough together in a hurry, cut off loaves to fit your greased pans, and put them in a warm place to raise."

The dough, once it has plumped out to double size, should be baked 50 to 60 minutes in a moderately hot oven or reflector baker that, preferably, is hottest the first 15 minutes. Baking should redouble the size of the loaves.

One tests "in the usual way," the old trapper added. He explained, probably because it seemed necessary, that the "usual way" is to wait until the loaves seem crisply brown, then to jab in a straw. If the bread is done, the straw will come out dry and at least as clean as it was when inserted.

Sourdough bread is substantial in comparison with the usual air-filled bakery loaf. It keeps moist for a satisfactorily long time. When the bread is made according to the preceding suggestions, the flavor is unusually excellent, being especially nutty when the slices are toasted. If your crew likes real tasty crust, bake the bread in long slim loaves to capitalize on this outstanding characteristic of sourdough.

BAKING IN A DUTCH OVEN

The Dutch oven will bake biscuits and bread deliciously both below and above ground. Heat the contraption first, setting the lid on a good solid fire and easing the pot atop that. When the pot is hot, you should be all set to go.

Say you want to bake a mess of baking powder biscuits. Drop a blob of butter, margarine, lard, bacon drippings, or other grease into the pot and work it around a bit. While it's melting, ready the biscuits. Put them into the pot and plant this solidly and evenly above a bed of coal and ashes. Clang on the lid. Heap additional coals onto that. The fact that the lid has been preheated to a higher temperature than the pot should balance the natural rising tendency of heat sufficiently to cook the tops and bottoms of the biscuits evenly.

Take a look after about ten minutes, if you want. If the biscuits aren't already taking on a healthy tan, rake the accumulating cinders and ashes from the lid and substitute more live coals. Dutch ovens require a certain amount of cooking experience, but the biscuits should ordinarily be ready in a dozen or fifteen minutes.

Bread, taking longer to bake, is better adapted to underground cooking. For this, start in the forenoon by digging a hole somewhat larger than the oven and filling it with a blazing hardwood fire. As a basic precaution, be sure this pit is in mineral soil, well away from roots and humus. When the blaze has burned down to coals, shovel or rake out about half of it. Set in the preheated and greased Dutch oven with a big round sourdough loaf bulging in it. Ease the oven around until it's setting evenly. Then move the embers and ashes back in until the utensil, except for its upraised bail handle, is hidden.

You need a certain amount of experience here, too. If it seems that the coals are going to be too hot, insulate the oven with an inch or so of ashes. In any event, seal in the heat with several inches of dirt. Then spend the afternoon getting enough trout or wild raspberries to go with those crusty hot slices that will be awaiting you at suppertime.

DUMPLINGS

Nothing sets off a hearty outdoor stew like steaming hot dumplings. These are a cinch to make, and they have the additional advantages of needing neither separate cooking nor extra washing. The following recipe should satisfy two ravenous campers. About a dozen minutes before mealtime take:

> 2 cups flour
> 2 teaspoons baking powder
> 1 teaspoon salt
> 2 tablespoons margarine or butter
> 1 cup milk

Mix the flour, baking powder, and salt. Work in the margarine or other solid shortening. Make a bowl-like hollow in the center. Have everything ready to go, for these dumplings should be cooked only 8 to 10 minutes, and then the meal should be served immediately. Have the broth simmering above enough meat and other solids so the dumplings will not sink below the surface.

Now pour the milk, which may be reconstituted from powdered milk, into the well in the middle of the dry ingredients. Mix quickly and gently with a folding, rather than a stirring or whipping, action.

Moisten a large spoon in the broth. Use it to place large spoonfuls, apart from one another, atop the stew. Cover tightly. After several minutes, you may, if you want, turn each dumpling carefully and speedily. Re-cover immediately and continue simmering until light and fluffy.

Then serve without delay. If any dumplings remain for second helpings, place them in a separate hot dish so they won't become soggy.

POTATOES

BAKED POTATOES

A good way to cook the most popular of American-grown vegetables, potatoes, is to bake the large ones in their skins in hot ashes, not glowing coals, until they become pretty well blackened on the outside. They're done when a thin, sharpened stick will run easily through their middles. Rake out, break in half, and serve at once with salt and melting butter or margarine.

BOILED POTATOES

Scrub enough potatoes, choosing those of equal size as far as possible so they'll cook uniformly. Cover with boiling water, seasoned with a teaspoon of salt for every three potatoes. Simmer, covered, 20-30 minutes or until a fork penetrates easily. Drain, peel if you wish, season with pepper and salt, and cover to keep warm and prevent sogginess.

Or, particularly if you're in a hurry, peel. Cut into uniform pieces. Drop into cold water for a short time to prevent darkening. Cook, covered, in a small amount of boiling salted water until done. Then handle as above.

FRYPAN POTATOES

Start 3 slices of bacon in a cold frypan and cook until crisp. Remove the bacon and pour all but about a tablespoon of the drippings into the camp shortening can. Add a chopped onion, forking the bits around until they have started to brown. Break up the bacon and return it to the pan. Slice in 4 potatoes.

Flatten out the slices and cover them at once with a minimum amount of water. Bring this to a simmer and keep the potatoes cooking until they've started to break to pieces and to thicken the liquid. Add hot water if any more is required. Salt, pepper, and eat as soon as the potatoes are done.

HASHED BROWN POTATOES

Heat 4 tablespoons margarine, cooking oil, or other shortening in the frypan. Add enough potatoes, peeled and cut very fine. Salt and pepper. Then press down and cook over low heat until brown and crisp on the bottom. Loosen this crust with a knife. Then cover the frypan with a plate and invert it with the frypan quickly so the potatoes will come out with the brown underside on top.

HASH

You can hustle together hash by chopping cooked meat with an equal volume of boiled potatoes. Salt and pepper to taste, and add part or all of the following: chopped onion, fresh or powdered celery, and parsley flakes. Moisten the mixture with soup stock, bouillon, thin milk, or water. Spread thickly on a greased pan. Set over low heat 20 minutes until the bottom of the hash is well browned, or cook in an oven or reflector baker with moderate heat.

BOILED ONIONS

Peel the onions. These will cook more uniformly if all are about the same size. Large onions may be sliced before boiling. To avoid watery eyes, you can carry on these operations with the vegetables held under water.

Cover with salted boiling water. Cook, uncovered, 20-35 minutes or until the onions are tender but not broken. The water, incidentally, will be excellent for soups and such. Drain, add your idea of enough butter or margarine, and season with salt and pepper.

ROAST CORN

Sweet young corn is best for this. Carefully strip the husks down to the end of the ear, leaving them attached. Pull off the silk. Soak the corn in cold salted water for half an hour. Drain. Then brush the kernels with butter or margarine and sprinkle them with salt and a little pepper. Pull the husks back up around the corn and twist tightly together.

Make a hollow of coals at the edge of the campfire, cover it with an inch of ashes, lay in the corn, cover with more ashes and then hot coals, and roast about 30 minutes. After raking off the ashes and coals, peel the husks back again and use as handles.

If you're where there is green corn, probably aluminum foil is available, too. If you want, wrap and twist each ear tightly in foil before consigning it to the ash-insulated coals. This way you can poke the corn around occasionally to assure more even cooking, and even take a look while it is roasting to taste.

TREATS FOR THE SWEET TOOTH

ICE CREAM

Ice cream is one of the quickest and easiest of all desserts to make outdoors, especially after a fresh snow. Best for the purpose are dry flakes. You also can use the granular interior of the perpetual snowbanks found in the higher mountains, although the result will be more a coarse sherbet.

Just empty a can of evaporated milk into a large pot or bowl. A similar amount of dry milk, reconstituted with about half the usual amount of water, will do as well. Add 2 table-spoons of sugar, ⅛ teaspoon salt, and some flavoring. Vanilla or one of the other extracts will serve. So will cocoa, powdered coffee, and the like. Mocha? Balance 2 teaspoons of powdered instant coffee with a teaspoon of chocolate—enough, incidentally, for a quart of ice cream. If the flavoring, as, for instance, chocolate syrup, is already sweet, just omit the sugar.

Then quickly stir in fresh snow to taste. More sweetening and flavoring may be added at the end, if you want. For this reason it is safest to go light on these initially. Otherwise, you'll have to repair any mistake with more milk and snow—not that this isn't a good excuse.

Three varieties that come out especially well, if you happen to like them to begin with, are the universally favored vanilla, rich dark chocolate with overtones of peppermint extract, and banana ice cream made with banana extract.

TREELESS MAPLE SYRUP

The sugar maple grows only in North America. Like all green trees, it mysteriously changes water and carbon dioxide into sugar. So exceptional is the sugar maple's capacity for storing the sweet that this talent is a double boon. In autumn it produces some of the loveliest hues of the American forest; in spring, the amber succulence of maple syrup.

The only trouble many wilderness cooks have is that the availability of maple syrup is largely confined to eastern regions such as the St. Lawrence Valley, New Brunswick and Nova Scotia, and such New England states as New Hampshire and Vermont. But there's a slightly incredible way around. You'll need:

> 6 medium potatoes
> 2 cups water
> 1 cup white sugar
> 1 cup brown sugar

Peel the potatoes. Boil uncovered with 2 cups water until but 1 cup of fluid remains. Remove the potatoes for use any way you want. Stirring the liquid until the boiling point has again been reached, slowly add the sugar. Once this has entirely dissolved, set the pan off the heat to cool slowly.

See if that first spoonful you doubtfully try doesn't seem to justify your worst suspicions. But bottle the syrup and put it away in a dark place for several days to age. Taste it again at the end of that time and see if you aren't pleasantly amazed.

APPLESAUCE FROM DRIED APPLES

Dried apples vary considerably. It will pay to buy the best obtainable, although outdoors almost any dried apples taste delicious. Before using them, it is usually desirable to trim away any remaining portions of the core. Bruises should be cut out, too.

Brands differ, but on the average it takes about seven pounds of fresh apples to make one pound of dried. Dried apples cook up roughly to double bulk.

Applesauce, which may not get a second glance in the city, is relished in the open as a side dish with meat, as part of the stuffing for poultry, atop cereal, and in numerous forms as a dessert. When the thermometer threatens to contract out of sight, try mixing some applesauce with evaporated milk and setting it in the cold, covered against the intrusion of small wild folk. The result will be a super ice cream, crystalline enough to eat easily.

Applesauce is handily made by simmering 2 cups of dried apples, plus ⅛ teaspoon salt, in 4 cups of water, until tender. Stir 4 tablespoons of sugar and a teaspoon of nutmeg or cinnamon into the finished product, unless your palate dictates otherwise. Lemon juice, concentrated or dehydrated, is also generally favored when available.

STEWED PRUNES

Cover the prunes with cold water, bring to a bubble, and keep barely simmering until the fruit is soft.

Or let the prunes plump up overnight in enough water to cover. Cook slowly in the same fluid until done to your taste. Then add sugar, if you like. Some also like to include lemon when any is available.

Sometime when you want a particularly delectable syrup, try soaking and cooking the prunes in strong black tea. You won't be able to detect the tea taste, by the way. A little cinnamon and lemon will improve even this singular flavor.

STEWED APRICOTS

Cover the dried apricots with cold water. Bring this to a dancing boil for 15 minutes or until the fruit is tender.

Another way is to cover the apricots with hot water, set them away from the heat for 2 hours or so, and then simmer slowly in the same water until soft. During the final few minutes of cooking, add sugar to taste if you care for any additional sweetening. Many campers don't.

FRUIT AND DUMPLINGS

This is a cinch when you bivouac in blueberry, raspberry, blackberry, strawberry, saskatoon, or other berry country. Just pick enough berries for dessert. Stew them over the campfire, sweetening them the way you like them. Or stew dried fruit, instead. When you're ready to sit down to the main meal, drop on a white dome of dumplings, the recipe for which is given previously in this chapter. Cover the pot tightly.

HUDSON'S BAY COMPANY PLUM PUDDING

If you're going to be in the bush with a friend or two on Thanksgiving and want to have something a little special for that occasion, you may be interested in going prepared to make one of the Hudson's Bay Company aromatic puddings which, traditionally varying in accordance with what ingredients have been at hand, have crowned many a holiday feast in the silent places since the Company was founded three centuries ago.

The following components can be mixed at home and sealed in a plastic container:

    4   cups sifted flour
    4   teaspoons baking powder
    ½   teaspoon cinnamon
    ½   teaspoon nutmeg
    1   cup brown sugar
    ½   cup white sugar
    ¼   cup finely chopped glaceed fruit mix
    2   cups seedless raisins
    1   cup currants
    4   tablespoons dehydrated whole egg
    6   tablespoons dehydrated whole milk
    ¼   teaspoon powdered lemon juice
    2   cups finely minced suet
    2   cups water

When the memorable day arrives, shake and stir all these ingredients together. The suet can be either beef suet brought for the occasion or animal suet obtained on the spot. Add the water to make a cake batter. Wring out a heavy cotton bag in hot water and sprinkle the inside with flour. Pour the batter into this. Tie the top tightly, leaving plenty of room for expansion.

Place this immediately in a pot filled with boiling water sufficient to cover. Keep it boiling 3 hours, turning the bag upside down when the pudding starts to harden so all the fruit will not settle to the bottom. As the cooking continues, shift the bag occasionally so it will not scorch against the sides of the receptacle. At the end, dip this cloth container briefly in cold water and carefully remove the fabric so as not to break or crumble the pudding.

Serve this plum pudding with some appropriate sauce. Butter and sugar, flavored with some spice such as nutmeg or an extract such as lemon powder, will suffice. So will the thick juice from boiled, dehydrated fruit.

Voltaire acidly described the North two centuries ago as "a patch of snow inhabited by barbarians, bear, and beaver." He should have seen the top of this continent when it's in a holiday mood!

Chapter 17

SHOPPING FOR FRUIT
IN THE WILDS

THE PICK of the wild foods will upgrade your meals while you're camping, hiking, fishing, or exploring. That's not all. Back home they'll keep right on guaranteeing you some of the best eating there is, plus the continued incentive to get outdoors in the woods and fields, where the really healthy appetites are born.

With countless pesticides gradually poisoning the cultivated areas of North America, it's both healthful and pleasant to go into the open places and gather undefiled foods from Nature's own pure garden. Too, these wild delicacies have been uncontaminated by the dozens of human hands that handle and rehandle the fruits and vegetables sold by markets.

As for possible poisoning, it is just as easy to become poisoned by eating the leaves of garden rhubarb or the sprouts or greened skins or ordinary potatoes. There are thousands of edible wild plants in North America and only a limited number of poisonous plants.

Wild vegetables and fruits grow everywhere. If you pack far enough north, as a matter of fact, there is no non-edible vegetation whatsoever, with the exception of one breed of mushrooms. Some of the lichens are bitter, it's true. But when this acidity is soaked out, such a variety as the familiar Iceland moss is so nutritious that it's packaged and widely sold as food and tonic for convalescents.

If you will surely identify as edible everything before you pick it, and if you prepare it properly, you will never have any trouble. Start with just a few wild edibles, if you want, perhaps with those you've already known for years, although perhaps not as foods. Each year add a few more.

PICK INSTEAD OF PACK

A lot of times you want to get a few miles deeper into remote country where the fishing is better. The outfit you're packing is just too heavy, however. So, reluctantly, you settle for less. This usually means it's much harder to land even the small ones. As for those record-busting trophies, they're just not around.

The next time, you figure, you're going to travel lighter and farther. With careful planning you can save weight and space on nearly every item in your outfit. When it comes to grub, however, you're still going to need a minimum of 2¼ pounds of reasonably waterfree provisions each day to keep enjoying yourself under full power.

Yet there's a way to lop a pound a day off those basic food requirements and still have the rugged, tasty, healthy meals you need to make it a real vacation. This is a method once used by our frontiersmen and still employed today by sportsmen, explorers, and other experienced outdoorsmen who regularly journey into the most inaccessible regions of this continent. It's a technique you yourself can adopt with every assurance of success from the start.

The grubstakes most outdoorsmen pack on extended trips, when space and weight are at a premium, include such staples as flour, oatmeal, side bacon, oleomargarine, sugar, salt, rice, jam, tea, coffee, and either baking powder for bannock or baking soda for sourdough. For those days when the wilderness is going to keep them pretty well occupied, they add a few of the dehydrated vegetables and fruits.

What about the sacks of onions and spuds, that bag of oranges, the bunches of celery, old cabbages and cauliflowers, lemons, carrots, parsnips, and the occasional head of lettuce they used to try to keep in a moistened cloth bag just a couple of days longer? These stay where they are until the return to where transportation is no longer a problem. So do those heavy cans of berries. Why bother with the bulk, heft, care, waste, and expense of such vegetables and fruits when you can pick them as you need them?

Besides meaning the difference between an easy pack and a troublesome one, adding from season to season the recognition of a couple more wild edibles can become an engrossing and practical hobby, as well as a thrifty and healthful way of introducing new delicacies to the table. You don't even have to lug your pots and pans into wilderness country to begin finding wild eatables. They grow all over.

ROSE HIPS (*Rosa*)

Rose Hips (*Rosa*). *Left:* rose hip. *Right:* rose hips, stems, and leaves.

For example, there is a familiar berry that, although you've maybe never sampled it, has the flavor of fresh apples. More important, its juice is from six to twenty-four times richer in Vitamin C than even orange juice. Throughout much of the continent you can pick all you want the greater part of the year, even when temperatures fall a booming 60° below zero. As for recognizing the fruit, no one with a respect for brambles and a modicum of outdoor knowledge is going to get the wrong thing by mistake. It is the rose hip, the ordinary seed pod of roses everywhere.

These rose hips have a delicate flavor that's delectable. They're free. They're strong medicine, to boot. Three rose hips, the food experts say, have as much scurvy-preventing vitamin as an orange. You get the good from this cousin of the apple whether it's eaten off the bushes, cut up in salad, baked in bannock, or boiled with sugar into pancake syrup.

As a matter of fact, plain, dried rose hips are well worth carrying in a pocket for lunching on like raisins. To prepare them, just cut each in half. Remove the central core of seeds. Dry the remaining shell-like skin and pulp quickly, as in a kettle suspended above the fringes of a small campfire.

BLUEBERRY (*Vaccinium*) (*Gaylussacia*)

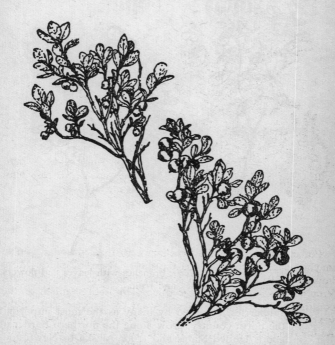

Blueberry (*Vaccinium*) (*Gaylussacia*). *Left:* branches with leaves and flowers. *Right:* branches with leaves and fruit.

Like numerous other members of the heath family, the blueberry tribe thrives in acid soil. You sometimes see bushes heavy with berries spreading over fire-blackened woodlands by the thousands of acres. Some thirty-five different varieties, from low shrubs to high bushes, grow throughout the United States and Canada, mostly in open woods and clearings. None is poisonous. Other names include huckleberries, whortleberries, and bilberries.

CRANBERRY (*Vaccinium*)

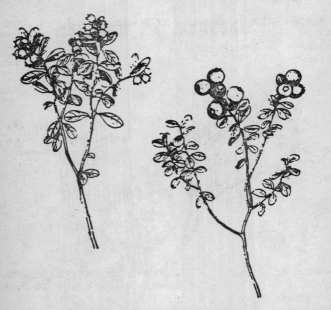

Cranberry (*Vaccinium*). *Left:* branches with leaves and flowers. *Right:* branches with leaves and fruit.

Wild cranberries, regarded by many as the most important berry of the north country, grow along the northern border of the contiguous United States and from Alaska to Newfoundland, south to Arkansas and Virginia. They have more flavor and color than domestic varieties.

Three species of this prime bear food liven bogs, marshes, rocky or dry peaty acid soil, and open coniferous woods across this continent where they are also known as lingenberries, low-bush cranberries, American cranberries, cow berries, rock cranberries, lingon, swamp cranberries, pommes de terre, and partridgeberries. Although they cling to the vines all winter, and when kept fresh by snow, are available many months as an emergency food, cranberries are at their best after the first mellowing frost.

HIGHBUSH CRANBERRY (*Viburnum*)

Despite the name, this shrub of the *Viburnum* family, some twenty species of which occur in the United States, is not a cranberry. A lot of people, too, object to the distinctively sweetish-sour odor and flavor. They do at first, that is. It has

Highbush Cranberry (*Viburnum*). *Top:* leaves and fruit. *Bottom:* blossoms.

become one of the favorite berries of numerous outdoorsmen, especially when they let a few frozen fruit melt on their tongues like sherbet in late fall and winter.

The juicy red highbush cranberries, which often have an attractive orange hue, also are sometimes called squashberries and mooseberries. They are at their best for cooking just before the first softening frost, although they continue to cling to their stems throughout the winter and are thus one of the more useful emergency foods in Alaska, Canada, and the northern states, where they are to be found usually the year around. Even when soft and shriveled in the spring, they are particularly refreshing when you're thirsty, and once you get to recognize the clean but somewhat musty odor, you're never going to get the wrong berry by mistake.

PAPAW (*Asimina*)

Papaw (*Asimina*). *Left:* bud and leaf scar. *Center:* stem with leaves and flowers. *Right:* fruit.

This fruit so relished by opossums and raccoons, sometimes called "false banana" because of its appearance, also is widely known as "custard apple" in deference both to its deliciousness and its family. Like the highbush cranberry, papaws usually call for an acquired taste. But once you come to like their creamy sweetness, they can become one of your favorite fruits. They are at their best harvested when ripe, which, in the North, may mean after the first frost.

Despite the nuisance of several large dark seeds, the papaw has a wealth of bright yellow pulp whose mellow sweetness makes it really something to feast on outdoors, as the hungry members of the Lewis and Clark expedition discovered on their homeward journey. They are quickly gathered, often from the ground. You also can pick them slightly green and put them out of the way in a dark, dry place to ripen.

RASPBERRIES AND BLACKBERRIES (*Rubus*)

Raspberry (*Rubus*).
Stems with leaves
and fruit.

Blackberry (*Rubus*).
Branch with stems,
leaves, flower, and
fruit.

Even expert botanists have trouble trying to tell the numerous members of the raspberry and blackberry families apart. In fact, they can't even agree how many varieties there are in the United States, the estimates varying from about 50 to 390, including the raspberries, the hordes of true blackberries, the cloudberries, bakedapple berries, salmonberries, dewberries, thimbleberries, and a lot more. Most woodsmen don't try to distinguish between all the varieties. They just eat them.

The tender young peeled sprouts and twigs of raspberries and blackberries also are edible, being something pleasant to chew on when you're in the woods and fields. The leaves provide one of the many wilderness teas.

SERVICEBERRY (*Amelanchier*)

Serviceberry (*Amelanchier*). *Left:* branch with stems, leaves, and fruit. *Right:* branch with stems, leaves, and flowers.

Also known as Juneberries, the numerous members of this family are used like the blueberries they resemble. Millions were once gathered to flavor pemmican.

Four or five species of serviceberries, which are primarily North American shrubs and trees, are native in the East and up to about twenty in the West. Bearing delicious fruit from Alaska to Newfoundland and south to California and the Gulf of Mexico, they thrive in such habitats as open woods, rocky slopes and banks, and swamps. Various other common names include saskatoon, shadblow, shaberry, sugar pear, and Indian year. Incidentally, some frontiersmen still make an eyewash from the boiled green inner bark.

MAY APPLE (*Podophyllum*)

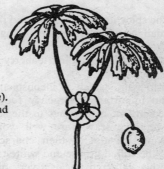

May Apple (*Podophyllum*). *Left:* stem with flower and leaves. *Right:* fruit.

Springtimes these attractive plants poke up like miniature forests of little opening umbrellas. Preferring moist, rich woods and banks, their creamy-white flowers are later familiar from southeastern Canada to Florida and west to Minnesota and Texas. These produce sweetly scented, lemon-yellow fruits which, when delectably ripe, are relished by many.

This native perennial, a member of the barberry family, is also known as mandrake, wild lemon, and raccoon berry. Only the fruit is edible. The root, which Indians collected soon after the fruit had ripened and used in small quantities as a cathartic, is poisonous. So are the leaves and stems.

WINTERGREEN (*Gaultheria*)

Wintergreen (*Gaultheria*). *Left:* with flowers. *Right:* with berries.

Both the spicy little red berries and the wintergreenish leaves of this small evergreen plant are among the most widely known of all the wild North American edibles. The some twenty-five names accorded it, including teaberry and checkerberry, support this conclusion.

The firm fruit, which is inconspicuous though bright red, can be an important emergency food when found in great enough quantities, as it clings to the stems all winter.

The evergreen leaves are well worth chewing, especially when young, because of their characteristic flavor, and are a food of the ruffed grouse and white-tailed deer. These leaves, when freshly gathered, make a very palatable tea, a teaspoon to a cup of boiling water.

ELDERBERRY (*Sambucus*)

You can use the flowers of the common elderberry in your cooking, feast on the berries, and make flutes from the limbs. As a matter of fact, some Indians knew this member of the honeysuckle family as "the tree of music" because of the way they made wind instruments from the straight stems. These were cut in the spring, dried with the leaves on, and then the soft pith of their interiors was poked out with hot sticks. In fact, this is a way to make spouts for gathering sap from maples, birches, and other trees.

Elderberry (*Sambucus*)

Quantities of the purplish black, round, juicy berries can be picked in a hurry. But even when at their ripest, they are none too palatable when fresh, although some of the game birds feast on them eagerly. However, there's an easy way to improve the flavor if you're camping in one spot. Just pick and clean the mature berries as usual. Then dry them in the sun.

STRAWBERRY (*Fragaria*)

Strawberry (*Fragaria*)

Everyone knows the wild strawberry, similar to domestic varieties but usually far smaller and always infinitely sweeter. Some four species sweeten the air from the Arctic Circle to Florida and California, growing wild nearly everywhere except in arid country. Deer like to browse on these juicy members of the rose family which you'll find in open woods, fields, clearings, and along dry hillsides and shaded banks, often so abundant that you can sit in one place and quickly fill yourself. The stems and stalks of this popular perennial are also tasty.

CURRANTS AND GOOSEBERRIES (*Ribes*)

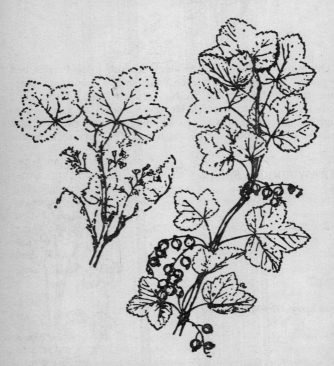

Currant (*Ribes*). *Left:* with flowers. *Right:* with fruit.

Gooseberry (*Ribes*)

Some eighty species of currants and gooseberries grow across the United States and Canada, from Alaska and Labrador to North Carolina, Texas, and California. Although differing considerably, they closely resemble cultivated varieties. All produce fruit that is edible raw and particularly when cooked, although the bristliness and odor of some of the berries call for an acquired taste, especially when they are eaten directly from the bushes. Important Indian foods, they were among those soon adopted by the settlers and frontiersmen.

PARTRIDGEBERRY (*Mitchella*)

Partridgeberries are so easily recognizable that they make a good emergency food. Too, they are available from autumn to spring, clinging conspicuously to the trailing evergreen shrubs throughout the winter. You will find them in moist woodlands

Partridgeberry (*Mitchella*)

and clearings from Nova Scotia and New Brunswick to Florida, west to Minnesota, Arkansas, and Texas. Other names
include twin berries and checkerberries.

MULBERRY (*Morus*)

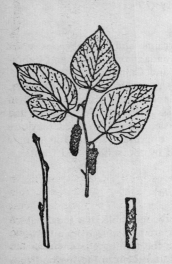

Mulberry (*Morus*). *Left:*
winter twig. *Center:* branch
with leaves and fruit. *Right:*
bud and leaf scar.

Mulberries ripen in early summer and at this time of the year are one of the favorite foods of songbirds and small game. A standby of Indians and of early European explorers and settlers, they are now widely popular in jellies and pies, especially when their sweetness is modified by a touch of lemon. You often can gather them by the gallon just by shaking a heavily laden branch over an outspread tarpaulin.

WILD CHERRIES (*Prunus*)

Rum Cherry (*Prunus*). *Top left:* blossom. *Top right:* branch with leaves and fruit. *Bottom:* branch with leaves and flowers.

Chokecherry (*Prunus*). *Left:* flowering branch. *Center:* branch with leaves and fruit. *Right:* winter twig.

Some fourteen native species of wild cherries, ranging in size from shrubs to large trees, are widely distributed across the United States and Canada. Game birds and songbirds feast on their fruit summers and falls when it ripens, and even before, and animals feed on the cherries that have dropped to the ground. Deer, elk, moose, and mountain sheep are among those supplementing their diet with the foliage, twigs,

Pin Cherry (*Prunus*). *Top left:* blossoms. *Right:* branch with leaves and fruit.

and tasty bark of wild cherries. Chipmunks often store large quantities of the seeds for their winter food supply.

KINNIKINIC (*Arctostaphylos*)

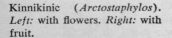
Kinnikinic (*Arctostaphylos*). *Left:* with flowers. *Right:* with fruit.

As for kinnikinic, after old-timers have filled up on the sustaining if blandly dry red berries, they sometimes make themselves a smoke with the leaves. Dried and pulverized, these have been a frontier tobacco substitute for centuries.

The widely distributed and easily recognizable kinnikinic should be better known, if only for possible use as a sustaining emergency food. Some of the other names that have become attached to it are mealberry, hog cranberry, upland cranberry, arberry, and especially bearberry. In fact, one of the best places to look for black bear after they have come out of northern hibernation in the spring is on a sunny hillside patch of kinnikinic.

Kinnikinic is luxuriant across Canada, Alaska, and the tops of Asia and Europe. Preferring a sandy or gravely upland habitat, this member of the heath family is found south to Virginia, New Mexico, and California. Grouse and other game birds pick its small berries. Deer browse extensively on its green, leathery foliage.

One of the most important things about the berries, especially when considered as a potentially important emergency food, is that, hard and dry, they cling resolutely to the prostrate shrubs all winter. Otherwise, although mealy, they are rather tasteless. Cooking improves them considerably, however. Too, people depending on wild fruit sometimes pick them in poor berry years and mix them with blueberries.

Chapter 18

BEING YOUR
OWN GREENGROCER

IF YOU have ever sat down to a well-prepared meal that included wild vegetables, maybe you've noticed that many of them seem to taste better than domesticated varieties. You may as well know the trade secret. They *are* better.

Green leafy vegetables, to give just one example, deteriorate very quickly. Even when purchased as fresh as obtainable from the finest nearby market, they'll already have lost a sizable proportion of vitamins.

Some of the food values of greens diminish as much as one third during the first hour after picking. But gather them fresh from nature's own garden and eat them while they're at their tastiest, and you'll enjoy the best they have to offer.

DANDELIONS (*Taraxacum*)

Gathering wild greens is a happy way to sharpen a good-sized appetite, even if you go no further than to collect a sackful of common dandelions. Actually, this familiar vegetable, all too well known because of the way it dots many a lawn, is among the best of the wild greens.

The tender young leaves, available in the early spring, are among the first wild edibles to gather while camping, trout

Dandelion (*Taraxacum*).

fishing, horseback riding, or just plain hiking through the greening wilderness. At first they are excellent in salads. Later, when the plants start blossoming, they develop a toughness and bitterness. Changing the first boiling water into which they are crammed will remove much of this bitter taste, if you want, although many find it clean and zestful. Incidentally, when you can, include as many buds as possible, as they liven both the color and the flavor.

Although they contain a laxative, the roots, when young, are often peeled and sliced, like carrots or parsnips, for boiling as a vegetable. To remove the characteristic tinge of bitterness, change the salted water once. Serve with melting butter or margarine. Being particularly nourishing, these roots are a famous emergency food, having saved people from starving during famine.

Although the woods afford a multitude of teas, they are short on coffees. The dandelion will provide one of these latter. Roast the roots slowly in an open oven or reflector baker all morning or afternoon until, shriveling, they will snap crisply when broken, revealing insides as brown as coffee beans. Grind these roots, as between two stones, and keep tightly covered for use either as regular coffee or for mixing to expand your normal supplies. Dandelion roots may be used the year around for this purpose.

LAMB'S QUARTER (*Chenopodium*)

Lamb's Quarter
(*Chenopodium*)

In a lot of camps the acknowledged pick of the edible greens is lamb's quarter. The tender tops of this wild spinach, which has none of the strong taste of market varieties, are delicious from early spring to frost-withering fall. They are good as salad greens and as a potherb.

The entire young plant is good from the ground up. Even from the older ones a quantity of tender leaves can usually be stripped. However, the pale green leaves with their mealy-appearing underneaths and slim stalks are not the only taste-tempting components of this green, also widely known as pigweed and goosefoot.

Indians long used the ripe seeds, 75,000 of which have been counted on a single plant, for cereal and for grinding into meal. These tiny gleaming discs, which develop from elongated dense clusters of small green flowers, also are handy for giving a pumpernickel complexion to biscuits and bannock.

STRAWBERRY SPINACH (*Chenopodium*)

Strawberry Spinach (*Chenopodium*)

Strawberry spinach, also known as Indian strawberry and as strawberry blite, is similar to its close cousin, lamb's quarter. The major difference lies in the bright red masses of pulpy fruits which often, when you're traversing the north woods in the fall, will stain your boots like dye, making this edible easily recognizable. It is common across Alaska and Canada, southward into the northern states.

The young stems and leaves, and later the young tender leaves by themselves, may be used like those of lamb's quarter, either raw in salads or cooked like spinach, which they considerably excel in taste, at the same time providing nutritious amounts of vitamins A and C.

PLANTAIN (*Plantago*)

Plantain (*Plantago*)

Plantain is almost as good as lamb's quarter. Furthermore, plantain is as well known to most as are the similarly prepared and eaten dandelions, although not usually by name.

It is the short, stemless potherb whose broadly elliptic leaves rise directly from the root about a straight central spike. This singular spike blossoms, although you've possibly never noticed it, with minute greenish flowers that later turn into seeds. At any rate, plantain is found all over the world, even growing through sidewalks in New York City, Boston, and San Francisco.

Plantain leaves make excellent greens. The fact is, the greener they are, the richer they are in vitamins A and C and in minerals. Many like them boiled. What holds for plantain, when it comes to this common, if often murderous, method of cookery, goes for the other wild greens as well. Unless it means standing over a riled trail cook with a cleaver, try to see that all these are cooked only until just tender and slightly crisp. This usually takes a surprisingly brief time.

SOW THISTLE (*Sonchus*)

Sow Thistle (*Sonchus*)

Nearly everyone knows the sow thistle, with its prickly or bristly but otherwise dandelionlike leaves, best handled with gloves. Its top clusters of yellow flowers resemble those of the dandelion, but are much smaller. They later develop a multitude of seeds that are one of the favorite foods of goldfinches, those cheerful little cousins of pet canaries.

Like the dandelion, the sow thistle is characterized by a milky sap. This sap is bitterish, again like that of the dandelion, and this is a reason why some users prefer to boil the leaves in two changes of salted water.

PURSLANE (*Portulaca*)

The reason for purslane's worldwide distribution is its tremendous production of seeds, relished by birds and rodents.

Purslane (*Portulaca*)

Although purslane does not become large, 52,300 seeds have been counted on a single plant. Indians in our Southwest used these for making bread and mush.

"I learned that a man may use as simple a diet as the animals, and yet retain health and strength. I have made a satisfactory dinner off a dish of purslane which I gathered and boiled," Henry Thoreau noted in Massachusetts over a century ago. "Yet men have come to such a pass that they frequently starve, not for want of necessaries, but for want of luxuries."

SCURVY GRASS (*Cochlearia*)

Scurvy has gathered more explorers, pioneers, woodsmen, and prospectors to their fathers than can ever be counted, for it is a weakening killer whose lethal subtleties through the centuries have too often been misinterpreted and misunderstood.

Scurvy, it is known now, is a nutritional deficiency disease. If you have it, taking Vitamin C into your system will cure you. Eating a little Vitamin C regularly will, indeed, keep you from having scurvy in the first place. Fresh vegetables and fruits will both prevent and cure scurvy. So will the long misused lime juice and lemon juice, but, no matter how sour, only if they, too, are sufficiently fresh. The Vitamin C in all these is lessened and eventually destroyed by age, by oxidation, and, incidentally, by salt.

Scurvy grass, of which there are several species belonging to the *Cochlearia* family, was one of the first wild greens used by frontiersmen and gold diggers across the northern portions of this continent, from Alaska to Newfoundland, to combat scurvy; hence the name. It so happens, too, that other greens throughout the New World have been similarly used and similarly named, this being one reason for the use of distinguishing Latin names in this book.

Scurvy grass is not only succulent in spring and early summer, but young lower leaves also can be found in the fall. Although it has a distinctive deliciousness whether eaten raw

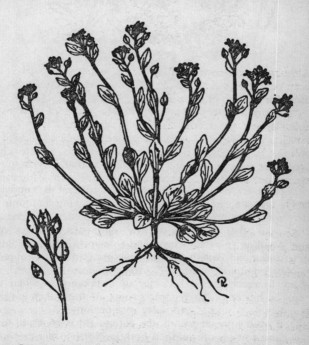

Scurvy Grass (*Cochlearia*). *Bottom left:* seed pods. *Right:* entire plant with flowers.

or after being briefly simmered in a small amount of water, scurvy grass furnishes the utmost in nourishment when served in salads or eaten raw between slices of buttered bread or bannock.

ROSEROOT (*Sedum*)

Roseroot (*Sedum*). *Bottom left:* root. *Right:* stems, leaves, and flowers.

Roseroot is another of the wild greens that is known as scurvy grass because of the often life-saving amounts of Vitamin C it has provided for explorers, bushmen, prospectors, sailors, and other venturers on this continent's frontiers. Also sometimes known as stonecrop and rosewort, it may be found from Alaska and British Columbia across Canada to Labrador and Newfoundland, south to North Carolina.

Easy to recognize, it becomes unmistakably so when you scrape or bruise the large, thick roots, as these then give off the agreeable aroma of expensive rose perfume.

Good from summer to fall, the perennial roseroot and some of its close cousins are relished both in North America and in Europe as a boiled vegetable and as a salad plant. The succulent young leaves and stems, which are at their tenderest just before the plants flower, become pretty tough by the time the red and purple seed-filled capsules appear.

But then, where the plants are abundant, you can boil up a feed of the big, rough roots, season them with butter and pepper and a little salt, and enjoy them with your meat or fish.

GLASSWORT (*Salicornia*)

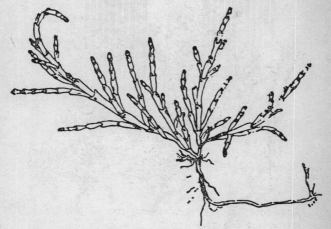

Glasswort (*Salicornia*)

Also called beach asparagus, glasswort bears the additional names of chicken claws, pickle plant, and samphire. At least four species grow in saline regions from Alaska and Labrador southward along the Pacific and Atlantic coasts, and around the Gulf of Mexico. Typical of seashores, brackish marshes, and glistening tidal flats, these members of the beet and spinach family also pop up on the alkaline mud flats rimming western lakes. All in all, they thrive in salty surroundings, taste salty, and appropriately are also called saltworts.

Because the raw tops remain tender and tasty from spring until fall, and especially because this wild edible is so very easy to identify, the glasswort can be a life-saving food in an emergency. It loses some of its sprightliness when cooked as a potherb, although this is done in Europe.

NETTLES (*Urtica*)

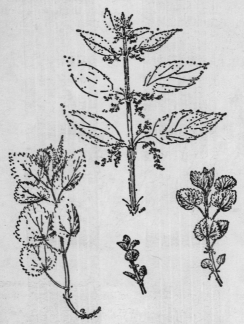

Nettle (*Urtica*)

Nettles are best gathered with leather gloves and a knife because their stem and leaf surfaces bristle with a fuzz of numerous fine prickles that contain irritating formic acid.

Don't overcook your wild vegetables. Even with such a formidable green as young nettles, once the salted water has reached the boiling point and the dark green nettles have been dropped in, they'll be tender almost immediately and ready for that crowning pat of butter or margarine as soon as they are cool enough to eat.

Because they are so easily and positively identified, nettles may be an important emergency food. Too, in a pinch, the stems of the older plants will yield a strong fiber, useful for fish lines.

CLOVER (*Trifolium*)

Clover (*Trifolium*)

Everyone who as a youngster has sucked honey from the tiny tubular florets of its white, yellow, and reddish blossoms, or who has searched among its green beds for the elusive four-leaf combinations, knows the clover. Some seventy-five species grow in this country, about twenty of them thriving in the East.

Bread made from the seeds and dried blossoms of clover has the reputation of being very wholesome and nutritious and of sometimes being a mainstay in times of famine. Being so widely known and plentiful, clover can be invaluable in an emergency.

The young leaves and flowers are good raw. Some Indians, eating them in quantity, used to dip them first in salted water. The young leaves and blossoms can also be successfully boiled, and they can be steamed, as the Indians used to do before drying them for winter use. The sweetish roots also may be appreciated on occasion, some liking them best when they have been dipped in oil or in meat drippings.

MUSTARD (*Brassica*)

Mustard (*Brassica*)

Mustard, which flourishes wild over most of the globe, is universally recognizable because of its brilliant yellow flowers that become almost solid gold across many a field and hillside. Five species are widely distributed over the United States. Most important of these is black mustard, an immigrant from Europe and Asia, which has become so much at home on this continent that it now grows over most of the United States and southern Canada. The young leaves and flowers are enjoyable raw. The flowers can be boiled quickly in salted water to make a broccolilike dish.

WATER CRESS (*Nasturtium*)

Available the year around except when the waters in which it flourishes are frozen, water cress is found over much of North America. The plants with their glossy green leaves prefer clean, cold water, but with civilization spreading the way it is, you can't always be sure that those streams, pools,

Water Cress (*Nasturtium*)

wet places, and even springs are not contaminated. A reasonable precaution is to soak the well-washed leaves and tender shoots in water in which a halazone tablet or so has been dissolved, using two of the little pellets to a quart of water and letting stand a half-hour (see Chapter 13 for use of halazone tablets in purifying water).

SHEPHERD'S PURSE (*Capsella*)

Shepherd's Purse (*Capsella*). *Top:* stalks with leaves and flowers. *Bottom:* rosette.

Shepherd's purse is valuable to wild food seekers in that it is one of the more common of the weeds, being found the greater part of the year wherever civilization has moved throughout the world. It is quickly recognizable, and the tender young leaves which, like others of the mustard family, are pleasingly peppery, may be enjoyed either raw or cooked. Indians even made a nutritious meal from the roasted seeds.

This wild green is easily identifiable because of its flat, triangular, or heartshaped seed pods which, their broad bases uppermost, ascend the top parts of the stalks on short stems. These are a favorite food of the blue grouse.

The leaves, bursting with vitamins, toughen as shepherd's purse matures. They then can be relegated to a small amount of boiling salted water, cooked until just tender, and dished out with the usual butter, margarine, vinegar, oil, hard-boiled egg, or other supplements.

MINER'S LETTUCE (*Montia*)

Miner's Lettuce (*Montia*)

The clinching feature of the well-known miner's lettuce is the way pairs of leaves grow together part way up some of the short stems and form cups through whose middles the stalks continue. The stems and leaves are estimable salad fodder when young and a better than average spinach substitute when older.

When the Forty-Niners stampeded up California's streams and into its deserts and mountains in their search for gold, the lack of fresh food brought scurvy to some camps. It was the Indians and Spanish who helped some of these argonauts cure the vitamin deficiency disease by introducing them to the succulencies of miner's lettuce. Those miners who didn't care for salad, or who gathered the edible so late in the season that it was tough, settled for boiling it, ideally briefly, in a small amount of salted water.

WILD CELERY (*Angelica*)

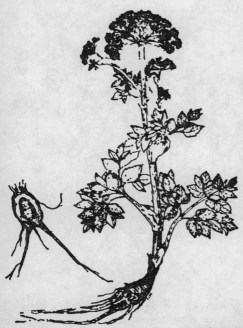

Wild Celery (*Angelica*)

Wild celery, also known as seacoast angelica, is even juicier and tastier than the celery you buy in stores. It grows in damp fields, beside moist roadsides, and along rocky or sandy coastlines from New England and eastern Canada to Alaska and British Columbia. It is at its best in late spring and early summer, while still tender.

Both the stems and leaf stalks are gathered when young, peeled, and their juicy interiors eaten with the same relish that is accorded the choicest celery. They often are boiled, too, sometimes in two changes of water if the user prefers a more subdued taste. Wild celery also imparts a piquant flavor to boiled fish. You'll probably like it, too, in soup.

SCOTCH LOVAGE (*Ligusticum*)

Scotch Lovage (*Ligusticum*)

Scotch or sea lovage, another of the wild celeries, grows in wind-swept sandy and gravelly stretches along the northern seacoasts from New York to Alaska. It has long been a favorite green and cooked vegetable among the coast-dwelling Scots who early discovered it here during their excursions to the New World. Rich in vitamins A and C, it is particularly tasty with fish.

MOUNTAIN SORREL (*Oxyria*)

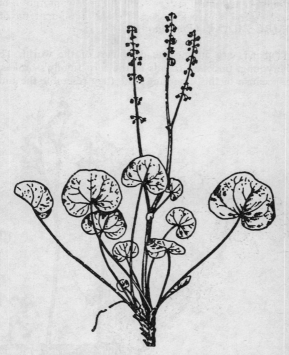

Mountain Sorrel (*Oxyria*)

Mountain sorrel, a member of the buckwheat family, grows from Alaska and Greenland to Southern California. Also widely enjoyed in Europe and Asia, it is known in different parts of this country as sourgrass, scurvy grass, and alpine sorrel.

The juicy leaves, which are at their best before the plant flowers, have an agreeably acid taste which somewhat resembles that of rhubarb. In fact, mountain sorrel looks to some like miniature rhubarb, although it so happens that the leaves of domestic rhubarb, whether raw or cooked, are poisonous. Those of mountain sorrel, on the other hand, are delicious for salads and as a potherb. Where this wild edible grows in the Arctic, Eskimos both in America and Asia ferment some of it as a sauerkraut. The tender young leaves also give a zip to sandwiches.

PASTURE BRAKE (*Pteridium*)

Fiddleheads are among the delicacies of the world. These are the young, uncoiled fronds of the fern family's brakes, so called because in this emerging state they resemble the tuning

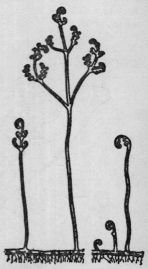

Pasture Brake (*Pteridium*)

ends of violins. They also are known in many localities as crosiers because of their resemblance to the shepherds' crook-like staffs of bishops, abbots, and abbesses.

Although some other similar fronds also are edible, it is the fiddleheads from the widely familiar and distributed pasture brake, *Pteridium aquilinum*, that are most commonly enjoyed. These grow, often luxuriantly, throughout the Northern Hemisphere, in Europe and Asia as well as in North America. You find them, sometimes in waving acres that brush your knees when you ride through on horseback, from Alaska across Canada to Newfoundland, south through the states to California and Mexico.

These are edible, however, only while still fiddleheads and therefore young. Later the full-grown fronds toughen and become poisonous to cattle as well as humans. While still in the uncurled state, on the other hand, they are found very acceptable by some of the wildlife, including the mountain beaver.

Fiddleheads are best when not more than five to eight inches high, while still rusty with a woolly coating. Break them off with the fingers as low as they will snap easily, remove the loose brown coating by rubbing them between the hands, and they're ready for eating raw or cooking. If you like vegetables which, like okra, are mucilaginous, you'll probably enjoy a few of these raw.

DOCK (*Rumex*)

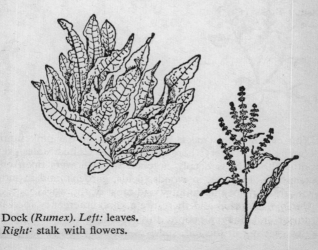

Dock *(Rumex). Left:* leaves.
Right: stalk with flowers.

The more than a dozen docks thriving on this continent from the Arctic Coast of Alaska southward throughout the United States provide hearty greens which were widely eaten by the Indians, some tribes of which used the abundant seeds in grinding meal. The Eskimos still put up quantities for winter use. This wild edible, also eaten in Europe and Asia, has a more rugged flavor than some of the other wild vegetables. Having overtones of both sourness and bitterness that vary with the different species, it is often preferred when mixed with other greens. Dock leaves can be boiled in a small amount of salted water only until tender and eaten with butter or margarine. Young dock leaves make a better than average salad.

COMMON CHICKWEED (*Stellaria*)

Common Chickweed (*Stellaria*)

You can find this meek little member of the pink family blooming almost everywhere in the central United States every month, although its deeply notched white flowers open only in sunshine. It grows in woods, fields, gardens, and in moist places throughout this country and most of the world.

Easily recognized and therefore a good emergency food for stranded and hungry people, this annual is unique in that it begins growing in the fall, survives the severities of cold even in the North, starts blossoming in late winter, and often finishes its life cycle and valuable seed production in the springtime. These numberless tiny seeds in their papery capsules, and the plant's tender leaves, are enjoyed by many game birds.

There's nothing fancy about common chickweed, but it is an abundant green that boils up wholesomely in a little salted water. If only the top stems and leaves are used, these will become tender in a very short time.

FIREWEED (*Epilobium*) (*Chamaenerion*)

Fireweed (*Epilobium*)
(*Chamaenerion*)

Fireweed, which in summer gives an unforgettable amethyst hue to vast fire-blackened wildernesses, is another wild vegetable difficult to mistake. Thousands of square miles of burned lands from the Aleutians and Greenland to Mexico soften to magenta annually, so showily do these tall perennials flame into spikelike clusters of flowers.

Two species of fireweed enhance most of the wooded sections of the continent from the Far North south to California, Kansas, and the Carolinas. These gaunt, pink- to purple-flowered members of the evening primrose family spring up in otherwise unsightly areas bared by logging operations, forest fires, and road clearings, stretching skywards from one to eight feet.

Try cutting the young stems into sections and boiling them in a small amount of salted water until tender. This way they resemble asparagus. In fact, French Canadians on the Gaspé Peninsula in Quebec sometimes call this edible *asperge*—wild asparagus.

DWARF FIREWEED (*Epilobium*) (*Chamaenerion*)

Dwarf Fireweed (*Epilobium*) (*Chamaenerion*)

This close cousin of the spectacular fireweed is also known as river beauty, riverweed, rock rose, prostrate willow herb, and broad-leaved willow herb. It grows in colorful expanses across the northern half of the continent, from the Gaspé Peninsula and Labrador to British Columbia and the Aleutians, preferring sandy and gravelly banks and slopes, roadside ditches, and wet places.

This perennial makes a better green before it flowers, although the addition of a few buds gives it added succulency. The new shoots and fleshy young leaves boil up in salted water even more deliciously than fireweed itself. Being very common in much of the North, it is an excellent emergency food.

WILLOW (*Salix*)

Willow (*Salix*). *Left:* branch with leaves.
Right: winter twigs.

This favorite browse of deer, elk, and moose is included here because, being so widely distributed and so easily identified, it is a food that, in time of crisis, could save your life.

Between two hundred and three hundred varieties of willow grow in the world, about one-third of them thriving all over this country. They prefer damp, fertile bottom lands, stream edges (which they often hold in place), and lake and pond rims, but some are seen also in high, rocky country. They vary from big graceful trees to tiny shoots and shrubs, only a few inches high, in Arctic and alpine regions.

Often the first spring source of Vitamin C, the buds and sprouts of these latter species provide the main subsistence of ptarmigan. Several species of grouse look to willow buds and tender portions of the twigs for food, while rabbits and many of the hoofed browsers seek twigs, foliage, and bark for nourishment.

Young willow shoots can be gathered at the beginning of warm weather, peeled of their outer bark, and their tender insides eaten raw. The tender young leaves, some of which have been found to be up to ten times richer in Vitamin C than oranges, also are edible raw.

So is the thin layer of inner bark which, after the outside bark has been removed, can be scraped free with a knife. This is tastiest at the start of the growing season. Bitterish in many species of willow, in others it is surprisingly sweet. Too, this inner bark is sometimes dried and ground into flour.

WILD RICE (*Zizania*)

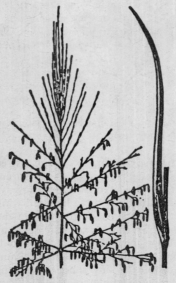

Wild Rice (*Zizania*). *Left:* stalk. *Right:* leaf and stem.

The two native varieties of wild rice, which are tagged with surprisingly high prices in markets, but which, flavorwise, are worth nearly every penny of it, grow free for the eating through much of the East from southern Canada to the gulf of Mexico. This notable Indian food reaches its most opulent abundance in the north country from Maine and New Brunswick to the eastern reaches of the prairies and in lush freshwater marshes along the Atlantic seaboard. It also has been widely transplanted as a duck food.

This coarse, large, plume-topped grass grows luxuriantly on mucky or silty bottoms in shallow water where there is enough circulation to prevent stagnation. Its slender seeds become dark and rodlike, expanding in husks that are stiffly tipped with a hairlike growth.

These husks are loose, however, and not difficult to remove. Spread out the rice and let it dry. Then parch it in a moderately warm oven or reflector baker for three hours, reaching in a hand and mixing it occasionally so it will dry evenly without burning. The husks then can be freed by beating, or, if you have only a small amount, by rubbing the seeds between the palms. The easiest way to blow away the chaff is by pouring the rice back and forth between two receptacles in a good breeze. Store in a dry place in well-closed containers.

A more important consideration is harvesting the crop during the latter half of summer or in early autumn when, depending on the local climate, it will be ripe and waiting. The mature seeds soon fall from the plants, but on the other hand, they adhere too tenaciously for easy gathering while still green. The Indian way of getting in wild rice is still a good one. Spread a large canvas over the bottom of a canoe, paddle among the plants, bend the stalks over the canoe, and beat the seeds out on the tarpaulin with a stick.

Chapter 19

GETTING THE BEST
FROM WILD ROOTS
AND TUBERS

INSTEAD of potatoes, carrots, parsnips, radishes, beets, and turnips as we now know them, Indians often relied on wild roots and tubers, especially in those parts of the arid West where the lack of rainfall made gardening nearly impossible. When frontiersmen, prospectors, and others later began daring the plains and deserts, many of them starved amidst abundance because they didn't know what to eat or how to prepare it.

Breadroot, with its sweet turniplike flavor, was not only an important food among many Indians, including the Sioux, but it was vital to the knowledgeable plainsmen who first opened our Great Plains. During their first hard years in Utah, the early Mormons relied to a great extent on the bulbs of the mariposa lily, now the state flower.

Tuberous arrowhead roots, cooked like potatoes by boiling or roasting in hot ashes, were relished by a number of tribes. When Père Marquette journeyed with his followers from Wisconsin to near the present Chicago, their chief nourishment was wild onions. In fact, the name *Chicago* is taken from an Indian word for a locality where wild leeks are abundant. During Colonial days, the Swedes who brought their log cabins to the Delaware River depended on groundnuts because of the lack of bread.

GROUNDNUTS (*Apios*)

Groundnut (*Apios*)

The Pilgrims, shown the groundnut by friendly Indians, relied on them to a large extent their first rugged winter in Plymouth. Other Indians along the eastern seaboard regularly ate these potato-like vegetables. Thus they became known to early white settlers, many of whom found them very acceptable substitutes for bread. Today they provide interesting supplements to the most modern of meals, while in an emergency they still can prevent starving.

The perennial vines of this member of the pea family twine across low, damp places and along the edges of swamps and streams, climbing where they can. They are found from New Brunswick and New England to Florida and the Gulf of Mexico, west to Ontario, Kansas, and Texas. Other names include Indian potato, hog potato, and wild bean.

The groundnuts grow in a chain of tuber-like enlargements, sometimes as big as eggs, on the long roots. Lying in strings just beneath the surface, these can be easily uncovered by hand unless the ground is frozen. Edible raw, groundnuts are better boiled until a fork passes through them easily, then eaten, unpeeled, with melting butter or margarine.

ARROWHEAD (*Sagittaria*)

Arrowhead   (*Sagittaria*). *Top:* stalks, leaves and flowers. *Bottom:* tuber.

Indians from the Pacific to the Atlantic ate the potato-like roots of the arrowhead, usually either boiling them or roasting them in the hot ashes of campfires.

The arrowhead is one of the most valuable native food plants and, nutritious and delectable, is well worth eating. Today, however, it is mostly idly observed by fishermen whipping their lines along the edges of ponds and sluggish streams from the southern half of Canada, throughout most of the United States, to deep into Mexico. Starving men, too, sometimes stumble over it where it grows in fresh, marshy ground.

There are some twenty or more species of *Sagittaria*, all bearing edible tubers, scattered in wet, non-saline places throughout the continent. About seven of these have large, starchy roots. The differences in the plants usually are minor, and there is no need to try to separate them. Other names include arrowleaf, duck potato, and swan potato, as well as the Indian cognomens of wapatoo and katniss. Ducks, geese and muskrats feast on the tubers when they are not too large or buried too deep. Ducks also eat the small, flattish seeds.

The hard little tubers, looking much like potatoes and varying in size from the most usually used size of eggs to that of BB shot, grow at the ends of often long subterranean runners, sometimes a few feet beyond the plant. Mature after midsummer and in the fall, they also are toothsome throughout the winter. During these seasons, wading Indians used their toes to dislodge the bulbs, which then floated when freed of root and mud.

Arrowhead tubers can be eaten raw in a pinch, but they taste better cooked. They require more cooking than white potatoes of the same size, and they are the better for peeling afterward.

CHICORY (*Cichorium*)

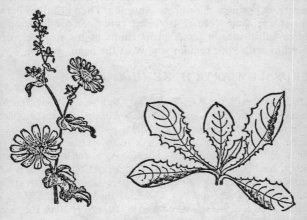

Chicory (*Cichorium*). *Left:* branch with flowers. *Right:* rosette.

Chicory, millions of pounds of whose roots have been used as an adulterant and as a substitute for coffee, also provides greens for salads and for cooking whose excellence gives them prime positions on the vegetable counters of many markets.

Resembling the dandelion both in appearance and taste, it has, however, usually bright blue flowers which, except in cloudy weather when they may stay shut all day, generally open only in the morning sunshine and shut by noon. These beautiful wheel-like blossoms, which sometimes spread like soft blue mist along roadsides and across grassy pastures and fields, give the plant its other common name of blue sailor. It also is known as succory.

Although pleasantly bitter at first and hard to equal for salads, maturing and toughening chicory leaves all too soon become excessively bitter, even when boiled in several changes of salted water. So get them before they flower.

Much of the chicory root used in this country as a coffee substitute, flavorer, and stretcher is imported from Europe, but exactly the same thing grows right here at home. If you'd like to make your own, just dig some of the long roots, scrub them with a brush, and then roast them slowly in a reflector baker or partly open oven until they break crisply between the fingers, exposing a dark brown interior. Then grind, as between two stones, and store in a closed container for brewing as a coffee substitute, in lesser proportions as it's stronger, or for blending with your regular supply of the bean.

JERUSALEM ARTICHOKE (*Helianthus*)

Jerusalem Artichoke (*Helianthus*). Left: stalk with leaves and flowers. *Right:* tubers.

Jerusalem artichokes, distinctively flavored tubers of a native wild sunflower, were cultivated by Indians and much used by early settlers.

Wild Jerusalem artichokes, which should be harvested no sooner than fall, are native to the central parts of the United States and Canada. Their popularity among Indians and arriving Europeans, plus their cultivation in different parts of the country, helps explain why this native has long since escaped its original bounds and is now often found in abundance elsewhere, such as east of the Appalachians.

The long, somewhat flat tubers are good just scrubbed, simmered in their skins in enough water to cover until just tender, and then peeled and served like potatoes. They then afford a byproduct, too. When cold, the water in which they were boiled becomes jelly-like, providing a flavorful and substantial foundation for soup.

Many also like the crisp sweetness of the peeled tubers, which have somewhat the same texture as that of cabbage stalks, just sliced raw and added liberally to tossed salads.

BURDOCK (*Arctium*)

Burdock (*Arctium*)

This member of the thistle family marched across Europe with the Roman legions, sailed to the New World with the early settlers, and now thrives throughout much of the United States and southern Canada. A topnotch wild food, it has the added advantage of being familiar and of not being easily mistaken.

The somewhat unpleasant associations with its name are, at the same time, a disadvantage when it comes to bringing this aggressive but delicious immigrant to the table. Muskrats are sold in some markets as swamp rabbits, while crows find buyers as rooks. But, unfortunately, on this continent burdock usually is just burdock, despite the fact that varieties are especially cultivated as prized domestic vegetables in Japan and elsewhere in the Eastern Hemisphere.

No one need stay hungry long where the burdock grows, for this versatile edible will furnish a number of different delicacies. It is for the roots, for instance, that they are grown by Japanese throughout the Orient. Only the first-year roots should be used, but these are easy to distinguish as the biennials stemming from them have no flower and burr stalks.

The tender pith of the root, exposed by peeling, makes an unusually good potherb if sliced like parsnips and simmered for twenty minutes in water to which about one-fourth teaspoon of baking soda has been added. Then drain, barely cover with fresh boiling water, add a teaspoon of salt, and cook until tender. Serve with butter and margarine spreading on top.

If caught early enough, the young leaves can be boiled in two waters and served as greens. If you're hungry, the peeled young leaf stalks are good raw, especially with a little salt. These also are added to green salads and to vegetable soups and are cooked by themselves like asparagus.

TOOTHWORT (*Dentaria*)

These slender members of the mustard family flourish in moist woods and along streams. The medium-small white or pinkish flowers grow in clusters, their four petals sometimes arranging themselves in the shape of crosses. The crisp whitish roots taste like peppery water cress and mild horseradish. Some dozen species grow, often abundantly, across the continent, one western variety whitening the meadows of the Coast Range in the springtime when it blooms.

Toothwort (*Dentaria*). *Left:* root. *Right:* stems with leaves and flowers.

The refreshing pepperiness of the long roots makes them pleasant to nibble on while hiking or fishing. They also make a very palatable addition to meat sandwiches, whose salt helps bring out their flavor. Chopped, they give character to green salads.

Or you can just scrape or grate a couple of tablespoons or so of these pungent, fleshy rootstocks, moisten with a little vinegar, and set on the table in a small covered cup. You haven't really lived until you try this sometime with fresh fat meat, roasted or boiled over a campfire.

SPRING BEAUTY (*Claytonia*)

Thousands of frail little spring beauties, a very close cousin of the succulent miner's lettuce, carpet sunny stream banks and moist open woods from Alaska to Nova Scotia, south to Florida and Texas. They also are known as fairy spuds because of their starchy roots, which were a favorite Indian food.

These small, potatolike roots lie several inches below the surface and require a certain amount of digging, although where they are abundant you can amass a respectable number with just a pointed stick. These roundish tubers range in diameter from one-half to two inches, becoming more and

Spring Beauty (*Claytonia*). *Left:* root. *Right:* stalk with leaves and flowers.

more irregular in shape the larger they grow. They are easily cleaned by scouring them in the hands or with a brush. Because they are boiled with the jackets on, though, this is not too critical a task.

Fifteen minutes of boiling in salted water usually does the job, although up to five extra minutes may be required for the larger ones. They're done when a fork shoves through them without any difficulty. Then just peel and eat, dipping each first into a pool of melted butter or margarine.

CATTAIL (*Typhaceae*)

Who does not know these tall, strapleaved plants with their brown sausagelike heads which, growing in large groups, are exclamation points in wet places throughout the temperate and tropical countries of the world? Sure signs of fresh or brackish water, cattails also are known as rushes, cossack asparagus, bulrushes, cat-o'-ninetails, and flags.

Although now relatively unused in the United States, where four species thrive, cattails are deliciously edible both raw and cooked from their starchy roots to their cornlike spikes, making them prime emergency foods. Furthermore, the long

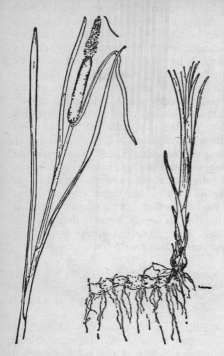

Cattail (*Typhaceae*). *Left:* leaves, head, and flower spike. *Right:* basal leaves and root.

slender basal leaves, dried and then soaked to make them pliable, provide rush seating for log cabin chairs, as well as tough material for mats. As for the fluff of light-colored seeds which enliven many a winter wind, these will softly fill pillows and provide warm stuffing for comforters.

Another name for this prolific wild edible should be wild corn. Put on boots and have the fun of collecting a few dozen of the greenish young flower spikes before they start to become tawny with pollen. Husk off the thin sheaths and, just as you would with the garden vegetable, put into rapidly boiling water for a few minutes until tender. Have plenty of butter or margarine handy, as these will be somewhat roughly dry, and keep each hot stalk liberally swabbed as you feast on it. Eat like corn. You'll end up with a stack of wiry cobs, feeling deliciously satisfied.

These flower spikes later become profusely golden with thick yellow pollen which, quickly rubbed or shaken into pails or onto a cloth, also is edible. A common way to take advantage of this gilded substance, which can be easily cleaned by passing it through a sieve, is by mixing it half and half with regular flour for breadstuffs, including pancakes.

It is the tender white insides of about the first one or one and a half feet of the peeled young stems that, eaten raw or cooked, gives this worldwide delicacy its name of cossack asparagus. These highly palatable aquatic herbs can thus provide important nutrition in the spring.

Later on, in the fall and winter, quantities of the nutritiously starchy roots can be dug and washed, peeled white still wet, dried, and then ground into a meal which can be sifted to get out any fibers. Too, there is a pithy little tidbit where the new stems sprout out of the rootstocks that can be roasted or boiled like young potatoes. All in all, is it any wonder that the picturesque cattails, now too often neglected except by nesting birds, were once an important Indian food?

Chapter 20

BUILDING A HOME
IN THE WOODS

EVERYONE talks about building a log cabin. Very few, however, ever get around to it, as Henry David Thoreau did. This is too bad in a lot of ways, for log cabin living is a delightful experience that is absolutely unique.

"Near the end of March, 1845, I cut down some tall pines by Walden Pond and hewed timbers, studs and rafters with my axe," wrote Thoreau. "By the middle of April, for I made no haste in my work but rather the most of it, my house was ready for raising.

"I dug my cellar in the side of a hill where a woodchuck had formerly dug his burrow, down through sumach and blackberry roots. In May, with the help of acquaintances—rather to improve as good an occasion for neighborliness than from any necessity—I set up the frame of my house and as soon as it was boarded and roofed, I began to occupy it."

Thoreau's home in the woods cost him $28.12.

"I intend to build me a home that will surpass any on the main street in grandeur and luxury, as soon as it pleases me as much," he wrote, "and it will cost me no more than my present one."

Cabin building itself is very simple. The job takes work but no particular skill. Best of all, it proceeds with satisfying speed.

Any reasonably able-bodied boy or man can put up a comfortable cabin by himself. If he has help, the construction will go all the faster. You don't even have to swing an ax if you don't want. All the necessary cutting and trimming can be done with a saw, with occasional assistance from mallet and chisel.

BUILDING MATERIALS

CHOOSING AND SEASONING LOGS

Straight, smooth cedar, lodgepole pine, fir, and similar evergreens make the best logs. About 50 of these, averaging 8 to 10 inches in diameter, will make a cabin.

Ideally, these should be cut in the late fall or early winter and allowed to season on skids, up off the ground, for at least six months. For all practical purposes, however, generally you can do well enough right away with whatever may be at hand. It will pay, though, to scout around and find some sound standing dead dry wood for at least the foundations and the ridgepole.

Logs should be peeled. Even when one goes to a tremendous amount of care, unpeeled cabin logs almost always turn out to be dirty or otherwise unsatisfactory. Ideally again, the best procedure is to hew or shave off two narrow strips of bark the length of each log, top and bottom, when you fell it. These strips should follow the straightest length of the log. This is so the cracks, that will largely concentrate here as the logs dry and shrink, can be hidden in the walls. When the bark eventually loosens in the spring, while the logs are still on skids, just pry it off.

If you're going to build right away, get the bark off in the easiest way possible when you drop the trees. If you're building in the springtime, the bark will strip off in great rolls.

MANUFACTURED MATERIALS

Although it is possible to build a cabin entirely with such wilderness materials that may be at hand, you'll do better to buy planed lumber for floor, window and door frames, shelves, bunks, tables, and the like. Rough lumber and roll roofing will save time and trouble when you come to topping off the structure. Some two-by-fours, especially for use as floor joists where they'll be hidden, are quicker to fit than poles. You'll also need an assortment of spikes and nails, a thimble for the stovepipe outlet, windows, hinges, etc.

In the semiarid interior of the country, cabins are often put up with their lower logs actually resting on the ground. Many such cabins stay sound for twenty years or more. In wet country, though, unless the bottom logs are kept dry, they'll begin to rot the first year.

Where decay is a problem, as in coastal regions, it may be feasible to use a preservative on the logs. Local inhabitants can give you a line on these, as homemade mixtures are compounded for the purpose. An excellent commercial product is pentachlorophenol. Directions accompany this preparation, commonly known as "penta."

PICKING THE SITE

A good way to visualize your future wilderness cabin is to mark its proposed outline with stakes and strings. When these are in place, look over the location from every angle, both inside and out. Consider every point that may be important to you: sunlight at different seasons, view, wind, drainage, access, etc. If the answers aren't satisfactory, keep moving your markers until the best possible site is located.

Before you do any actual building, get your plans and measurements down on paper. It is possible to get along quite happily in a very small, easily heated area. But every inch of space must be utilized to the fullest.

The dimensions of your log cabin will be determined to a large degree by your personal needs and by the materials at hand. For one or two people, a cabin about 20 feet long and 12 feet wide is an agreeable size. Room can be saved effectively by massing all the windows in one of the long walls. No matter what else you do when building in the woods, make sure that the cabin interior will get plenty of cheerful light. You'll appreciate this, especially in the north woods, during rainy weather and the long, darkish days of winter.

FOUNDATIONS

Four large stones, solidly embedded with the flat surfaces up, will serve for cornerstones. If the locality is at all wet, however, you'll get a far better foundation by laying another slab loosely without cement atop each base stone. Moisture which will climb the first stone by capillary action will then be checked by the second. Similar supports should be placed about every six feet beneath the foundation logs.

Then get the four bottom logs into position. These should be the sturdiest of the lot. Lift the two long logs into place first, if you want. Then roll up the two short logs. These should set half a log higher than the side logs. This can be accomplished by notching them, as will be considered in a moment. These four bottom logs should be solid, square, and of nearly equal height at the corners. When you get them ready, spike them together.

KEEPING THE LOGS PLUMB AND LEVEL

The inside measurements are what you use when building a log cabin. Keep the insides of the wall logs plumb, that is, straight up and down. One way to do this is to spike guide boards upright inside the four corners. Check these with a plumb line to make sure they're perfectly vertical. A string with a stone at its end will serve for this purpose. Or, if such guides are going to be in your way, keep checking the logs with the plumb line as you proceed.

The logs should be kept as level as possible, as each tier rises into place. You'll then have a reasonably level base for your roof, door, and window frames. These levels are very easily regulated by the deepness of the various notches.

The logs can be kept reasonably level, too, by alternating each round of logs so the thin end of one log will always contact the thick end of another. Four kitchen matches will illustrate this point. Lay them with the four heads resting upon one another. You get a fan effect. Then switch every other match so no two tops touch. A reasonably square rectangle is the result.

A flat bottle, filled with contrasting tea with an air bubble in it, will serve as a level. As a matter of fact, you can pretty well improvise throughout. The cover of this book, for example, could be your square. But a good steel tape is one refinement that will save you considerable time.

It's not necessary to become too particular in the matter of getting everything straight and level. When you're working with logs, you can only approximate these ideals at best. However, it's just about as easy to keep everything fairly true and thus allow yourself the widest possible margin for error. You'll end up with a better looking and more substantial cabin. Also, there will be less work when you get around to putting up shelves and cabinets.

CORNERS

Unless you've actually notched in a corner, this is the part of the log cabin building that probably will loom up as the stumbling block. Actually, corner work is simple in the extreme.

The main reason for this is that log walls are not built to fit with any of the tightness of frame buildings. As a matter of fact, you'll end up with a warmer, tighter cabin by making sure that the wall logs remain up to two inches apart. This will make the later chinking considerably easier and more effective.

You can, if you want, avoid notching by spiking the wall logs directly between corner posts. But either of the two corners suggested here will give you a better cabin. If they happen to be new to you, after you've studied them a bit, why not saw a few straight saplings into short lengths? Then experiment with a knife until you have a sound working knowledge of exactly how your corners will fit together.

The general procedure is to get the log into position and move it around until it is resting on its straightest length. Then make sure that the better of the other two sides will be on the inside of the cabin. Now you're ready for your notch.

SADDLE NOTCH

The saddle notch is quickly made. It is good-looking, and it's practical in that no cut is left upturned to gather moisture. The drawing, "Measuring Saddle Notches in a Wall Log," is pretty much self-explanatory. Succeeding notches are made in similar fashion.

Measuring Saddle Notches in a Wall Log

As the walls go up, first of all you measure. The notch at its widest spot will, of course, be open only enough to cup the log beneath it. The notch's depth, also governed by the log it is to fit, customarily will be a little less than half the diameter of the log in which it is cut.

Each log should be notched so it will lie fairly level. Suppose the unnotched log lies an inch high on one end? Then either cut the notch on that end an inch deeper or cut the opposite notch an inch shallower.

All this is simplified by the fact that you have a couple of inches to play around with. Wall logs may be laid that far apart at their widest gaps.

It usually takes a few tries before everything fits to satisfaction. Make your notches, roll the log into place, mark where some more cutting is needed, roll the log off, make the cuts, and try again. When the corners are right, spike them.

TENON CORNER

This type of corner can be cut with a saw. It is fashioned by flattening the top and bottom ends of each log so the resulting tongues will ordinarily be a little more than half as wide as the log ends in which they are made. Leveling and measuring are the same as with all corner construction.

The drawing, "Marking a Tenon Cut," practically explains itself. Each tongue can be made with two vertical and two horizontal cuts. A swiftly working Swede saw or a crosscut saw will take care of all these. Or you can saw down the two vertical marks, then quickly split out each slab with a chisel and mallet.

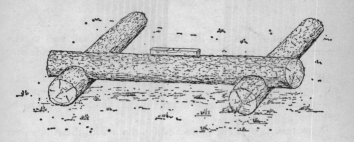

Leveling Wall Log Held in Saddle Notches

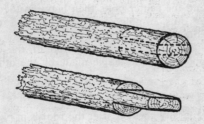

Marking a Tenon Cut

Tenon Corner

RAISING THE LOGS

The handiest way to lift logs is with a block and tackle, generally available for the borrowing. Leaning pole skids into place will facilitate the raising of the logs even more.

A pole tripod is handy for suspending a block and tackle for lifting cabin logs. Line up three poles on the ground with the bottoms together, and mark where the lashing is to be centered.

Now take two of the poles and lay them with their tops over a log so you can tie them conveniently. Place the third pole between them with its end in the opposite direction. Line up the marks. Separate all three poles with small blocks.

Start the lashing with a clove hitch around one of the outside poles, all the time heeding the marks. Take a half dozen or so loose turns around all three poles. Remove the blocks and take two tight turns around the lashings between one outside pole and the center pole, then between the center pole and the other outside pole. Finish off with a clove hitch around the center pole.

When you set up the tripod, the top of the center pole should be supported by the angle made by the other two.

FLOOR

The floor generally goes on after the roof is in place. There's an easy way to provide for it. Spike milled two-by-fours, with their narrow sides up, the length of the two longest bottom logs. Make sure they're level and parallel. Then lay two-by-fours across these from wall to wall, about a foot apart. Spike these joints, which also should have their narrow sides uppermost.

Unless you are able to obtain seasoned flooring, it will be better not to nail it permanently until the second year. Most of the drafts in log cabins swirl in around the feet. You can guard against such cold as much as possible by banking the cabin every fall just before freeze-up. It will also be worthwhile to put in a double floor at the start, laying the second layer at right angles to the first, with heavy, waterproof building paper in between. The covered surfaces can be left rough.

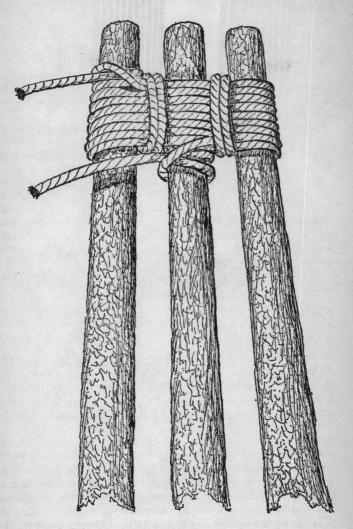

Tripod Lashing

WINDOWS AND DOORS

Quickest Way to Cut Openings

Where there is no shortage of logs, the quickest procedure is to build solid walls and then saw out the openings.

When you come to the top of the future opening, just frame it inside and outside with perpendicular boards, carefully measured and squared. Then saw out the top log inside these guiding supports. Later on, you can insert a crosscut saw in these openings and complete the work. Milled lumber will simplify the framing.

Doors should be built on the spot and should be made solid and massive. A practical door can be constructed of two or more thicknesses of planks, with waterproof building paper between. The exterior layer should be put on vertically so there will be no horizontal cracks exposed to trap moisture.

ROOF

Once the walls are up, the next procedure is generally to put on the roof and make it waterproof. Log construction is rugged, and most cabin roofs are small. Except in very heavy snow country, a steep roof is unnecessary.

A gable roof with a 25 per cent pitch is usually excellent. To determine this pitch, measure between the side walls. Say this

Roof Purlins Set in Gables

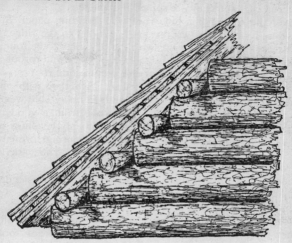

distance is ten feet. Then the top of the ridgepole should be roughly five feet higher than the tops of the side walls.

With some five or six short logs, build the two ends of the cabin up to the necessary height. Then center the ridgepole in place.

You'll next need purlins. These are straight, slender logs the same length as the ridgepole. The handiest way to put them up is to cut off the end of each short gable log just enough to allow the purlin to be positioned atop the log below.

The purlins should follow the slant of the roof in such a way that they will support boards or poles laid from the ridgepole to the top of the side walls. When all fitting has been done, spike everything down.

POLE ROOF

The pole roof is the most beautiful of cabin roofs, something to appreciate when you are dreaming up at it from inside your wilderness retreat. For this type of roof, you'll need a quantity of peeled poles, long enough so they'll butt together atop the ridge and then reach down to the eaves. These poles can be readied all at once on the ground. Butts and tops will be alternated when they are spiked into place.

Cover the top of this pole roof with building paper. Spike on two-by-fours some two feet part, parallel to the ridge. Fill in between them, if you want, with the dry moss to be found in many woods. Nail on boards and cover with waterproof roll roofing. That will make a warm and picturesque roof.

If, for some reason, you don't want to bother with poles, lumber may be used throughout instead. In really cold weather in the North, it's easy to tell a poor roof from a good roof at a glance. The poorly insulated roof not only becomes bare and icy, but heat waves can be seen shimmering through it. Look around and see who have warm roofs. Then ask how they insulated them.

One fast way to insulate a board roof is to provide a dead-air chamber. Cover the initial layer of boards, nailed to the purlins, with roofing paper. Spike two-by-fours along the edges and parallel to the ridge about three feet apart. Nail on another layer of boards. Cover this with waterproof roofing according to the directions accompanying the product. The result, besides being warm, is trim and clean.

CHINKING

The walls will be completed as soon as they are caulked and chinked. Many wilderness builders take care of the caulking by stringing sphagnum moss, common in numerous localities, liberally between logs and in all joints as the construction proceeds. Oakum, which can be purchased in bulk, is even better.

The chinking usually is an annual matter of mixing up a thick mud, slapping and pressing it into the cracks, and then smoothing it with a flat stick or a small trowel. The numerous ways of chinking also become subjects of considerable local interest, being heatedly discussed and debated through the years. Some earths stay in place better than others, especially if you drive a few nails upright in the cracks for anchors.

Plasters of cheap flour, salt, and water are common in some areas. One of the toughest and most harmonizing of all chinkings is made by mixing sawdust from the job with melted sheet glue.

Chapter 21

MAKING FURNITURE
PLAIN AND FANCY

"I WOULD rather sit on a pumpkin and have it all to myself," said Thoreau, "than be crowded on a velvet cushion."

Furniture for the wilderness home should be born, not borne, there. Possibilities range from such simplicities as table and stools to individualities like four-poster beds. The particular cabin should be the arbiter.

Rainy afternoons can be enlivened by satisfying your inherent creative urge in the fashioning of seats and other necessities for the forest abode. Furniture is fun.

MATERIALS

BEST WOODS

Unpeeled birch is a favorite material for indoor furniture. Cedar is a top choice for all kinds of work, the rough sticks being particularly picturesque. Pine certainly is in tradition. The undisputed excellence of such hardwoods as oak and chestnut is tempered only by the increased difficulty in working with them.

Seasoned wood is preferable, not only because it is lighter, but because subsequent shrinkage of undried pieces is apt to cause warping and wobbling. Many find it a profitable practice to store choice sticks to dry for future furniture demands.

LUMBER

Planks can be given a hand-made look by having them roughened against a buzz saw at the mill. Or they may be touched up with a hatchet, then rubbed with coarse sandpaper, for a hewn effect. Wood may also be effectively raked with a wire brush, perhaps in conjunction with light charring with a blow torch.

Lumber is not to be passed up too lightly, therefore, for such roles as table tops and chair seats where smooth surfaces are mandatory. Knotty pine is a log cabin favorite. Boxwood is handy for concealed work such as shelves and drawers. It is more desirable if faced with slabs of other rustic materials, however, when used for cupboards and such.

Plywoods are available today in a wide choice of varieties, some of which will enhance both the plainest and the most elaborate wilderness homes. Well-made plywood has the advantage of coming in large, durable, light-weight, easily finished, exceedingly rugged panels which can be quickly and economically cut to any practical shape or size.

HIDES, FILLERS, AND DYES FOR UPHOLSTERY

Moose and similar hides not only impart a magnificence to log cabin furniture, but their smoky fragrance, if Indian-tanned, will recall many a flickering campfire. They may be used intact, or portions may be tacked to frames for chair seats and backs.

Hides also may be cut round and around with a sharp knife to form a continuous ⅜-inch or so lace for furniture making. An easy way to go about this is to stick the knife into a wide board. Drive a nail beside it the width away desired for the lacing. Then turn a piece of hide around and around this until it is reduced to a single long strip. This babiche or shaganappi, as it is called in the North Woods, should be soaked and then stretched under pressure a number of times.

It then should be resoaked and, while it is wet, tightly laced to a frame to make webbed chair seats or backs. A snowshoe needle, which can be interestingly made of a four-inch bone, sharpened at both ends and with a hole in the middle, will quicken the process. Or the babiche may be simply laced back and forth over a frame or in parallel lines through holes cut in a frame.

The webbing, when dry, should be given several coats of high-grade varnish, a process that may well be repeated yearly.

The making of varicolored cushions will brighten the log cabin and make it more comfortable. Native fillers, such as wild marsh hay, aromatic evergreen needles, and soft sphagnum moss, may be stuffed in to make them invitingly plump.

You may even like to experiment with natural dyes. Cloth immersed in liquid in which swamp maple bark has been boiled will come out a mountain-lake blue. To make it a professional job, you need only add a little iron sulphate to the solution first. If none is lying around the vicinity, a dime's worth may be purchased from a drugstore. Or you may obtain it from a cobbler's shop where it is known as copperas.

Alder bark when boiled gives off a tawny yellow dye that has colored many an Indian's garments. The rich hue of pioneer homespuns was often obtained by boiling the outer nut shells and inner bark of the butternut tree. Sunflower blossoms contain a sunny stain that has the exciting hue of gold.

GLUE

Waterproof glue in powder form is available for furniture building. When prepared according to instructions and applied thinly and evenly to tightly fitting, smooth joints, it may be counted upon to make a union stronger than the wood itself. Other satisfactory glues may be purchased at almost any variety or hardware store. Directions accompany them. Glued joints generally should be kept under pressure for some four hours and not subjected to strain for an additional twenty-four hours.

Nails will do for furniture. Screws are better. Countersinking the latter and topping them with glue-immersed pegs is finer still.

STOOLS

A short, upright log is the simplest stool. Place a slab, poles, or a hewn plank over two of these to make a bench. Start with taller blocks, and a table is the result.

Split a short log. Smooth the flat surface, using sandpaper to finish the job. Take a brace and bit, auger, or even a jackknife. Bore four holes in the underside.

Angle in four lengths of saplings or tree limbs, about two inches in diameter. The tops of these should be whittled until they fit snugly. They can be fastened with glue, or small nails may be slanted through them into the slab.

Simple Stool, Bench, and Table

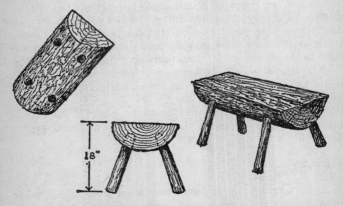

Stool Made from Split Log

An effective touch is to bore a small hole through the seat and each leg, then to secure the latter by driving in a wooden peg. Softwood dowels adapt themselves easily. Hardwood pegs have to be whittled with more precision. Both will fit more solidly if first dipped in glue.

Stools so made often bring extraordinarily high prices at auctions under the guise of antiques.

BENCHES, CHAIRS, AND TABLES

Handle a longer log similarly for a bench. Bore several holes in the flat surface to support a simple back, and a settee is the next step. Do the same thing with a stool to make a chair. Seat legs can be bored and rungs inserted.

Longer legs will make a table. It may be necessary to brace the legs. A slab shelf can be screwed into position to steady table legs.

Other tops may be substituted for the original split log. Slabs will do. So will planks. Holes will have to be bored all the way through thinner woods, of course. This should be done from the top downward. When the tip of the tool pricks through, the boring should be completed from the other side

Settee

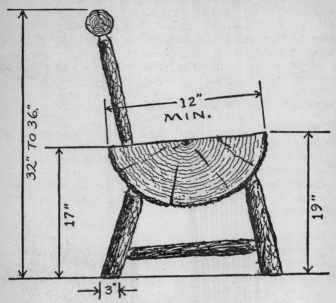

Settee Measurements

so the wood will not be unnecessarily torn and splintered. The legs, after being fitted, can be smoothed until entirely flush.

A spectacular table can be made from the naturally rounded end of a huge log that has been sawed some four inches thick. Effective companion tables may then be topped with similar slices from smaller logs.

DINING ROOM SET

The simplest eating arrangement for the camp is a table with benches attached. Six poles and several slabs will do the job, as the illustration shows. An additional H-support can be added to the middle, if this seems desirable.

Similar combinations are inviting when put up at outdoor vantage points. Four long posts are first driven solidly into the ground, and the piece is constructed around this nucleus.

Dining Room Set

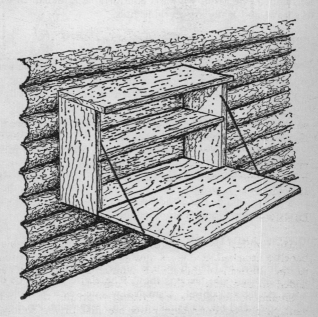

Drop Leaf Desk

DROP LEAF TABLE

Drop leaf tables, both movable and stationary, are space savers in the wilderness home. A frequently valuable provision, too, is a fixed cabinet whose door swings downward for use as a writing desk or typewriter stand.

PROPER PROPORTIONS

Tables and chairs, when used together, may be respectively thirty and eighteen inches high. If the table is slightly lower, the difference in height between it and the chair should still be one foot. The backs of such chairs should be somewhat more than twice the seat height. They should be practically straight.

If the seat and back are both pitched backward several inches, the seat lowered and widened, and a few rustic cushions added, the result will be a comfortable armchair in which to sprawl and lazily survey blue hills.

USING A MOTIF

Simplicity is the enduring ideal to be stressed above everything else in wilderness furniture building. Actual designs may vary. When one is chosen, it often is pleasing to follow it throughout.

Effective is the use of substantial peeled poles of the same wood as the cabin logs. Post tops need not be flat, but can be slanted at forty-five degree angles and touched up with a sharp hatchet to give a hewn effect.

Well-sandpapered slabs, left round on one side, will often fit in magnificently. Joints held by countersunk screws, boldly pegged, can, many times, add a final fine touch. Interlocking mortise and tenon joints are outstanding.

MORTISE AND TENON JOINT

The mortise and tenon joint is made with surprising ease, as the step by step illustrations show. The entire job can be done with a mallet and chisel. A small saw, such as a keyhole saw, and a brace and bit, will make the work even simpler.

A mortise is a slot, which, in this instance, is cut in a piece

1~ A MORTISE IS A SLOT

A

MARK

B

BORE HOLES
TO EASE WORK

C

CHISEL OUT
SLOT

2~ A TENON IS A TONGUE

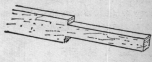

A— MEASURE TO FIT SLOT   B— SAW

Steps in Making a Mortise and Tenon Joint

of wood so that the tongue of another piece of wood can be inserted through the slot. A hole is made in the projecting end of the tongue and a wooden wedge driven in to pin the joint tightly together.

In the use of the interlocking joint suggested later on for a four-poster bed, each tenon may be marked on both sides of the wood with the aid of a try square, then sawed with a fine-tooth tool on the waste side of the guide lines. The wood may then be smoothed with sandpaper.

A slot just big enough to accommodate the tongue is then marked on one side of the piece of wood through which it is to be pushed. An additional location mark may be made on the opposite side, as well, by using the try square to assure accuracy.

The rectangular holes can be cut with a chisel and mallet, trimmed with a knife, and finally smoothed by sandpaper. The

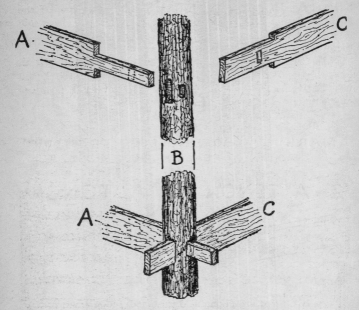

Fitting Mortise and Tenon Joints Together

wood will knock out more neatly if a number of holes are first bored side by side within the indicated slot. These holes should not extend the full width of the mortise. They should be made by boring through one side until the tool pricks through, then turning the wood and boring from the other side, thus avoiding splintering.

A small narrow slot is similarly marked and cut in the locking tongue. A wooden wedge, whittled to fit tightly, is then driven in to hold the assembled joint together. The distance between the inside of this final slot and the base of the tongue should, of course, equal the width of the main mortise.

BOOKCASE

A bookcase for a log cabin can be built in a very few minutes if lumber is at hand. Decide first on the size. Assemble the four outer pieces. Then, perhaps using the larger of the books that are to be stored as a guide, mark on one of the side boards the location of the shelves. Lay both of these side boards side by side and get the strips on evenly by putting them on in pairs.

Now fasten the frame together, nailing the top and bottom boards over the sides for greater strength. Then set this frame in place against the wall, preferably nailing it in position. Saw the shelves to measure and slide them into place.

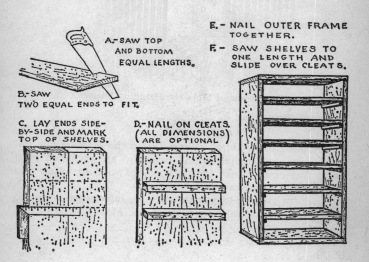

A.- SAW TOP AND BOTTOM EQUAL LENGTHS.

B.- SAW TWO EQUAL ENDS TO FIT.

C. LAY ENDS SIDE-BY-SIDE AND MARK TOP OF SHELVES.

D.- NAIL ON CLEATS. (ALL DIMENSIONS ARE OPTIONAL)

E. - NAIL OUTER FRAME TOGETHER.

F. - SAW SHELVES TO ONE LENGTH AND SLIDE OVER CLEATS.

Steps in Making a Bookcase

Blocks of shelves for any purpose can be speedily assembled in this fashion. Add doors, and the result will be a cabinet. A turning piece of wood can be nailed in place so it can be pivoted to hold the door closed.

A more professional way of installing shelves is by sliding them into slots. These slots may be made easily enough by sawing in each instance along two lines drawn the width of the shelf, and carefully knocking out the wood with chisel and mallet.

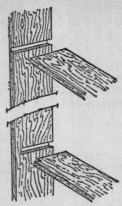

Two Kinds of Slots for Installing Shelves

PICTURE FRAMES

Quartered bits of birch salvaged from the kindling pile will do. Halved cedar saplings and such also are excellent. Neat rustic frames also may be made of boxwood to which thin strips of birch bark have been glued.

Covers of outdoor magazines often are interesting enough to hang. So are some calendar illustrations. Maps of one's locality are invaluable.

BEDS

BUNK

The bunk, as differentiated from the usually movable bed, is attached to the wall. The frame of the ordinary corner bunk requires no more than five poles at most. Since it has but one leg, which supports the only corner not fastened to the cabin logs, it may be put up in several minutes.

If the entire back of a narrow shelter is to be converted into a single large bunk, as is frequently done, the task is not much magnified. The oversize bunk in numerous fishing shacks, for instance, generally has a wooden bottom that is supported between a convenient log in the back wall and a single husky pole stretched across the front. This crosspiece often is spiked between the side walls and is prevented from sagging by one or more pole legs.

PROPER HEIGHT OF BUNK. The need for storage space is what usually governs the height of the bunk or bed constructed in the wilderness home. Such sleeping arrangements often are thirty or more inches high for this practical reason.

Corner Bunk with Pole Spring

The area beneath may accommodate drawers or shelves. It is many times found more convenient to store boxes or duffle bags loosely beneath.

The bottom of the frame can be closed in with boards or slabs in which doors or sliding panels are cut. Easiest, though, is curtaining the space.

TWO-STORY BUNK. The double-deck sleeping accommodation saves space in a way more commendable in cold weather than warm. Any cabin builder who has spent many nights in the top section of one will not make the mistake of adding frills which, although perhaps picturesque, will interfere with air circulation.

Two-Story Bunk

The frame for the upper half of a double bunk may be made similar to that of the lower half, except that posts need not extend between corners and floor, but can be spiked instead between corners and ceiling.

The upper story may be reached by a permanent or portable ladder. The former may be made of cross poles spiked between two vertical poles that are attached either to the bunks or to the cabin wall.

TRUNDLE BED

The trundle bed conserves space and, at the same time, preserves sleepers from hot upper climes. It may be built atop four posts braced with crosspieces, except along the inner length, so the stationary bed or bunk, under which the trundle is slid lengthwise, can also furnish a storage area. An end can be left open instead, of course, but then more floor space will have to be left unblocked.

Trundle beds for use in one room may be made to push endwise through wall holes under permanent sleeping accommodations in another room.

FOUR-POSTER BED

A handsome four-poster bed can be built entirely of seasoned wilderness materials in such a way that it can be taken apart in a few moments, then reassembled elsewhere in as short a time.

Dimensions will vary to accommodate whatever spring and mattress are used. A comfortable overall height, including these, however, may be set at two feet.

Four matched posts, about five or six inches in diameter, will be needed. These will be worthy of a painstaking search. Four planks about two inches thick will be required, too. These may be roughed against a buzz saw or touched up with a sharp hatchet so as to take on a handmade look. The posts should be carefully worked over with a hatchet or ax for the same reason. The wood then can be smoothed down somewhat with coarse sandpaper.

For the craftsmanlike effect shown in the illustration, this bed should be fitted together with interlocking mortise and tenon joints held by removable hardwood wedges.

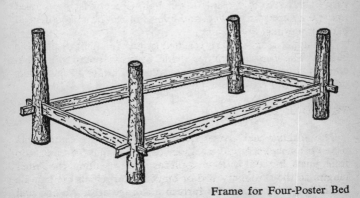

Frame for Four-Poster Bed

The bed springs, which can be improvised with ropes or saplings, may rest on slats supported by strips of wood preferably screwed near the lower interiors of the two longer sides. If the slats are made to fit tightly, their square ends will prevent their turning to slip off the supports and will, therefore, make fastening unnecessary.

RESTRAINT

Some care should be taken not to crowd the cabin too enthusiastically with furniture. Thoreau found three chairs sufficient in his wilderness home: "One for solitude, two for friendship, three for society."

Chapter 22

USING AND MAKING DISTRESS SIGNALS

LEARNING the skills and following the procedures and precautions outlined in previous chapters will minimize the chances of getting into serious outdoor trouble. However, the unforeseen and sometimes unavoidable occur, and it is best to be prepared for them. This chapter and the following two chapters suggest ways for coping with the emergencies most commonly encountered in the wilderness.

Very often the best procedure to adopt when lost, stranded or in trouble is to stay where you are, moving about as little as possible, especially if food is scarce, improvising the easiest shelter, and setting about to attract aid in the most effective ways available.

SIGNAL FIRES

A fire, in addition to its warmth and good fellowship, makes one of the better distress signals. In fact, if you are in any of the numerous areas where regular watches are being maintained from towers and observation planes, in an emergency you often have only to kindle a blaze to attract necessary help.

One way to send up the smoke that will make a conflagration most conspicuous during daylight is by throwing evergreen

337

or any green boughs into a hot fire. "If green boughs are available, cut plenty," the Hudson's Bay Company advises, "as when burning they make a lot of smoke and a good signal." Pouring oil from an auto crank case on a hearty blaze not only rolls up a tremendous surge of black smoke but makes a hot fire, too. Burning tires or other rubber articles will similarly send up black billows.

Water will give a white smoke, although, as everyone realizes, too much dampness will drastically quell and even extinguish the fire. A long-lasting smudge can be built, however, by covering hot coals with humid green foliage, wet dead leaves, slowly burning green wood, moist decayed wood, damp animal refuse, and similar substances.

If there is any scarcity of fuel, it may be preferable to keep only a small fire going, if that is necessary for comfort, and to concentrate on heaping up signal pyres to be lit at a moment's notice.

The smoke from a strong smudge fire can, incidentally, be invaluable for indicating wind direction to the pilot of a rescue craft.

THREE SMOKES

The distress signal most commonly used is made with three fires or three smokes. If these are built in a conspicuous location in a straight line, their intent will be the more apparent. You also can send smoke signals from a single conflagration by momentarily cutting off the smoke with something such as a wet blanket and releasing series of three puffs.

USING INGENUITY

When no natural fuel is available, a possibility if you are in a desert, for instance, improvise something appropriate to your particular circumstances, such as scraping a sign for help in the sand and, when a jeep or auto is nearby, filling the depressions with gasoline and cautiously igniting it by tossing lighted matches or debris. Be sure to stand well back. Of course, such measures should only be used in extreme emergencies.

The most universally recognized distress signals are based on the number three: three flashes, three shots, etc., even to the three dots, three dashes, three dots of the familiar SOS.

SIGNALING WITH FIREARMS

There is, unfortunately, no general agreement as to how signal shots should be spaced. Some advocate firing the three blasts as rapidly as possible, although obviously it is not unusual for a hunter to let drive in this fashion at game. The practice of separating each shot by about five seconds is more logical, especially as this gives a listener the time he may need to determine where the signal is coming from. In any event, an understanding on this point may well be reached in advance by members of a group.

WHISTLE

A whistle can be particularly handy for signaling in remote regions. The Hudson's Bay Company includes a whistle in its survival kits with the succinct instructions: "Use your whistle to gain or keep contact with other members of your party. It may also be used to notify anyone close enough to hear of your position. Don't shout or call. Blow the whistle."

MORSE CODE

Knowledge of a dot-and-dash code will enable the sending and receiving of messages with flag, flashlight, mirror, whistle, smoke, radio, and numerous other devices, including the primitive thumping on a hollow log or tree.

The International Morse Code, which is the most widely understood, follows:

Letters	Morse Code	Flag Movements
A	dot-dash	right-left
B	dash-dot-dot-dot	left-right-right-right
C	dash-dot-dash-dot	left-right-left-right
D	dash-dot-dot	left-right-right
E	dot	right
F	dot-dot-dash-dot	right-right-left-right
G	dash-dash-dot	left-left-right
H	dot-dot-dot-dot	right-right-right-right
I	dot-dot	right-right
J	dot-dash-dash-dash	right-left-left-left
K	dash-dot-dash	left-right-left
L	dot-dash-dot-dot	right-left-right-right

Letters	Morse Code	Flag Movements
M	dash-dash	left-left
N	dash-dot	left-right
O	dash-dash-dash	left-left-left
P	dot-dash-dash-dot	right-left-left-right
Q	dash-dash-dot-dash	left-left-right-left
R	dot-dash-dot	right-left-right
S	dot-dot-dot	right-right-right
T	dash	left
U	dot-dot-dash	right-right-left
V	dot-dot-dot-dash	right-right-right-left
W	dot-dash-dash	right-left-left
X	dash-dot-dot-dash	left-right-right-left
Y	dash-dot-dash-dash	left-right-left-left
Z	dash-dash-dot-dot	left-left-right-right

WIGWAGGING

Such signals transmitted by flag can be seen for miles under favorable conditions, particularly if the sender places himself in an unobstructed spot against a contrasting background. Reading with the help of glasses, it is then no feat at all to send messages from mountain to mountain.

The flag may be something such as a large handkerchief or shirt, knotted to the end of a light pole some six feet long so as to expose an easily manipulated area. It can usually be most easily used if the base of the staff is held at waist level in the palm of one hand and the stick gripped a dozen inches or so higher by the master hand.

All letters start with the staff held straight upward. The dot is made by swinging the flag down to the right and then back again. A way to fix this in mind is to remember that the word "right" has a dot over the "i." It follows that the dash is made by swinging the flag in a similar arc to the left and back. The easiest way to keep the flag flat for maximum visibility is to move it in tight loops. To send the letter "n," for example, swing left and back and then right and back in what is, when you look up at the tip of the staff, a narrow figure eight.

Hold the flag upright a moment to end a letter. Lower and raise it in front of you to finish a word. Swinging right-left-right-left-right signifies the conclusion of a message, although the important factor in any kind of emergency signaling is not correctness of form, but common sense.

PARTY SIGNALS

One of the simplest and most valuable precautions a party in a wilderness area can take is to agree beforehand on a set of signals for its own use. These should be both simple and brief. It will be well to set this code down on paper so each individual can carry a copy with him at all times, possibly rolled within his waterproof match case.

USES FOR A MIRROR

There is good reason for including a mirror with the equipment to be carried on the person in the bush, if only for the assistance thus afforded in removing the bits of bark and other particles that always seem to be getting in the eyes. A surface of ordinary metal, such as the back of a watch, is a poor substitute in this respect. Furthermore, an adequate mirror can be vital if you ever need to attract attention in an emergency.

The substantial Emergency Signaling Mirror, available for a few cents at some surplus stores, is a particularly useful article to have in a pocket. Its range under ideal conditions is limited only by the curvature of the earth, and with it, in bright weather, you have a good chance of attracting anyone you can see.

Even if no rescuer is visible, the practice of sweeping the horizon with an aimed beam of reflected sunlight is recommended, for, as most can testify, the way in which even a distant tiny flash from something as small as a dewdrop can catch the eye is startling.

The Hudson's Bay Company includes such a double-faced mirror in its emergency kits, with the following advice for attracting the attention of ships and aeroplanes: "If the angle of the sun and the aeroplane or surface ship is not too great (90° maximum), you can hold the mirror three to six inches from your face and sight at the plane through the small hole in the center.

"The light from the sun shining through the hole will form a spot of light on your face, and this spot will be reflected in the rear surface of the mirror. Then, still sighting on the aeroplane through the hole, adjust the angle of the mirror until the

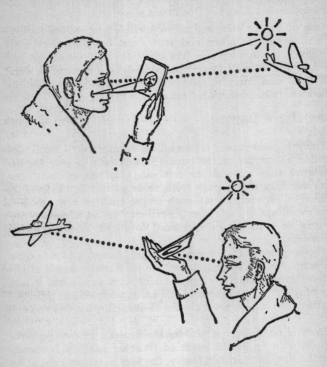

Signaling with Mirror at Plane. *Top:* When angle between plane and sun is 90° or less, hold mirror 3 to 6 inches from your face and sight at plane through hole in center of mirror. Still sighting at plane through hole, adjust angle of mirror until spot of sunlight reflected from your face to rear of mirror coincides with the hole and disappears. *Bottom:* When angle between plane and sun is more than 90°, sight at the plane through hole in mirror; then adjust angle of mirror until reflection of light spot on your hand in rear of mirror coincides with hole and disappears.

reflection of the light spot on the rear of the mirror coincides with the hole in the mirror and disappears. The reflected light now will be accurately aimed at the plane.

"If the angle between the target and the sun is great (more than 90°), sight the aeroplane through the hole, then adjust the angle of the mirror until the reflection of the light spot on your hand coincides with the hole in the mirror and disappears. This method will work where the aeroplane or ship is almost on one horizon and the sun almost 180° away on the opposite horizon."

The Hudson's Bay Company illustrations otherwise speak for themselves. The double-faced emergency mirror issued for the armed forces of the United States, made with a small open cross for facilitating aiming, can be employed in the same manner.

Any reflecting surface, even a flat piece of wood that is slick with moisture, can be used instead of a mirror. By punching a small hole in the center of something such as a flattened can, sufficiently shiny on both sides, you will be able to improvise a sight for aiming a reflected beam.

WHEN TO SEND RADIO SIGNALS

If you should happen to have a radio, the most likely times to send distress signals will be during the three-minute international silent periods which commence at fifteen minutes before and at fifteen minutes after every hour Greenwich time.

BODY SIGNALS

There are certain established body signals that will be recognized by most airmen.

Do you require urgent medical assistance? Then, as you probably already know, lie on your back with arms stretched straight behind you. Another widely used signal indicating severe injury is the crossing of the arms across the body.

Standing erect with the left arm hanging at the side and the right arm upraised signifies: "Everything is all right. Do not wait."

If, still leaving the left hand at the side, you hold the right arm horizontal, that means you will be able to proceed shortly and that the plane should wait if practical.

If you continue to stand erect and lift both arms to horizontal position, you need either mechanical help or parts, and there will be a long delay on your part.

Standing and holding both arms straight above your head means that you want to be picked up.

Swinging your hands sidewise back and forth above your head means that the observing plane should not try to land where you are.

To signal the pilot to come down, squat on your heels and point in the direction of the recommended landing place.

Perhaps you have a radio. If so, and if the receiver is working, this you can signify by cupping your hands conspicuously over your ears.

Body Signals Recognized by Airmen. (1) Medical aid urgently needed. (2) Everything all right; don't wait. (3) Can proceed shortly; wait if possible. (4) Mechanical help or parts needed. (5) Pick me up. (6) Don't land here. (7) Land at spot pointed to. (8) Have working radio. (9) Affirmative signal.

If, instead, you want the pilot to drop a message, swing the right hand in front of you to shoulder height several times.

To signal in the affirmative, wave something such as a shirt or handkerchief up and down in front of you.

Although signs vary with different groups of flyers, the plane can make an affirmative by dipping up and down the way the head is nodded. It can show negation by a slight zigzag motion comparable to shaking the head. Green flashes from a signaling lamp or the aircraft's rocking from side to side is an acknowledgment that the plane has understood the message; red flashes on the signaling lamp or a complete right-hand circuit indicate that it hasn't.

SYMBOLS

Symbols designed to be seen and interpreted from the air can be fashioned with boughs, stones, and lengths of various materials such as strips of cloth. They can be formed by such methods as digging or scratching lines, and by trudging back and forth in snow until trenches are made that will loom up black to a plane.

These impressions should be extended north and south whenever possible so as to be most conspicuous in sunlight strong enough to cast a shadow. Another way to capitalize on contrasting darkness in snowy terrain is to floor such trenches with evergreen boughs and to heap shadow-throwing snow on the southern sides of the symbols.

Any such symbol should naturally be put down in as prominent and conspicuous a location as is available. It's best to make them large, perhaps an easily visible ten feet thick and, depending on locality and expediency, possibly one hundred feet or more long. Color contrast can be vital.

An arrow with the point heading the way you intend to go will indicate you are proceeding in a particular direction. Perhaps you'll want the plane to show you which way to go. Then put out a large "K." The pilot probably will take note of it by waggling the wings, after which he'll head in the correct direction for a significant period of time.

A long, straight line means you need urgent medical assistance. Two long, straight lines denote that, although a doctor is not required, you do want medical supplies. A cross is the sign that you are unable to proceed by yourself, perhaps because of serious injury. A triangle: "Probably safe to land here."

Negation is indicated with a big "N." Yes is "Y." "L" means that all is well. Are you hungry and perhaps thirsty? Then make a big "F." A square will show that you would like a map and compass. Two "V's," one inside the other, request firearms and ammunition.

Chapter 23

CORNERING GAME
IN TIME OF NEED

STARVATION is not a great deal more pleasant than most would expect. The body becomes auto-cannibalistic after a few food-less hours. The carbohydrates in the system are devoured first. The fats follow.

This might not be too disagreeable, inasmuch as reducing diets seek to accomplish much the same result. But then proteins from muscles and tendons are consumed to maintain the dwindling strength their loss more gravely weakens.

No reasonable nourishment should, therefore, be overlooked if one needs food. Furthermore, if you are ever stranded and hungry in the wilderness, be sure, while your strength is near its maximum, not to pass up any promising sources of sustenance.

Practices ordinarily contrary to both game regulations and good sportsmanship are justified in extreme emergencies by the more ancient law of survival.

Under ordinary circumstances many of the methods of securing food here considered are illegal practically everywhere and reasonably so. Repugnance accompanies even the thought of some, while at best their successful commission during emergencies will not be joined by any satisfaction except that resulting from the thus answered instinct to stay alive.

OVERCOMING FOOD PREJUDICES

Few will disagree, at least not when the moment of decision is at hand, that there is a point when luxuries as such become relatively unimportant.

One of the luxuries which is valued most highly is the freedom to indulge taste prejudices. These taste prejudices are commonly based on two factors.

First, there is a human tendency to look down upon certain foods as being beneath one's social station. When grouse are particularly thick in the Northeast, for example, they are often scorned among backwoodsmen as a "poor man's dish." The same season, in the Northwest where there happens to be a scarcity of grouse but numerous varying hare, the former are esteemed while you hear natives apologizing for having rabbits in their pots. As it is everywhere in such matters, the lower the often self-designated station in life is, the more pronounced such evaluations become.

Second, it is natural to like the food to which you have become accustomed. Individuals in the United States and Canada have their wheat. The Mexican has his corn, the Oriental his rice. These grains Americans and Canadians like also, but it would seem a hardship to have to eat them every day as one does wheat bread.

One's fastidiousness, too, is sometimes repelled by the idea of a Scandinavian's eating raw fish, although at the moment you may be twirling a raw oyster in grated horseradish. The Eskimo enjoys fish mellowed by age. Many farther south regard as choice some particularly moldy, odoriferous cheeses.

INSECTS AND REPTILES

Grasshoppers are edible when hard portions such as wings and legs have been removed. So are cicadas. Termites, locusts, and crickets are similarly eaten.

Some natives have capitalized on ants' acidity by mashing them in water sweetened with berries or sap to make a sort of lemonade. The eggs and the young of the ant are eaten also.

Both snakes and lizards are not only digestible, but often are considered delicacies for which some willingly pay many times the amount they expend for a similar weight of prime beef. The only time snake meat may be poisonous is when it has suffered a venomous bite, perhaps from its own fangs. This also holds true with lizards, the only poisonous ones in North America being the Southwest's Gila monster and Mexico's beaded lizard. To prepare the reptiles, behead, skin, remove the entrails, and cook like chicken to whose white meat the somewhat fibrous flesh often is compared.

An ancient method for securing already cooked insects, reptiles, and small animals is to fire large tracts of grassland and then to comb them for whatever may have been roasted.

TURTLES

Turtle fat, from which no more heat than that from the sun renders a clear, savory oil, is so nutritious that the reptile is an unusually valuable food source. Blood and juices often are used to relieve thirst.

Occasionally it is possible to backtrack a female to a fresh nest of eggs, generally buried in sand or mud not far from water. Although not greatly esteemed for taste by those more accustomed to hen's eggs, these are nourishing at all stages.

A turtle can be killed by concussion or by beheading, care being taken even after it is dead to avoid both jaws and claws. If it is convenient, the turtle can be scalded for several minutes by being dropped into boiling water. The under shell then may be quartered and the entrails removed, whereupon the meat can readily be simmered free of the upper shell.

FISH

NUTRITIONAL VALUE

Freshly caught fish also provide a completely balanced diet when sufficiently fat and not overcooked. The main difficulty with subsisting exclusively on fish arises from the fact that in calories they often are far less nourishing than one might expect. This fact can be vital.

Suppose there comes a time when you have nothing to eat but, say, trout. You're stranded in the wilderness, for example, about two days east of the Alaska Highway. No one knows you're missing, and therefore no one is searching for you. You know the general lay of the country well enough, by map, to be confident of cutting the Alaska Highway if you keep heading west by compass.

The area seems barren of game, but by really working at it, you may reasonably expect to average catching a half-dozen one-pound trout daily. Should you remain where you are for a few days and live on fish, with the idea of building up your dwindling strength for the journey that still lies ahead?

An office worker undergoing very little physical exertion requires some 2,000 to 2,500 calories daily. It is reasonable to generalize that an individual living a rugged outdoor life needs at least twice as many of these energy units. Any not supplied directly by food will be taken from the body's own carbohydrates, fats, and proteins.

A one-pound rainbow trout when caught, Canada's Department of National Health and Welfare has ascertained, contains only slightly more than 200 calories. So to eat 4,500 calories daily, you'd have to catch twenty such trout each day. Instead of gaining vigor on six pounds or so of fresh trout daily, you'd be very gravely losing strength. You'd do better to finish the journey as soon as possible.

Other considerations, of course, could alter the situation. You might have unlimited fish. You might be able to supplement the fish with sufficient other wild nutriment. The fish might be some more nourishing species, such as, in many localities, fat salmon averaging closer to 900 calories per fresh raw pound.

Too, the wild food available might be yours so easily that you could conserve a decisive amount of energy by relaxing most of the time beside a warm blaze. For although the basal energy requirements of the human system decline but little even when one is starving, a man lounging comfortably beside a campfire may consume only about 100 calories an hour, whereas struggling through the bush he can burn six times as much.

EMERGENCY FISHING METHODS

Just because you do not happen to have a hook and line doesn't mean you can't catch fish. Unravel a bit of sweater, for example. Tie on a small strip of bright cloth, such as the corner of a handkerchief. When the fish closes its mouth over the cloth, give the line a tug. There is a reasonable chance, especially where fishing is virgin, that you'll flip the quarry out on the bank. This doesn't always work, of course. Fish won't always take regular bait, either.

HOMEMADE HOOKS. You can devise almost any number of different types of hooks. A bent pin really works, as many a youngster has learned, the only trick being to maintain pressure so the fish won't slip off. An open safety pin is a somewhat larger hook of the same variety. Bent nails have been used with considerable success.

It follows, therefore, that hooks can be made out of practically any workable metal of sufficient rigidity. To make a really rugged one, lash the blade of a pocket knife partly open against a wooden wedge. A second blade, so opened at an opposite angle, can form a barb of sorts. The knife, so prepared, then can be hidden in a gob of bait.

You also can cut hooks from wood, preferably wood that is hard and tough. Whittle the shank first. Lash one or more sharp slivers so they slant upward from the lower end. You can even add a barb by lashing another sliver even more acutely downward from the top. Thorns, if available, can be utilized. Fish bones, too, will furnish both serviceable points and barbs.

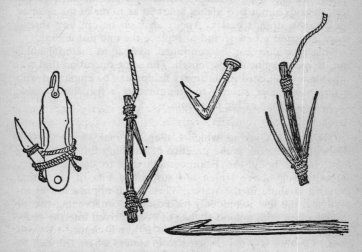

Improvised Fishhooks and Spear

PRIMITIVE FISHING DEVICE. One of the most primitive fishing devices, still used successfully if not sportingly, is made by tying the line to the middle of a sharp piece of wood or bone that has been sharpened at both ends. Hidden in bait, this is swallowed by the fish, whereupon a jerk of the cord pulls it crossways.

MAKING FISHING LINES. Fish lines can be improvised in numerous ways. One method is to unravel a piece of fabric and to knot lengths of four or so threads together at frequent intervals. Another is to cut around and around a section of leather, forming a continuous lace, as described in Chapter 3.

Line can be more scientifically made, after cutting or raveling any fabric or fiber that may be available so as to procure a number of long strands. Take four of these threads and fasten them at one end. Hold two threads in each hand. Roll and twist each strand clockwise between the thumb and forefinger of each hand, while turning those in the right hand counterclockwise around those held in the left. This twisting and winding must be done tautly, so the completed line will not unravel.

Depending on the lengths of thread, conclude each of the four strands about two inches apart so as to make the splicing on of new strands easier. About an inch before any thread stops, twist on a new strand to replace the one just ending.

This procedure can be continued, as long as material holds out, to make a line of any length. The same operation that will provide a small cord for ordinary fishing can be employed with a dozen or more strands to manufacture a fish line capable of landing a tuna or big lake trout.

GIGGING. Gigging, which is illegal in many localities and not without reason, is the practice of catching fish by hooking them in the body. An Eskimo method is to dangle a long, smooth hook above which are suspended bits of bone that flutter and shine in the water. When a fish approaches to investigate, the line is suddenly jerked up the intervening two or three inches, with a good chance of being driven into the prey, which is at once hauled up before it has a chance to work loose. Gigging is often resorted to in waters where fish can be seen but not readily induced to bite.

BUTTONS AND SPOONS. A button often is successful as a lure. So is any bright small bit of metal. In its emergency kit the Hudson's Bay Company includes a tablespoon with a hole drilled in it so a hook can be wired in place for trolling or gigging.

FINDING THE BEST BAIT. Various insects, and even fuzzy seeds resembling them, will catch fish. Widely effective are grasshoppers, which, when available, can themselves be harvested with particular ease at night with the aid of a light.

"Experiment with bait," the Hudson's Bay Company advises any of its employees who may be in distress. "Look for bait in water, for this is the source of most fish food. Insects, crayfish, worms, wood grubs, minnows, and fish eggs are all good. After catching your first fish, examine the stomach and intestines. See what it is feeding on and try to duplicate it. If it is crayfish (a form of fresh-water crab), turn over the rocks in the stream until you get one."

If you succeed in finding many crayfish, incidentally, there's your meal, for once they are cooked by being dropped into boiling water, the lower portions are easily sucked free of the shells. One way to catch these is by driving a school into a restricted pool and dipping them out with a net made either by tightly interlacing foliage to a frame consisting of a bent green sapling, or by attaching some porous article of clothing to such a loop.

FISHING WITH BARE HANDS. Fish such as salmon and herring throng up streams in such numbers at certain times of the year that one can catch and throw ashore large numbers of them with the bare hands. It also is possible, on occasion, to secure by hand alone quantities of such fish as smelt, when schools come up on beaches to spawn in the surf.

You also can find such fish as perch and trout wedged among rocks of fast little rivers. Still another way to capture fish with the bare hands is by feeling carefully among the nooks and cavities in stream banks. You can even catch fish, strange to say, by forming a sort of cave with your cupped hands held motionless against a bank. Trout in particular will investigate, whereupon, by the acquired art of closing the hands quickly enough but not too hurriedly, you'll have them.

When rations are short one sometimes can splash up shallow

brooks, driving any fish ahead of him. When these are cornered in a pool, he can, if he must, block their retreat with piled stones and go in and kill them with a club. Small streams, too, often can be diverted so as to strand fish in pools.

If one is really up against it in beaver country, occasionally it is possible to strand a life-sustaining catch by prying an opening in a beaver dam. Another technique is to wade in, riling with the feet the muck that amasses behind such a dam and catching with bare hands the temporarily mud-blinded fish.

BUILDING A FISH TRAP. Fish often can be trapped with considerable success in cases of dire need. One such basic trap, recommended by the Hudson's Bay Company for use under life-or-death conditions, can be built by driving sticks and branches into the bottom so their tops protrude above the water. The trap consists of a narrow-mouth enclosure into which the fish are led by a wide funnel-like V.

Attracted by some such bait as spoiled fish or decomposed meat, the prey guided into the pen through the slit at the apex are, in enough cases, unable to find their way out.

Materials used in making such a trap vary. Stretching a net around stakes will, if the former is available, save considerable energy. Stones can be utilized, perhaps leading into a natural fresh-water or tidal pool.

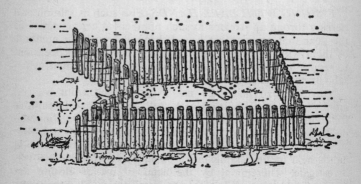

Fish Trap

SPEARING. You may have already experimented with making spears, perhaps sharpening a long dry stick for the purpose and hardening this point over the embers of a campfire. It's also possible to fashion a barbed spear by whittling the point in this instance at the joint of an inverted crotch, an inch or two of whose angle you have slivered into a sharply restraining projection. You also may test the efficacy of barbs and tips of bone, stone, or metal that you have lashed into place.

One procedure is to thrust the spear very slowly through the water toward the target, often to within inches of the fish before making the final jab. With the help of a light, perhaps a torch of flaming birch bark or a burning pine knot, you can, many times, spot a fish at night lying pratically motionless in shallow water. By advancing the spear cautiously, aiming low to counteract deceptive refraction, it becomes increasingly easy to pin a majority of such fish against the bottom.

DRUGGING. Certain Indian methods of fishing may prove life savers to the hungry wayfarer. One procedure is to crush the leaves and stalks of the mullein, or fishweed, *Croton setigerus.* These are dropped into a still pool or temporarily dammed brook. The fish therein, momentarily narcotized, will float to the surface where they should be immediately secured.

The bulbous root of the so-called soap plant, *Chlorogalum pomeridianum,* can be similarly used. Fish caught by these emergency means are as wholesome as if merely dazed by concussion.

OTHER MARINE FOODS

SEAWEEDS

All seaweeds are good to eat. You can munch them raw, simmer them in fresh water to make soup, boil them with meat or vegetables, and even dry them for a number of other future uses. Algae, of which seaweeds are one type, are, in fact, regarded by research scientists as potentially valuable sources of the gigantic amounts of protein-rich food that may be needed if the increasing world population becomes so burdensome that present supplies are inadequate.

SEA CUCUMBERS

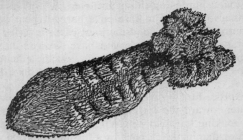

Sea Cucumber

Sea cucumbers are eatable boiled, fried, stewed, and raw. Actually an animal, the sea cucumber also is dried and smoked by some natives. The easily recognizable organism, so common along seashores, has a rough and flexible body about six to eight inches long when contracted and about twice that length when expanded. The five long white muscles, left after the insides have been discarded and the slimy outer skin scraped away, are what is used. Their taste is not unlike that of clams.

SEA URCHIN EGGS

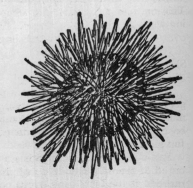

Sea Urchin. *Left:* spineless. *Right:* with spines.

The sea urchin, a marine animal related to the starfish, is a principal source of nourishment in many localities. Safe when found in the temperate and arctic waters of this continent where they often can be gathered in quantity at low tide, sea urchins are shaped like slightly flattened balls. They have thin, fragile shells that often bristle with movable spines. The lengths of eggs inside the top shell are edible both raw and cooked.

ABALONE

The abalone, a large, rock-clinging mollusk, is particularly well known along the Pacific coast of North America. There hundreds at a time, attached to boulders and ledges, are revealed by low tides. Also they are occasionally seen floating free in seaweed. Their flattened shells, which vary from black and green to red, are fantastically lined with mother-of-pearl.

By abruptly inserting a long, thin instrument such as a sheath knife or stick between the abalone and the rock and prying quickly, the shellfish can be detached, usually with little trouble, before it has a chance to adhere more tightly. The operation otherwise requires a heavier tool and considerable pressure.

The abalone then can be levered from the shell, which not infrequently has a diameter of ten inches or so and therefore considerable utility as a bowl. Or the shell can be cracked with a rock and picked off. The hard white meat is what is retained. This may be sliced into thin steaks and tenderized by pounding with the flat edge of a stone, then very briefly fried, broiled over open coals, or diced and simmered into chowder.

SHELLFISH

Any time we may be up against it for food, there will be, in general, no more promising areas in which to seek nourishment than those near water. Piles of shells beside a creek may be the clue to clams that often can be seen in clear water or felt beneath the bare feet.

Salt-water clams, although not so easily dug, may be secured at low tide. Evidence of these bivalves' presence is furnished by elongated siphons or the marks left by the withdrawals thereof. Along Pacific shores below the Aleutians, all dark portions should be discarded for the six months beginning with May and ending with October because of possibly dangerous concentrations of toxic alkaloids therein, the white meat alone then being eaten.

Snails are edible and, by some peoples, particularly relished. So are scallops, oysters, and shrimps. Eels also are very much eatable, in many localities being regarded as superior to any other fish.

Mussels, with one important exception, may be safely eaten if care is taken to avoid any that do not close tightly when touched. The small, bluish-black mussels found attached, usually in clusters, to seashore rocks become poisonous at certain times of the year along the Pacific Coast below the Aleutians. The poison, which, being alkaloid, cannot be destroyed by heat, is the result of a diet which includes venomous organisms that drift shoreward from about the end of April through October. If there is any doubt whatsoever about when, in any particular area, these mussels are fit for food, they should be avoided entirely.

Crabs are all good. Usually they can be immobilized in shallow water for a long enough time either to crush them or reach behind and pick them up. They will attach themselves readily to flesh lowered on a line. Although salt-water varieties may be eaten raw, land crabs are sometimes infected with parasites and should be dropped live into boiling water for at least twenty minutes.

BIRDS

All birds are good to eat. When they are moulting and unable to fly, it is not difficult to corner them on foot. Large flocks may occasionally be captured by driving them into nets or traps. Roosting or nesting birds can be secured by a noose fastened to the end of a pole. Birds also can be caught in fine snares placed where they nest, feed, or congregate. Deadfalls get them, too.

Even the riper eggs, or any eggs it may be possible to secure, are nourishing. If one has continued access to a large colony at nesting time, one way to be assured of fresh eggs is to mark whatever is already in the nests, perhaps removing all but a few, if conditions seem to justify it.

BAGGING BIRDS WITHOUT GUNS

Game birds such as ptarmigan and grouse promise feasts for anybody lost in the wilderness, especially as a few stones or sticks are often the only weapons needed. If one misses the first time, such fowl usually will afford a second and even a third try. When they do fly, they generally go only short distances and may be successfully followed, particularly if this is done casually and at such an angle that it would seem that you were going to stroll on past.

BIRD TRAPS. Traps also work well with birds. A stick fence, put up in a narrow spiral and baited, will sometimes catch in its center fowl such as quail. Geese can be bagged in a ditch some four feet deep into which they are led by bait such as wild grain. When one rushes suddenly at the geese, they try to fly but are unable to spread their wings.

Turkey also are taken by the use of bait, one ruse consisting of attracting them head down under a low fence. Once turkeys so pen themselves and, upon finishing their pecking, raise their long necks, it often takes them too long a time to figure how to retreat.

BOLA. One can improvise a bola, a primitive missile consisting of stones attached to the ends of thongs. Although the Spanish peoples generally are thought of in connection with the bola, Eskimos use a device of this type consisting of several cords about a yard long with a small weight at the extremity of each.

The bola is grasped at the center from which all cords radiate, and the weights are twirled above the head. Hurled at flying birds, the spinning strings often twist around one or more and bring them to the ground.

EASILY CAUGHT SCAVENGERS. Gulls and other scavenger birds can be easily although unsportingly caught by a man who is desperate enough for food. A short bone or stick sharpened at both ends is secured in the middle by a line, preferably tied to something limber, such as a sapling, and then concealed in some bait such as decomposed fish.

GAME

UTILIZING THE WHOLE ANIMAL

Some natives roast the bland young antlers of the deer family when these are in velvet. Others esteem the stomach contents of herbivorous mammals such as caribou, for such greens, mixed as they are with digestive acids, are not too unlike salad prepared with vinegar.

Some aborigines, as desirous of wasting nothing as those gourmets who cook and eat whole plucked woodcock, do not bother to open the smaller birds and animals they secure, but pound them to a pulp which is tossed in its entirety into the pot. Other peoples gather moose and rabbit excrement for thickening boiled dishes. Even such an unlikely ingredient as gall has, among other uses, utility as a seasoning.

Animals should not be bled any more than can be helped if food is scarce. Blood, which is not far removed from milk, is unusually rich in easily absorbed minerals and vitamins. Our bodies, for illustration, need iron. It would require ten ordinary eggs to supply one man's normal daily requirements. Four tablespoons of blood are capable of doing the same job. Fresh blood can be secured and carried, in the absence of handier means, in a bag improvised from the entrails. One way to use it is in broths and soups, enlivened perhaps with a wild vegetable or two.

The skin of the animal is as nourishing as a similar quantity of lean meat. Baking a catch in its hide, although ordinarily both a handy and tasty method of preparing camp meat occasionally, is therefore a practice to be avoided when rations are scarce.

Rawhide, incidentally, also is high in protein. Boiled, it has even less flavor than roasted antlers, and the not overly appealing look and feel of the boiled skin of a large fish. When it is raw, a usual procedure, naturally enough adopted in emergencies, is to chew on a small bit until that becomes tiresome, and then to swallow the slippery shred.

The mineral-rich marrow found in the bones of animals that were in good physical condition at demise is not surpassed by any other natural food in caloric strength. What is, at the same time, the most delectable of tidbits is wasted by the common outdoor practice of roasting such bones until they are on the point of crumbling. A more nutriment-conserving procedure is to crack them at the onset, with two stones if nothing handier is available. The less the marrow is cooked the better it will remain as far as nutrition is concerned. All this is something to consider if anyone desperate for food happens upon temporary salvation in the form of a skeleton of a large animal.

When food supplies are limited, nothing should be cooked longer than is considered necessary for palatability. The only exception is when there may be germs or parasites to be destroyed. The more food is subjected to heat, the greater are the losses of nutritive values.

Nearly every part of North American animals is edible. An occasional exception is the polar bear and ringed- and bearded-seal liver, which become so excessively rich in Vitamin A that they are poisonous to some degree at certain times and are usually as well avoided. All fresh-water fish are likewise good to eat.

You will probably want to eat most of any animals you can secure if short of food. Some parts, as, for example, the liver, whose abundance of Vitamin A has caused it to be recognized even among primitive tribes as a specific for night blindness, contain in more concentrated form certain of the necessary food elements. But any section of plump fresh meat is a complete diet in itself, affording all the necessary good ingredients even if you dine on nothing but fat, rare steaks for week after month after year.

CAPTURING SMALL GAME

HOW TO USE DEADFALLS. For the capture of food animals, the Hudson's Bay Company recommends the use of deadfalls by any of its employees who may be stranded without adequate sustenance in the northern wilderness. The Company of Adventurers' pattern of the deadly figure-four trigger is effective.

Essentially, you might prepare a deadfall by lifting one end of a heavy object such as a log. Prop up this end with a stick, doing so with such studied insecurity that any animal or bird who moved the support would knock it loose. You can encourage this by affixing some bait to the prop. It's possible to go

Figure-Four Trigger

even further, arranging a few branches so that, to reach the bait, the victim would place himself so as to receive the full weight of the dislodged deadfall back of the shoulders.

SNARES. Even if you have a gun, you may want to set a few snares, the principles of which are as simple as they are primitive. With a strong enough thong or rope, you can snare deer and larger animals. With nothing huskier than light fishline or horsehair, squirrels and rabbits can be caught.

A snare is, in effect, a slip noose placed with the object of tightening about and holding a quarry if the latter inadvertently moves into it.

The size of the snare depends on the size of the animal to be trapped. For example, on a rabbit trail the loop should be about four inches in diameter and hang 1½-3 inches above the ground.

Suppose you want to snare a rabbit for the pot. It's evident that they, like other animals, follow regular paths. Try, therefore, to hang the slip noose so the rabbit will run headfirst into it and quickly choke itself.

It helps to go one step further and narrow the trail at that particular spot. This can be accomplished in one of several ways. You can drop a branch or small tree as naturally as possible across the track, making a narrow slit in it in which to suspend the noose and shove a few sticks into the ground to serve as a funnel. You can block the top, bottom, and sides of the runway with brush except for a small opening where the loop awaits.

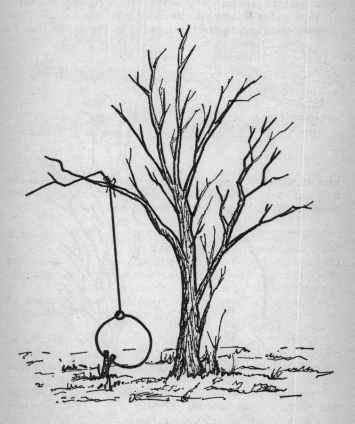

Snare

All possible guile should be bent to make everything seem as natural as possible. The necessity for this increases in direct proportion with the intelligence of the prey sought. Trappers customarily prepare snares months ahead of time and leave them, with the nooses harmlessly closed until fur season, to blend them with the surroundings. Small pot animals, however, usually can be snared by beginners with a minimum of artifice.

A quick way to collect squirrels, for instance, is to lean a pole against a conifer under which there is considerable squirrel sign, and at six or so points on the pole attach small, closely lying nooses. A squirrel scampering up the incline runs his

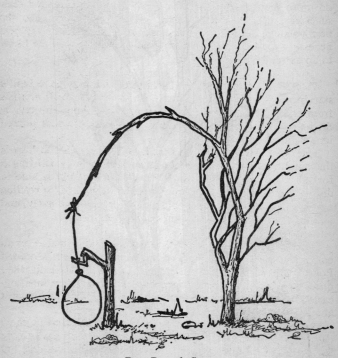

Bent-Branch Snare

head into the waiting loop and falls free. Its dangling there
does not seriously deter other squirrels from using the same
route and being so caught themselves.

You can tie one end of any snare to a stationary object such
as a pole or tree. You can tie it, particularly if snow makes
tracking easy, to a drag such as a chunk of deadwood. Preferably, you can bend a sapling and arrange a trigger so the animal will be lifted off its feet and, if not choked as humanely
as possible under the conditions, at least rendered unable to
exert direct pressure.

OTHER WEAPONS. Both slingshots and bows and arrows
are so familiar that, inasmuch as you will be limited in any
event by the materials at hand, there is probably no need to
do more than suggest them as survival weapons. As for their
successful use, this will depend largely on practice. Do the
best you can. If you have the ingenuity and resourcefulness
necessary for survival under extreme conditions, you are likely
to do extremely well.

SMOKING OUT GAME. Distasteful as it may be to him, a
starving man is occasionally forced to smoke small animals
from places of concealment. Sometimes an animal also can be
driven to within reach of a club by quantities of water poured
into a burrow.

The opening may be such that it will be possible to impale
the creature on a barbed pole or to secure it by twisting a
forked stick into its hair and skin. One frequently is able to
dig with success. One also may have some luck by spreading
a noose in front of the hole, hiding a short distance away, and
jerking the loop tight when the quarry ventures out.

LEMMINGS. Lemmings have been found valuable as an
emergency food by members of the Royal Canadian Mounted
Police on extended patrols. Lemmings are the little stub-tailed
mice that, when reaching the ocean on their migrations, occasionally start swimming in the possible belief that it is just
another pond or lake.

"In winter they rest on or near the ground, deep in snow
drifts," say Mounted Police sources, "and you will have to dig
for them. In summer you can find them by overturning flat
rocks. You can get them by setting snares of very fine wire

along the runways. Lemming are constantly preyed upon by shrews, weasels, foxes, and owls."

PORCUPINES. Porcupines, like nettles and thistles, are better eating than it might seem reasonable to expect. The sluggish rodent is the one animal even the greenest tenderfoot, although weak with hunger, can kill with something no more formidable than a stick.

Porcupines cannot, of course, shoot their quills, but any of these that are stuck in the flesh by contact should be pulled out immediately, for their barbed tips cause them to be gradually worked out of sight. This danger from quills is one reason why it is poor practice to cook a porcupine, as is sometimes done, by tossing it into a small fire. Very often all the quills are not burned off. Even if they are, a considerable amount of the valuable fat will be consumed as well.

The best procedure is to skin out the porcupine, first turning it over so as to make the initial incision along the smooth underneath portion. Many who've dined on this meat consider the surprisingly large liver especially flavorful.

FROGS. Frog meat is one example of the often disdained foods, sometimes so expensive in the more fashionable dining salons of the world, that nature furnishes free for the taking. The amphibians can be hooked with fishing tackle and small fly. They can be caught with string and bit of cloth, the former being given a swift yank when the latter is taken experimentally into the mouth.

Frogs can be secured with spears of various types. A sharpened stick will do. They can be so occupied at night by a light that you'll be able to net them and even, if you go about it slowly, to reach cautiously around and clamp a hand over one.

Most of the delicately flavored meat is on the hind legs which can be cut off in pairs, skinned, and in the absence of cooking utensils, extended over hot coals on a green stick for broiling. If rations were scant, you'd use the entire skinned, cleaned frog, perhaps boiling the meat briefly with some wild greens (see Chapter 18).

LETTING PREDATORS HUNT FOR YOU

If you are ever stranded and hungry, it may be worthwhile to watch for owls, for spying one roosting in a quiet, shadowy place is not unusual, and it may be possible to steal close enough to knock it down. Although not so large and plump as might seem from outward appearances, an owl nevertheless is excellent eating.

What is more likely, however, is that you may scare an owl from a kill and thus secure yourself a fresh supper. You may also have such good fortune, perhaps earlier in the day, with other predatory birds such as hawks and eagles. It is not uncommon to come upon one of these which has just captured a partridge, hare, or other prey that is proving awkward to lift from the ground, and, by running, to drive the hunter away with its talons empty.

Wolves, coyotes, and foxes also may be surprised at fresh kills that are still fit for human consumption. Such carnivora will seek new whereabouts at the sight or scent of an approaching human being.

Coming up to a bear's kill may be something else again. A wild bear probably won't dispute your presence. Then again it may. Although the chances are very much against this latter probability, that is all the more reason not to take disproportionate risks.

If you are unarmed and really need the bear's meal, you must plan and execute your campaign with all reasonable caution. This probably will mean, first of all, spotting in the minutest detail preferably at least two paths of escape in case a fast exit should be advisable. This should not be too difficult where there are small trees to climb.

You'll then watch for your opportunity, and if, for instance, the kill is a still warm moose calf, perhaps build a large fire beside it, discreetly gathering enough fuel to last for several hours—until morning if night is close at hand. Take care, in any event, to be constantly alert until well away from the locality, realizing that bears, especially when they have gorged themselves, have a habit of dropping down near their food.

If you have a gun, you will be able to judge for yourself if the best procedure may not be to bag the bear itself. Fat becomes the most important single item in almost every survival diet, and the bear is particularly well fortified with this throughout most of the year. Usually, except for a short period in the spring, bear flesh is particularly nourishing.

Many people, most of whom have never tasted bear meat nor smelled it cooking, are prejudiced against the carnivore as a table delicacy for one reason or another. One excuse often heard concerns the animal's eating habits. Yet the most ravenous bear is a finicky diner when compared to such offerings as lobster and chicken.

It is only natural that preferences should vary, and if only for this reason, it may be interesting to note that many who live on wild meat most of the time relish plump bear more than any other North American game meat with the single exception of mountain sheep. Furthermore, these individuals include a sizable number who, after long professing an inability to stomach bear meat in any form, found themselves coming back for thirds and even fourths of bear roast or bear stew, under the impression that anything so savory must be, at the very least, choice beef.

Chapter 24

WHEN THE WILDS BITE BACK

WHAT would be a very minor accident in a city, with assistance as near as the telephone, could be an extremely serious and even fatal misstep in the wilderness. So, both consciously and subconsciously, most individuals are wholesomely careful to sidestep trouble when in remote areas. Away from the masses, too, one is not so apt to become involved in the lapses and shortcomings of others.

All this is a major reason why among able-bodied men the probability of an accident or serious physical trouble in the deep wilderness is extremely small. In the comparative cleanness of the silent places, furthermore, there is correspondingly little likelihood of infection.

The exception to this latter circumstance has to do with the progressive lessening of built-up immunities when you are not in continual contact with the ills of civilization. An example is the common cold. This is a gradual matter and, being important only on recontact, is at most a minor consideration unless you are going to remain in remote country for months or years.

FIRST AID KITS

Anyone who goes more than a half a day from civilization and a doctor should, whenever possible, be armed with an adequate first aid kit and the working knowledge of how to use it. This precaution he owes, at the very least, both to himself and to any who accompany him. No more than a reasonable measure, it sometimes can mean the difference between an easily repaired disability and one that lasts a lifetime.

The ready-packed commercial kits, fine as they are for many purposes, seldom are satisfactory for the individual who wanders far from beaten trails. One reason is that their assembly is based more or less on the assumption that the patient can be placed under a doctor's care within a comparatively brief period. Furthermore, these kits do not always include provisions for those accidents most likely to occur in wild country. As for the Army first aid kit, this is designed for the emergency treatment of battle wounds.

It is not necessary that such an emergency aid kit be carried on the person, although it should be readily available at the camp, canoe, cabin, or other base of operations. Even a small and compact affair attached to the belt soon becomes an unwarranted nuisance, however, particularly as, at best, one would be useful in no more than a disproportionate few emergencies. Something can always be extemporized on the spot to do for a short time. Even a functional splint, for example, can be improvised from a thick live roll of birch bark peeled from a tree whose circumference is similar to that of the injured limb.

BASIC WILDERNESS MEDICINE KIT

Medical Supplies	Treatment Uses
1 triangular 40″ sterile bandage, with 2 safety pins	Direct application while sterile over wounds, covering sterile dressings, padding, splint and traction ties, tourniquet.
6 gauze roller bandages of assorted widths in individual sterile packages; 6 gauze compresses, 3 inches square, each in sterile packing	Direct application over wounds, direct pressure to stop bleeding, holding compresses in place.

Medical Supplies	Treatment Uses
1 package small adhesive compresses with plastic tape and plain sterile pads	Cover minor wounds, tape abrasions to guard against irritation and infection, protect blisters, draw cuts together, etc.
1 small bar soap	Cleanse hands before applying first aid, scrub wounds.
50 or less aspirin tablets, 5-grain	Counteract pain, relieve shock, lower temperature.
2 rolls adhesive tape, 2" wide	General taping, holding compress in place, emergency repairs.
2 elastic bandages, 4" wide	Applied fully stretched over compress, one or more of these as needed to control severe bleeding while, unlike the dangerous and temporary tourniquet, permitting circulation. Furthermore, these can be used anywhere, while tourniquets will serve only for the extremities. Even here, application will many times permit the gradual and fairly immediate removal of an already applied tourniquet. Good for strapping chest to exclude air in puncture wounds, for bandaging of fractures and dislocations, and for pressure bandages when applied at half stretch for strains and sprains.
1 snake bite kit	In bad snake country, each individual should have a personal kit on his person at all times.
1/4-oz. tube of antiseptic-anesthetic eye ointment	Soothing and treating eye injuries and minor infections, deadening eye prior to removing imbedded particles, treatment of pain and irritation of snow blindness.
1 good fever thermometer	Average normal temperature is 98.6, fluctuations of one degree not usually being regarded as significant.
1 small high-quality scissors, pointed	Spreading in preference to slashing the incisions indicated in snake bite treatment. Such disruption of the tissues, although painful, will more safely avoid injury to blood vessels and tendon.
1 sharply pointed tweezers or splinter forceps	Removing thorns and splinters. Forceps also valuable for spreading open, rather than cutting, certain incisions.

Medical Supplies	Treatment Uses
2 curved surgeon's needles, with ligature and needle holder	For emergency sewing, when sterilized, of wounds not easily closed by other means. Cleanse wound first, as by flushing liberally with sterile water. Pick out any debris and scrub with soap if that seems necessary.
Oil of cloves	To treat toothache. Dip bit of cotton in oil and insert in freshly cleaned cavity that is causing toothache. More modern treatment may well be favored by your doctor.
Vitamin B complex and Vitamin C in high-potency, stress doses	To replenish body supplies being drained by severe accident or illness. It is then important to maintain adequate nutrition, emphasizing B Complex, C, and protein.

In addition to the items in the list above, be sure to take along on wilderness treks a first-aid guide, supplemented, preferably by marginal notes made with your doctor's help, with information about the additional steps that may become necessary in remote areas. The terse, compact booklet put out by the U. S. Forest Service is excellent. It is available for twenty cents (stamps not accepted) from the Superintendent of Documents, U. S. Government Printing Office, Washington, D. C.

VERSATILE HOUSEHOLD PHARMACEUTICALS

There are other odds and ends that you may want to put in the emergency aid kit, as for example something such as salve for lips chapped by wind and sun. Items available elsewhere in your outfit can frequently be made to perform double duty, however.

BAKING SODA. Baking soda, according to the medical and dental professions, is as good a dentifrice as most and far less expensive than any of the manufactured products.

A paste of baking soda and water applied to insect stings and bites often will help to reduce the swelling and irritation. Soaking in water when possible is even simpler. Daubing on mud will do, too, in a pinch. The itching from hives, skin irritation caused by chafing, allergies, and so on, can often be relieved by patting on a paste of baking soda and water or by applying bandages or compresses soaked in a saturated solution of sodium bicarbonate.

For indigestion, ¼ teaspoon of baking soda in ½ glass of water, not to be repeated more than two or three times any day and definitely not to be used habitually, often helps ease the discomfort of acid indigestion and heartburn. If the necessity for an antacid is prolonged, one of the inert alkalis should be used, instead.

Half a teaspoon of baking soda in a glass of water will serve as a gargle or mouth wash.

SALT. Half a level teaspoon of salt in a glass of water is regarded by many doctors as equal to commercial mouth washes. No larger a proportion of salt should be used, for when a solution is employed that is stronger in salt than the body fluid, its tendency is to draw natural moisture out of the system, dehydrating tissue and causing irritation.

Plain ordinary table salt, a rounded teaspoon in a quart of warm water taken preferably before breakfast or at any rate on an empty stomach, will serve as a purge if you ever need one, passing through the digestive system in about half an hour. A quart of cold spring water, enjoyed while one is washing up the first thing in the morning, is also often effective as a laxative.

SNAKE BITE KIT

Taking up only slightly more space than a 12-gauge shotgun shell, one of the efficient little snake bite kits that can be tucked easily into a pocket should always be on the person in poisonous snake country. Especially handy are the Cutter Compak suction snake bite kits, devised by Robert K. Cutter, M.D. Sporting goods dealers and drug stores handle these. Each contains three suction cups, a sharp blade, antiseptic, lymph constrictor, and a calmly presented completeness of plainly illustrated directions.

The four kinds of poisonous snakes in the United States and Canada are the rattler, coral, moccasin, and copperhead. The dangerousness of these is, in general, considerably overrated, mortality from properly treated snake bite being very low. The mortality from bites treated with the kit mentioned above is less than 1 per cent. Even without treatment of any sort, mortality runs only 10 to 15 per cent; hence the mistaken acclaim given such useless and often harmful "remedies" as

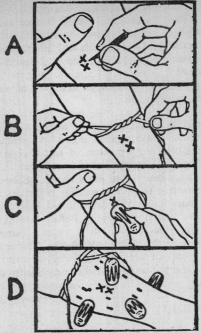

Treating Poisonous Snake Bite. Paint knife blade and fang marks with antiseptic. Make cross incisions ¼-inch long and ⅛- to ¼-inch deep at fang marks, as in *A*. (Don't make incisions if bite is on fingers, toes, or very large visible veins.) Tie lymph constrictor (cotton tape or string) 1½ inches above bite, just tight enough to dent skin, as in *B*. Never tie around a finger or toe. Squeeze cup and place over incisions, as in *C*. Every 10 minutes, remove constrictor for at least a minute; then apply again slightly higher so that it will be just beyond the extending swelling. If bite is serious and no physician available for 24 hours you may elect to make single lengthwise cuts, ¼-inch long and not more than ¹⁄₁₆-inch deep, as in *D*. Then apply suction cups as directed in kit.

tobacco juice, whisky, kerosene, freshly killed fowl, and the brilliant and effective-looking potassium permanganate. Searing likewise is ineffectual.

If you are unfortunate enough to be bitten by a poisonous snake, keep as quiet and calm as possible. You'll thereby avoid to the greatest possible degree any unnecessary quickening of the circulation, which would speed absorption of the poison into the general system.

During all cutting, be extremely careful to avoid tendons, arteries, nerves, and large veins. Because of the very real danger all these impose, safer although more painful than slashing is the spreading and working of the tissue apart with the sterilized points of scissors or, even better, splinter forceps. Cut the skin just enough to allow entry of these points. The tissue beneath the surface also can be parted with a single blunt edge.

COPING WITH INSECT HAZARDS

Insects are considerably more dangerous in the wilderness than any wild animals. In fact, mosquitoes and black flies become so thick in many regions of the United States and Canada that they can actually kill a full-grown man in good health who is lost or stranded without sufficient knowledge or ingenuity to protect himself. Modern insect repellents can solve the problem more quickly and easily than anything else. The best products now available are those in which diethyl toluamide is an active ingredient, preferably in compounds in which it is found in 75 per cent strength.

When used correctly, Cutter insect repellent is, at this writing, probably the most effective on the retail market. Be sure not to use over two drops for each side of your face and one hand. To use more simply defeats the purpose of having the cream rubbed into the pores, and leaving the skin without any sticky or greasy effect.

Smoke, too, will help discourage the pests when one is camped. Mud plastered on exposed parts will afford protection during travel. Plugging the ears lightly, as with cotton, will often make buzzing insects a lot more bearable. Inadequate clothing can be reinforced with some natural substances, a sheath of birch bark beneath the stockings, for example, adding protection for the legs. The best way to avoid insects is to keep, whenever possible, to windy stretches such as bare ridges and wide shores.

WHAT ABOUT TICKS?

Some ticks, especially in certain areas, carry Rocky Mountain spotted fever, an infection formerly more dangerous than it is now. If you are going into such a region, prior immunization is recommended. Too, chloromycetin and aureomycin have been found to control this heretofore too often fatal fever within one day.

Ticks usually are only annoyances, fortunately. Penetration of an egg-heavy female at the base of the skull can be dangerous, however. This is especially true, as she is apt to remain hidden in the hair until perhaps an increasing stiffness of the neck causes a close inspection. If all parts of the tick are not found and removed, respiratory paralysis and even death are serious possibilities.

What can be developing into a bothersome tick bite may be lanced one-eighth of an inch deep and suction applied for twenty minutes. A hot salt or wet grain poultice, if not too irritating to the individual, may help if left on from one-half to three-quarters of an hour. You also can wash with soap, allow to dry, cover with a sterile compress, and bandage.

An antihistamine ointment affords relief to many if applied early enough and if sensitivity exists. At the discretion of your doctor, inclusion of some such antihistamine, if only for specific allergies such as poison oak and for alleviation of burns, might well be warranted.

Ticks generally do not dig their heads in and begin to suck blood for a few hours and can be detected by daily afternoon inspection and removed by sliding a keen knife between them and your epidermis. The heat from a match or campfire embers occasionally will encourage them to back out from your body, as will touching them with coal oil, gasoline, or something alcoholic, such as shaving lotion.

Trying to pull or to unscrew them is not so good, sometimes leaving parts of the head behind to cause irritation, if not serious infection. Such parts should be cut out. Ticks should never be crushed during removal. Even after they have been taken off uninjured, the common technique of squashing them with the fingers is dangerous because of the thus released organisms that may be absorbed by the human system. Tossing them into the campfire will explode them instantaneously.

REMOVING OBJECTS FROM THE EYE

If back in the bush, anything becomes lightly imbedded in the cornea, that transparent outer coating of the eye through which light is admitted to the iris and pupil, it soon can become so unbearable that if skilled medical assistance is days away, some careful local action may be warranted. This is one reason for including in the kit a small tube of an antiseptic and anesthetic eye ointment suggested by your doctor, which will be of potential value, too, in soothing an irritated eye or treating a superficial infection. A possibility, for example, is a half-ounce tube of 2 per cent Butyn and Metaphen.

In removing a foreign object, first deaden the eye by using the ointment as directed. Then sterilize a needle. Fire will accomplish this, and if you keep the tip in the blue portion of a match flame, carbon will not form. If there is any remaining blackness, however, wipe the point clean with something sterile, such as cotton dipped in alcohol. This is particularly important, as otherwise an obscuring fleck of black might be left in the cornea.

Approach the foreign body very cautiously and steadily from the side with the sterile needle, holding it parallel to the eye rather than point first. Very often the object thus can be touched at its edge and flicked out, much in the fashion of playing tiddledywinks.

CLEANING WOUNDS

Alcohol, tincture of iodine, Merthiolate, and similar antiseptics have no place on a cut or scrape. These substances do kill germs. However, they also kill tissue. Because germs grow best in dead tissue and because some germs are always present, even in the primitive wilderness, such antiseptics set the stage for infection. At the very least, they delay healing.

The best way to handle such a wound is to wash it thoroughly with plenty of soap and water, dry it well, and if it is severe enough, apply a dressing.

CARBON MONOXIDE POISONING

Carbon monoxide, odorless and colorless, is a potential danger in any closed area where heating or cooking is being done with wood, gasoline and any other oil product, alcohol, fat, coal, and, in fact, anything that contains carbon. It kills by combining with the red blood corpuscles which are thus prevented from taking necessary oxygen from the air that is breathed. Being cumulative in effect, it often so weakens a victim that by the time he is aware something is wrong, he no longer has the strength to do anything about it. There is not even any prior difficulty with breathing to warn him. Fatal results can occur from inhaling small amounts of the unsuspected poison day after day, for these will remain combined with more and more hemoglobin until one more perhaps inconsequential dose is disastrous.

PREVENTION

The best precaution against carbon monoxide poisoning is good ventilation. You'd presume, therefore, that a tent would be safe. But when, for example, fabrics have been sealed by waterproofing in some instances, and by frost or rain in others, small heaters or stoves going overnight have sometimes killed all occupants.

The fact that log cabins are seldom tight affords a certain insurance, which is fortunate, for even a fire in a tight new stove with sufficient drafts can be perilous, inasmuch as the heat-glowing metal itself is able to release dangerous amounts of carbon monoxide. The hazard is increased, of course, as cold becomes more intense. Fires are not only increased at these times, but it is only natural to restrain ventilation.

A particular danger lies in wait for outdoorsmen whose automobiles are held up in cold weather by a storm. The tendency is to keep the cabs tightly closed and the motor going so as to operate the heater. The peril, especially if snow is drifting around the car, is that carbon monoxide can, and too often does, collect inside the unventilated vehicle in fatal quantities. Even when one is driving down the road, it is a good idea to maintain some ventilation.

TREATMENT

The treatment for carbon monoxide is to provide plenty of fresh air with the least possible delay. Get the victim out of the enclosure if you can. At any rate, smash or slash a way for fresh air to enter the enclosed space, if that is the best you can do at the moment. Keep him warm. Have him relax as much as possible, perhaps by lying quietly in a sleeping bag. Breathing deeply will help rid the blood of the effects of the gas. Stimulants such as coffee, tea, and hot chocolate are good.

If a victim has stopped breathing, or is having difficulty in breathing, artificial respiration may be necessary. When oxygen inhalators are available, they should be sent for without delay.

As soon as it can be done safely, the cause should be eliminated. The best way to protect yourself from the gas is to hold your breath while in its presence. Breathing through a handkerchief, wet or otherwise, is no protection. Incidentally, smoke such as that from a forest fire often carries dangerous amounts of carbon monoxide.

ARTIFICIAL RESPIRATION

Immediate action is necessary whenever breathing stops as a result of drowning, smoke inhalation, or electric shock, as from lightning.

First, check the mouth, making sure that the air passage from the mouth and nose to the lungs is not blocked. Remove mucus, water, and any other foreign substances. If the tongue has fallen back over the windpipe, hook it free with a forefinger.

Next, lay the victim face downward, with his feet higher than his head. Loosen clothing. Bend elbows and place hands one atop the other. Turn face to side, chin well up and cheek on hands.

Then kneel on one or both knees at the victim's head, facing him. Place the heels of your hands just below the line between the arm pits, with thumb tips touching and with your fingers downward and outward.

Rock forward on straight elbows, maintaining steady pressure on the victim's back. Rock backward, sliding your hand to the other's arms just above the elbows. Continuing to rock backward, grasp the arms. Raise arms until tension is felt, then lower the arms.

This completes the cycle, which should be repeated twelve times a minute for several hours if necessary. If the victim starts to breathe of his own accord, adjust your timing to his. Once the victim has been revived, treat for shock. If possible, keep him lying comfortably in a quiet, warm place for twenty-four hours.

If this method does not seem to be working, mouth-to-mouth resuscitation must be resorted to.

MOUTH-TO-MOUTH RESUSCITATION

This is currently considered to be superior to any other method, particularly if there is chest damage or if the surroundings are such that other procedures cannot be used. It is not pleasant, but it often will save a life.

Lay the victim on his back. Clear his mouth, as previously suggested. Pull his chin well forward until the head is fully tipped back.

Now place your mouth firmly over the victim's mouth. Pinch his nostrils closed. Exhale sharply. With a small child, place your mouth over both his nose and mouth while blowing. The chest of the victim should expand during this procedure.

Adequate chest motion and good skin color indicate that this procedure is being effective. Failure of the chest to move and a blue cast to the flesh point to the immediate need to recheck the victim's head and jaw position. His tongue may be blocking his air passage.

If you still get no chest action, turn him on his side and slap him sharply several times between the shoulder blades in an attempt to dislodge any foreign matter in the throat. If the victim is a child, hold him briefly head downward while you do this. Wipe the mouth clean and resume the mouth-to-mouth breathing.

With adults, blow one vigorous breath twelve times a minute. For small children, blow shallow breaths twenty times a minute. Don't give up, within reason, until the victim starts to breathe. Success sometimes takes hours of artificial respiration.

DEALING WITH WINTER HAZARDS

FALLING THROUGH THE ICE

One tool to have within easy reach during ice travel is a sheath knife, particularly when other safeguards, such as a pole, are lacking. On especially dangerous stretches, it is a good idea to hold this knife ready in hand. Then, if you do go through, you'll have the immediate chance to drive the point into solid ice and with its aid to roll yourself out and away.

Another method in cold weather of obtaining traction is, as quick as thought, to reach out to the fullest extent of your arms and to bring down your wet sleeves and gloves against firm ice where, if temperatures are low enough, they will almost instantly freeze.

If weather conditions are more temperate, you may have to break away thin ice with your hands to reach a surface strong enough to hold your full weight. It is usually possible, in the meantime, to support yourself by resting a hand or arm flatly on fragile ice. Then, if there seems to be no better way, get as much of your arms as you can over the edge, bring your body as nearly horizontal as is possible with the help perhaps of a swimming motion with the feet, get a leg over and roll toward safety.

MINIMIZING EXPOSURE
AFTER SUBZERO DRENCHING

If you can, after breaking through ice into water and quickly scrambling out again, roll at once in preferably soft and fluffy snow. If the outer clothing is somewhat water-repellent, the snow will blot up much of the moisture before it can reach the body.

In very cold weather any remaining dampness will freeze almost immediately. One advantage of this will be that the resulting sheath of ice will act as a windbreak.

Among the disadvantages will be the weight thus added. Another will be that this ice, depending on its thickness, can turn garments into something not too gently resembling armor. Most hazardous will be the clothing's losing part or most of its ability to keep the body warm.

If a boot becomes immersed in overflow, as is a common occurrence, you often can step into a snowbank quickly enough so that sufficient water will be absorbed to prevent any from penetrating to the foot. Sourdoughs occasionally treat their footwear this way deliberately.

Usually you proceed on ice as you do when traveling anywhere in the wilderness—with the assumption that the worst may happen. In this case, you realize that ice may give way beneath you any moment. The result is that if you do get wet, this does not usually extend beyond the outer clothing, except perhaps where moisture may run down into the footwear.

You can then at least change your stockings. Otherwise, squeeze them as dry as possible, pour and wipe away, perhaps with dry moss, any water that is inside the boots, warm the feet, if necessary, against some other portion of the body such as the thighs, dress, and continue as normally.

Suppose the more unusual happens and you become thoroughly drenched? You roll as quickly as you can in the most absorbent snow at hand, but not even this action is sufficient. If extra clothing is available, and if the weather isn't too cold, you may be able to get the wet garments off before they freeze. Some of them, particularly if a companion is there to help, you can squeeze reasonably dry and put back on. If alone in extreme cold, however, it will be safer first to build a fire, if that is feasible.

If you are going to build a fire, this should be attended to immediately, before hands become too numb. With a campfire blazing and with plenty of fuel at hand, it follows that no matter what you decide to do next, you can take your time. You may want to dry out thoroughly, in which case the quickest and most comfortable way to go about it may be with the clothes on. Or you may prefer to rig a windbreak, employing the drying garments themselves.

It is a slow and prolonged job for one alone to dry an outfit by an open campfire when temperatures are much below zero, particularly as the new danger to beware is that of damaging necessary gear by attempting to complete the chore too rapidly.

WHAT THE STRANDED MOTORIST SHOULD DO

Individuals halted by storm or other troubles when traveling by motor vehicle often have enough coverings to keep them

safe until help arrives. Too many add needlessly, and sometimes finally, to their difficulties by running motors so as to heat
unventilated cabs, thus risking carbon monoxide poisoning.
Others, prompted by fear of such an unlikely event as that of
starvation, leave in entirely inadequate clothing whatever sanctuary they have and stake everything against unreasonable
odds in an attempt to walk they're not sure where.

PREVENTING AND TREATING FROSTBITE

You need to pay constant attention to all parts of the body
to prevent freezing during intensely cold weather, examining
exposed areas in particular so as to make sure they have not
become stiff or numb. Unprotected portions of the head,
especially the ears, are particularly vulnerable.

If the hands are kept warm, by shoving them inside the
clothing against the flesh whenever necessary, such a frostbitten part can be thawed by holding the palm against it for a
few seconds. If this is attended to promptly, frost nip need be
no more serious than chapped skin.

If you were to ask almost anyone what is the most common
cause of accidental death in the North, the reply you'd most
often get would be freezing. As a matter of fact, the correct
answer is fire.

Every possible care should be taken not to freeze the feet.
These are susceptible because of poorer circulation and because of cold's reaching them by conduction and thus speed-
ing condensation. But once this vulnerability is recognized, it
can be so offset that there seldom will be any good reason for
such a predicament.

How should you act if a foot is actually frozen? First of all,
do not delay. If you can build a fire at once, do that. Then
you very possibly can thaw the foot in the heat of the blaze.
Better still, you may be able to keep yourself comfortable
while thawing the foot against some part of your own body
such as the bare thigh. Or you may be able to warm it sufficiently by contact with the abdomen of a human companion,
or with an animal.

WHAT NOT TO DO. Anyone not sure of the best procedure in any emergency will probably do better to let common sense be his determinant, rather than to follow blindly

some unreasonable procedure about which he may have heard.

When you lack the personal experience that may enable you to make your own evaluation, it is natural for you to accept the opinions of others. The unfortunate thing about this is that many popular beliefs are definite and positive in reverse ratio to their lack of foundation in fact.

Before anyone reading this rubs snow on a frostbitten ear, it is to be hoped that he will ask himself how the application of one frozen thing to another can be anything but a good way to extend the freezing.

The way to lift the temperature of an area to above freezing is, reasonably enough, to apply warmth. To thaw an ear, for example, cup it with a warm palm.

You soon learn not to rub, certainly. Chafing a frozen ear with snow in very cold weather is, you find, comparable to scrubbing a warm ear with sand and gravel. As for heating frozen flesh by friction sufficiently to thaw it, this not only is a slow process, but it can cause additional injury by tearing the sensitized skin.

Some disastrous results have followed the attempts, incredible as they may seem, of trying to thaw parts of the body with alcohol, gasoline, oil, salt water, and other liquids whose temperatures have been below 32° Fahrenheit. The erroneous theory has been that because these were not frozen, they were just the things to use to thaw something else. All one has to do is to glance at the ordinary thermometer on a subzero day to be reminded that, although alcohol may not be frozen, it still can be cold enough to be expected to solidify in the very brief time a foot is immersed in it.

FAST VERSUS SLOW THAWING. If part of the body is seriously frozen, should it be thawed gradually or as quickly as possible? Medical doctors disagree on this, although opinion continues to shift more and more toward speed.

Those favoring rapid thawing, as by soaking a foot in water as hot as can ordinarily be borne, believe that danger from gangrene becomes more of a possibility the longer the circulation is shut off. They also are of the opinion that the greater the length of time a part of the body is allowed to remain gravely frozen, the deeper the freezing may extend.

Those authorities favoring gradual thawing, by heat not much if any greater than normal body temperature, opine that there is less hazard of permanent damage to severely frozen tissues if only moderate heat is gently applied. This is the only treatment necessary, of course, in mild cases.

ESCAPING FROM SNOWSLIDES

Anyone caught in a snowslide has a good chance to walk away from it, especially if he can keep on top of the swirling and billowing avalanche. One way to accomplish this is by a swimming motion. The backstroke, particularly effective if it can be managed, has saved numerous lives in such emergencies.

TREATMENT AND PREVENTION OF SNOW BLINDNESS

Snow blindness is a painful and watery inflammation of the eyes resulting from overexposure to certain light rays, particularly when these are so diffused by water particles, frozen or otherwise, that they seem to strike the eyeball from every direction. The same symptoms result from exposure to glare from sand.

Treatment lies in avoiding all sunlight as much as possible. Eyes should be bandaged in a case of severe irritation, as the closed eyelids do not afford sufficient protection. This is true even inside a tent, as those who at some time have collected a sunburn through canvas can appreciate.

Sourdoughs occasionally use cold weak tea to bathe the eyes when they first seem to be filled with harsh, gritty soap powder. Some find cold compresses of the steeped tea leaves soothing. If you have it in your medicine kit, here is where an antiseptic, anesthetic eye ointment will really be appreciated.

Snow blindness can be prevented by keeping excessive light from the eyes. The most convenient way of accomplishing this is with sunglasses. Large lenses, well fitted not too far from the face, are advisable because of the additional protection they afford from side glare.

Cheap sunglasses usually are fragile, seldom give sufficient eye protection at any time, are frequently uncomfortable, and are prone generally to have lens shortcomings and defects that may injure eyesight. Plastic is not recommended, particularly when replacement may be difficult, because of its susceptibility to scratches and abrasions. Sunglasses that clip into place may damage regular glasses, and furthermore, do not exclude sufficient glare except directly in front.

Eye protectors can be improvised from strips of wood, bark, or bone, in which narrow slits have been cut. These have an advantage of not frosting under ordinary conditions. They have the disadvantage of severely restricting the vision. When the sun is high enough, shades such as those that can be fashioned from birch bark will help to cut down light, especially if their insides are darkened, perhaps with charcoal from the fire. Blacking about the eyes, as with soot, will also decrease reflected light.

MIRE

You occasionally find dangerous quagmires where mud, decaying vegetation, or both, are mixed with water in proportions not solid enough to support your weight.

That is all there is to it. No suction or evil influence exists within to draw one downwards. As a matter of fact, all that operates is gravity assisted by any unwise struggling. If you try to pull one of two imprisoned legs loose while putting all the resulting pressure on the other leg, the action will, of course, force this leg deeper.

A horse is caught quickly, for example, because of the comparative smallness of its feet. A moose of similar weight often will walk across the same quagmire without difficulty because of the way its hooves spread apart to present a larger surface. The human foot, like the horse's hoof, is a comparatively small area pressed downward by a correspondingly heavy weight.

If, when you feel the instability, you get to solid land by running, that will be the end of the matter. If you cannot do this, fall to your knees, for generally it will be possible to make it that way.

If you are still sinking, looking around quickly will often disclose some branch or bush to grab. Or a pack or a coat may support your weight. If not, flatten out on your stomach, with your limbs as far apart as possible, and crawl. You may have to do this anyway.

One finds quagmires in all sorts of country. Areas where water remains on the surface, and particularly where water has so lain, may be treacherous. You should watch out for tidal flats, swamps, marshes, old water holes which tremble beneath a topping of dried mud, and certainly for muskegs.

QUICKSAND

Quicksand is similar to quagmire, being sand that is suspended in water. It may drop you a lot more quickly, but methods of extrication are similar. There is not as much time, however, and you're in more potential danger unless you keep your head.

Unless help is nearby or there is some support to grasp, you may be able to throw yourself immediately full length and either crawl or swim free. You may have to duck under water to loosen your feet, digging around with the hands and perhaps quickly sacrificing footwear. Avoid, as much as possible, any sudden and abrupt motions that would serve to shove you deeper.

Rest but do not ever give up, for quicksands and quagmires often occupy a hole no larger around than a sofa or large chair. Another inch or two of progress, in other words, may well bring your fingers either to solidness or to where you can loop a belt, or perhaps a rope made of clothing, over a bush. If you can reach a spot where vegetation is growing, you will almost certainly find sufficient support to get you loose.

ANIMAL ENCOUNTERS

Wild animals which have been handled enough by man to lose their natural fear of human beings, as, for example, a fawn brought up on a bottle, may occasionally become dangerous.

Males of the deer family as a whole sometimes prove truculent during rutting seasons, while later a mother may try to send an intruder away if she thinks her young are threatened. So will a bear. So will a tiny swallow. And if someone then runs, apparently frightened, then the often-followed impulse of both bear and swallow is to chase.

Sometimes, too, an animal will flee at a sound or odor, and not seeing an individual, may appear to be charging him. An animal who is, or who believes himself cornered, may try to wipe a man out of the way. As for wounded animals, even a little squirrel will bite and scratch.

Suppose you come face to face with a large animal that shows no disposition to sift into the shadows. The best thing to do is to stand perfectly still and to talk in as calm and even a manner as possible. The choice of words makes no difference, for an unexcited and not unfriendly human monotone appears to have a soothing effect on an animal. Any you so meet in the open probably will, unless they bolt immediately, regard you for a brief time and then move away, usually slowly and, in any event, without sign of overmuch excitement.

If you have a firearm, you will naturally get that in position as calmly and smoothly as possible, particularly if the animal is at such close quarters that any abruptness may provoke a similar reaction. Any movement should, therefore, be so extremely gradual as to be almost imperceptible. Unless absolutely necessary, it will seldom be wise, under such circumstances, to shoot.

Suppose the animal shows no indication that it will give ground? Then you may prefer to leave with as much of an appearance of casualness as you can manage, continuing to avoid any sudden movements and still talking quietly.

FAVORITE RECIPES

TIPS ON SUPPLIES